BARBED WIRE

A call to transform the way we think about property, this book examines how capitalism has from its origins sought to enclose or privatize the commons, or land and other forms of property that had been viewed as communally owned, and argues that neoliberal economic policies and the corporate takeovers of urban spaces, prisons, schools, the mass media, farms, and natural resources have failed to serve the public interest. A study of corporate globalization and the continuation of empire after the era of political decolonization, it begins with the fencing of the West starting in the 1870s, and moves to examine recent phenomena such as urbanization, mass incarceration, financialization, and the treatment of people as commodities in the context of the longue durée of land enclosures, empire, and capitalism. Highlighting the threatened elimination of the public domain as a result of corporate efforts to privatize public utilities, prisons, schools, forests, seeds, and just about everything else that can yield a profit, *Barbed Wire: Capitalism and the Enclosure of the Commons* asks what it would mean if, instead of either private or public property, our most fundamental conception of property were communal. Would a redefinition of property from a community perspective lead us beyond the military-industrial complex?

Patrick Brantlinger is James Rudy Distinguished Professor (Emeritus) in the Department of English and Cultural Studies at Indiana University, USA.

"This is an expert tour of the many borders, past and present, that parcel up our collective existence; a deeply engaged, historically informed guide to privatization drives and their moral implications. Patrick Brantlinger, as always, probes deeply and uncovers truths with eloquence. An outstanding read."

Jan Nederveen Pieterse,
University of California Santa Barbara, USA

BARBED WIRE

Capitalism and the Enclosure of the Commons

Patrick Brantlinger

LONDON AND NEW YORK

First published 2018
by Routledge
2 Park Square, Milton Park, Abingdon, Oxon OX14 4RN

and by Routledge
711 Third Avenue, New York, NY 10017

Routledge is an imprint of the Taylor & Francis Group, an informa business

© 2018 Patrick Brantlinger

The right of Patrick Brantlinger to be identified as author of this work has been asserted by him in accordance with sections 77 and 78 of the Copyright, Designs and Patents Act 1988.

All rights reserved. No part of this book may be reprinted or reproduced or utilised in any form or by any electronic, mechanical, or other means, now known or hereafter invented, including photocopying and recording, or in any information storage or retrieval system, without permission in writing from the publishers.

Trademark notice: Product or corporate names may be trademarks or registered trademarks, and are used only for identification and explanation without intent to infringe.

British Library Cataloguing-in-Publication Data
A catalogue record for this book is available from the British Library

Library of Congress Cataloging-in-Publication Data
A catalog record for this book has been requested

ISBN: 978-1-138-56437-4 (hbk)
ISBN: 978-1-138-56439-8 (pbk)
ISBN: 978-1-315-12238-0 (ebk)

Typeset in Bembo
by Swales & Willis Ltd, Exeter, Devon, UK

For Andy, Susan, and Jeremy

CONTENTS

Acknowledgments   *viii*
Introduction   *ix*

1   Modern fencing   1
2   Urban spaces   17
3   Caging people: from schools to prisons   34
4   Thinking inside the box   49
5   Corporations as greed machines   65
6   Globalization and empire   80
7   Manufacturing disposable people   100
8   The real tragedy of the commons   119
9   What is to be done?   139

Bibliography   *149*
Index   *162*

ACKNOWLEDGMENTS

Over the years, many friends and colleagues have provided me with information and new ideas, offered advice, and inspired me. Foremost among them is my late wife, Ellen Brantlinger, author of *Dividing Classes* and many other works on education and equity. Our countless discussions about economic inequality, racism, feminism, and social justice make her virtually a co-author of *Barbed Wire*. There are too many others to name them all, but those who have been most important as I have worked on this project include Todd Avery, Purnima Bose, Milton Fisk, Todd Kuchta, Sara Mauer, Jim Naremore, Jan Nederveen Pieterse, and Joe Varga. I thank as well the many students who have taken my Victorian and Cultural Studies classes and whose dissertations I've been privileged to read and evaluate. I have always learned a great deal from those I have taught, much more than they realize. And I am grateful to a number of organizations that have been supportive. Besides Indiana University, these include the Midwest Victorian Studies Association, the Midwestern Conference on British Studies, the CUNY Graduate Center, and the University of Kansas Humanities Center.

INTRODUCTION

"They claim this mother of ours, the Earth, for their own use, and fence their neighbors away from her, and deface her with their buildings and their refuse."
— Sitting Bull

When I started this project, I guessed that no one had ever written a book about barbed wire. I soon discovered that there are several books and many articles about it. Henry and Frances McCallum's *The Wire That Fenced the West* contains everything anyone would ever want to know about the invention of barbed wire and its use in enclosing much of the Western US.[1] Barbed wire may evoke fencing the West, but it just as readily evokes prisons, zoos, junkyards, power plants, and ruined cities. Alan Krell's *The Devil's Rope* deals with many of its literary and artistic representations, such as W. H. Auden's "Memorial for the City": "The barbed wire runs through the abolished City." Auden wrote his poem shortly after World War II, so he had plenty of "abolished" cities to choose from. The most haunting artistic and photographic images of barbed wire that Krell discusses are those featuring Nazi concentration camps. Reviel Netz's *Barbed Wire: An Ecology of Modernity* also goes well beyond fencing the American West to examine the uses of barbed wire in military and penal contexts from the time of the Spanish-American and Anglo-Boer wars to the 2000s.[2]

This book, however, is not primarily about barbed wire. It is, as the subtitle says, about capitalism and the enclosure or privatization of what had been communally owned land and other forms of "the commons." Many inventions have contributed to capitalist modernization, but few capture the ambiguity of that process as sharply as barbed wire; it serves here primarily as a metaphor for that process. Barbed wire is a recent invention, dating from 1874, a decade after the Civil War.[3]

Capitalism is much older, of course, emerging gradually in Europe from late medieval feudalism, gathering force through empire-building, slavery, and the Industrial Revolution. Besides covering an immense span of history, capitalism has involved many different processes, including the development of the corporate form, and also treating just about everything as potentially private property and extracting as much "surplus value" or profit as it can from labor.

Much has been written about the early stages of capitalism and the "enclosure movement" or the "enclosure of the commons" in Europe. Marx saw that movement as the main form of "primitive accumulation," which was the basis for the development of capitalism out of feudalism.[4] He also interpreted Western imperialism starting in the late 1400s in terms of primitive accumulation:

> The discovery of gold and silver in America, the extirpation, enslavement and entombment in mines of the indigenous population of that continent, the beginnings of the conquest and plunder of India, and the conversion of Africa into a preserve for the commercial hunting of black skins, are all things which characterize the dawn of the era of capitalist production. These idyllic proceedings are the chief moments of primitive accumulation.

Marx noted that as imperialism spread, so too did "commercial war . . . which has the globe as its battlefield." That war began "with the revolt of the Netherlands from Spain, assume[d] gigantic dimensions in England's Anti-Jacobin War, and is still going on in the shape of the Opium Wars against China" (*Capital* 1: 915).[5]

Besides Marx, R. H. Tawney, E. P. Thompson, Raymond Williams, and many other historians have linked the early enclosure of the commons in Britain to the origins of capitalism and also to imperialism. Studies about the commons today, including this one, have been influenced by the work of Nobel laureate Elinor Ostrom, who taught as I did for many years at Indiana University. Ostrom and her husband Vincent, together with their numerous students and colleagues, investigated the governance of "the commons" or of "common pool resources" around the world. Although I met the Ostroms on a couple of occasions, I did not until recently recognize the importance of their work for my own thinking about empire, capitalism, enclosures, and the commons. Their general finding is that land and other resources treated as commons, or community-owned property, are often well-managed, environmentally sustainable, and sometimes long-lasting. This may seem unsurprising, but neoliberal economists have treated the fallacious idea of "the tragedy of the commons" as scientifically sound. According to it, any version of the commons is doomed to failure through overuse and freeloading.

From the late Middle Ages forward, the enclosure movement in Europe involved landowners appropriating small farms and areas that had long been understood as commons and relied on by the peasantry for foraging, hunting, and small fields and pastures. Many of the landowners wanted much larger pastures for raising sheep, providing wool for the textile industry. Peasants themselves often enclosed land, which usually meant surrounding a small area with stones or hedges to keep livestock in or out. A commons was not viewed as land open to anybody, but was rather territory that by custom or law came under the collective ownership of a specific community or group of peasants. Small-scale enclosures by the peasantry were usually regarded as unproblematic. The problem arose from the rich and powerful seeking to increase their holdings, which often involved evicting entire villages of peasants from land they had considered belonging to their families and communites for many generations. In one major episode between 1814 and 1820, the Duchess of Sutherland "swept" thousands of peasants off nearly 800,000 acres in Scotland, destroying their villages and turning their fields into sheep farms. The Scottish "clearances" "all seemed designed to overturn the old system and bring capitalistic values . . . to the Highlands" (Richards 8). "By 1825," writes Marx, "the 15,000 Gaels [in the Highlands] had . . . been replaced by 131,000 sheep" (*Capital* 1: 892).

Defenders of enclosures such as Adam Smith and Arthur Young saw them as increasing agricultural productivity and profits; opponents saw them as disrupting communal ways of life and increasing rural poverty. As Karl Polanyi notes, enclosing the commons amounted to class warfare waged by the rich and powerful against the rural poor. The same version of class warfare continues today, as corporations and their supporters engage in massive "land-grabs" and other forms of "accumulation by dispossession" (see, for example, Alexander Ross, *Grabbing Back*). It is not often noted, however, that the activities of corporations today are a continuation of what the first corporations such as the British East India Company were created to do, and that was to help the rich and powerful in the Western European nations build empires abroad.

Including the enclosure of land, there are by now countless conversions of what had been open, communal, or public—"the commons"—into private property, and especially into private property owned or controlled by corporations. Numerous critics of today's corporate capitalism, moreover, treat "enclosure" as a synonym for "privatization." To take just one example, in *Revitalizing the Commons*, C. A. Bowers writes:

> Even the airwaves have become enclosed, as corporate ownership now allows them to be used largely by inane television programs to hold the attention of the viewing public long enough to present a blitz of commercial advertising . . . . The privatization of the commons is now being extended to include what was previously the public's right to water . . . .
>
> *(5)*

If the airwaves and water are today subject to corporate enclosure or privatization, just about everything else is up for grabs.

In his analysis of "inverted totalitarianism," Sheldon Wolin summarizes the "privatization of public services and functions" going on today in the US. He attributes privatization to "the steady evolution of corporate power into a political form, into an integral, even dominant partner with the state." Donald Trump's appointment of corporate billionaires to his cabinet illustrates Wolin's point. Trump's presidency might easily be dubbed a government by ExxonMobil, Goldman Sachs, and Trump Inc. Privatization, Wolin continues:

> marks the transformation of American politics and its political culture, from a system in which democratic practices and values were, if not defining, at least major contributory elements, to one where the remaining democratic elements of the state and its populist programs are being systematically dismantled.
>
> *(303)*

He might also have said that the "democratic elements of the state" are being systematically enclosed, if not altogether closed down.

The general purpose of corporate enclosure or privatization is of course to make money. And where money accumulates, so does power—up to a point. In "Marxism and the Dialectics of Ecology," John Bellamy Foster and Brett Clark cite "the Lauderdale Paradox," according to which "the accumulation of private riches (exchange value) under capitalism generally depends on the destruction of public wealth (use values), so as to generate the scarcity and monopoly essential to the accumulation process. Under these conditions, accelerated environmental degradation destroying the commons is an inherent consequence of capital accumulation," just as it also undermines the democratic elements of the state.[6] They add that, according to Marx, "capitalism undermine[s] 'the original sources of all wealth—the soil and the worker'" (Foster and Clark 5–6).

Lauderdale's Paradox is related to the law of diminishing returns. Even in financial speculation, that law works its negative magic. As with the dot-com bubble of 1997–2000 or the housing and mortgage crisis of 2007–2008, under capitalism economic bubbles expand until they burst. Just like economic bubbles, moreover, empires also can "overstretch," weaken, and collapse, following their own versions of the law of diminishing returns.[7] *Barbed Wire* recognizes how, from the Renaissance forward, capitalist corporations helped the major European empires grow through territorial enclosures overseas. Along with transnational corporations, the major power centers today are of course nation-states, several of which, despite the era of decolonization that followed World War II, maintain empires. Since the demise of the Soviet Union, the US has emerged supposedly as the lone superpower. Its imperial might is largely economic, but it possesses the largest, most advanced—most lethal—military in history, including a huge nuclear arsenal and approximately 800 military bases around the world.[8] Recent television ads for the U.S. Navy mark sites where it operates to defend "all we hold dear," and those sites span the globe.

After the downfalls of the communist regimes in Eastern Europe and of the Soviet Union, in the 1990s, it appeared that the United States, and capitalism along with it, might reign supreme far into the future, or at least for decades to come. Free trade, prosperity, and democracy would spread throughout the world.

Today, however, just 16 years later, there are many predictions of the demise of capitalism, or at least of its main ideological prop, economic neoliberalism. These predictions reflect the economic crisis of 2007–2008 and the slow recovery—if it is a recovery—that has followed. They also reflect the recent realizations that global warming is occurring at a far more rapid rate than even climate scientists expected; that "the war on terror" has no end in sight; that poverty and inequality are increasing, not diminishing; and that technological advances are creating a "jobless future."[9]

Meanwhile, despite its unsurpassed power, the U.S. military is dependent on some of the world's largest corporations—Lockheed Martin, Boeing, Halliburton, Raytheon, to name just a few—who produce everything from fighter jets and submarines to uniforms and meals for the troops. And of course, it is dependent on Big Oil. The "military-industrial complex," as President Eisenhower dubbed it in 1961, exemplifies the many ways governmental and corporate powers are today interdependent both in the US and in other major nation-states.[10] Recent news reports indicate that under President Obama, who won the Nobel Peace Prize in 2009, the US sold more military weapons and dropped more bombs than at any time in history. Further, even though the world has supposedly passed beyond the stage of formal colonization, empires are and always have been the largest forms of territorial enclosure ever devised. Besides the US, Russia, China, Britain, France, South Africa, and Israel continue to dominate weaker polities through economic, political, and military means, so ours is by no means a "postcolonial" era. Despite their power and often vast domains, however, empires do not last forever. But perhaps imperial domination of some sort or other does.[11]

Much discourse about the enclosure of the commons today refers to natural resources and the environment, including land and water. Corporations are on the prowl to enclose or privatize anything that can be made profitable. As Jonathan Rowe says in *Our Common Wealth*, "Everything is up for grabs, everything is for sale" (32). Ideological modes of thinking—neoliberal economics is a prime example—naturalize corporate behavior, making it difficult if not impossible to imagine alternatives to the shrinkage of the public sphere happening everywhere in the world today as globalizing capital continues its forward—or backward—march. If progress means enclosing more and more of the commons, then it is not progress.

All of the essays in *Barbed Wire* deal with aspects of the commons and of corporate privatization or enclosure, ranging from ghettos and gated communities to corporate globalization and the current version of the American empire. The essays are not intended to provide a chronological history of capitalism, of the enclosure movement, or of Western imperialism. Though connected by the theme of corporate enclosure or the privatization of the public domain, they can be read separately and in any order. Under capitalism and its current main ideological prop, neoliberal economics, globalization has involved enclosing much of the planet within a new imperial structure. In *Empire*, Michael Hardt and Antonio Negri argue that this structure is radically different from older versions of imperialism. I do not think, however, that there is that much difference between new and old patterns of domination and enclosure. Because of new means of communication, transportation, and warfare, the rapidity with which Max Weber's iron cage of modernization is closing in on us is accelerating. But the basic nature of capitalism and the empires it has fostered has not changed greatly over several centuries.

Before the fifth World Social Forum in Porto Alegre, Brazil, in 2005, on one of Global Exchange's "reality tours," I visited a number of encampments and villages established by the Landless Workers Movement, or the MST, in that country.[12] Since the mid-1980s, landless workers and their families, with governmental support, have set up "black tent" encampments next to the boundaries, often fenced by barbed wire, that enclose *latifúndios* or large, privately owned estates.[13] After the government determines that some amount of such an estate is not being used productively, the workers can move onto it and establish small farms, cooperatives, and villages. By 2005, out of a total population of 4.5 million landless peasants, the MST had established farms for some 300,000 formerly propertyless families. This process reverses the immense land enclosures that resulted from conquest, colonization, and slavery. Land reform efforts throughout Latin America have been met by violence, and yet the MST has made some progress in undoing some of the worst effects of imperialism and slavery in Brazil.[14]

The sort of resistance to enclosure represented by the MST in Brazil is going on in many parts of the world. But corporations and the wealthy today make opposition seem quixotic. What is the solution? Democratic socialism? A United Nations that can take real, reformative action to halt both war and the greed and excesses of the rich and powerful? Revolution? A rebirth of communism, though not of the top-down, dictatorial sort that failed so spectacularly during the Soviet era? The American and French Revolutions had happier outcomes than did the Russian Revolution of 1917, but in general the violent overthrow of governments can end up in bloody chaos and outcomes as bad as, or worse than, before. The results of the Arab Spring may be relatively positive in Tunisia, for example, but they have so far hardly proved positive in Egypt, Libya, or Syria.

A starting point for positive solutions to counteract today's global corporate enclosure movement must be the recognition of the value and necessity of defending what is left of "the commons." Their protection and restoration from the ravages of unregulated capitalism are desperately needed. Several steps short of some sort of global revolution seem possible. These include land reform as exemplified by the MST, reversing the trend toward the privatization of everything, curtailing the size and power of corporations, ending the casino economy caused by financialization, insisting on diplomacy rather than war to solve international problems, turning to green energy sources, advancing the cause of labor and union organization, supporting workers' co-ops and other forms of worker, local, and communal ownership, encouraging the creation of land trusts and other alternatives to increase the collective or public possession and management of nature and natural resources, and making democracy work again in the US and elsewhere. In my view, these and other reforms must happen quickly, before capitalism encloses—rather, devours—the entire planet.

Notes

1 In the introduction, Henry McCallum writes: "Most people are of the opinion that all there is to be said on the subject of barbed wire could be put into one paragraph—or, more than likely, into one exclamation, such as, 'Of all things to write a book about—barbed wire!'" The MacCallums are collectors of barbed wire—all types and varieties. It seems an eccentric thing to do, but during its peak in the 1960s and 1970s, the fad of collecting specimens of barbed wire was quite popular. There may still be as many as 65,000 collectors of it in the US. They call themselves "barbarians." Besides books, there are journals, catalogues, songs, and poems about barbed wire, as well as the Devil's Rope Museum in McLean, Texas, and a similar museum in Lacrosse, Kansas, a town that bills itself as the "Barbed Wire Capital of the World."

2 I cite here only books about barbed wire that I have read. Some of the other books about it include Sir Hal Caine, *Barbed Wire* (1927), Elmer Kelton, *Barbed Wire* (2006), Joanne Liu, *Barbed Wire: The Fence That Changed the West* (2009), and Olivier Razac, *Barbed Wire: A Political History* (2003).

3 There were precursors to James Glidden's invention of barbed wire in 1874. Peter Linebaugh notes that 1867, when Karl Marx traveled from London to deliver the manuscript of *Capital* to its German publisher, was the year that barbed wire was first invented, "a means of enclosing cheaper, speedier, and nastier than any other" (*The Magna Carta Manifesto* 85). Linebaugh remarks that 1867 was also the year that Alfred Nobel patented his invention of dynamite, that David Livingstone set the stage for the Scramble for Africa, and that the Ku Klux Klan was established—a year of enclosing, bombing, racism, and imperialism. It was also the year that the British parliament passed the Second Reform Bill, granting the vote to a sizable portion of the male working class. If political democracy was on the rise, so was immigration from Europe to North America, as millions of the poor streamed across the Atlantic. The enclosure movement in Europe was a major factor leading to immigration. As land was increasingly privatized in Europe, land in North America seemed wide open, available for enclosure by "the huddled masses" from abroad, impoverished by enclosures in the lands of their origins.

4 Besides the land enclosure movement in Britain and elsewhere in Europe, there were other points of origin of capitalism, including the growth of finance and banking in Venice and Genoa, and of the spice trade that led to the expansion of the Dutch empire in the East Indies (e.g., see Linklater 65).

5 By "England's Anti-Jacobin War," Marx is referring to the multiple wars England waged in the 1700s against both Spain and France.

6 The Lauderdale Paradox is named after James Maitland, the eighth Earl of Lauderdale (1759–1839).

7 By now, there have been numerous studies of America's "imperial overstretch" from the Vietnam War to the invasion of Iraq and its bloody, chaotic aftermath. See, for example, Roger Burbach and Jim Tarbell, *Imperial Overstretch*.

8 See Chalmers Johnson, *The Sorrows of Empire*, and David Vine, *Base Nation*.

9 See, for example, Samir Amin's *The Implosion of Contemporary Capitalism*, Michael Hardt and Antonio Negri's trilogy starting with *Empire*, Naomi Klein's *This Changes Everything*, Paul Mason's *Postcapitalism*, Robert McChesney and John Nichols's *People Get Ready*, and Slavoj Žižek's *Living in the End Times*.

10 In *The Great American Stickup*, Robert Scheer comments on "the dance of the private with the public that is the norm in what we naively refer to as our 'free enterprise system'—be it agribusiness, the defense industry, telecomunications, or ... the financial sector. All of these industries operate in an environment of government rules that their lobbyists get to help write, and all succeed through an ability to negotiate the regulatory environment that results from those laws" (176).

11 Several of the books I published before *Barbed Wire* deal with British imperialism, race, and genocide: *Rule of Darkness*, *Dark Vanishings*, *Taming Cannibals*, and *Victorian Literature and Postcolonial Studies*. Besides the authors I mention, other writers on "the commons"

recognize the connection between the early enclosure movement in Europe and corporate enclosures today. These include Peter Linebaugh, Robert Marzec, and the authors of *The New Enclosures* produced by Midnight Notes Collective.
12 Movimento dos Trabalhadores sem Terra.
13 They are called "black tent" encampments because of the black tarpaulins the government provides them with for shelter.
14 See Wright and Wolford, *To Inherit the Earth*.

1
MODERN FENCING

"All this Americanising and mechanising has been for the purpose of overthrowing the past. And now look at America, tangled in her own barbed wire, and mastered by her own machines."

— D. H. Lawrence

From Greenville to Mad Art

Driving by the federal prison outside Greenville, Illinois, I started thinking about barbed wire and other modes of enclosure. The Greenville lockup is surrounded by barbed wire, topped by its perfection, spirals of concertina or razor wire. It occurred to me that the entire history of capitalism could be written in terms of enclosures, with prisons as an extreme version. I recalled Michel Foucault's account in *Discipline and Punish* of the rise of the penitentiary and "the carceral society." Perhaps I was also remembering Vijay Prashad's comment in *Fat Cats and Running Dogs* that "the story of Enron . . . is the tale of the Second Enclosure Movement, and follows from the earlier movement to enclose land with barbed wire and other fencing" (7).

In college, I had studied the first enclosure movement that began centuries before the invention and first manufacturing of barbed wire in the 1870s. Throughout Europe starting in the late Middle Ages, aristocrats and other wealthy landowners enclosed large areas that had previously been viewed as "commons" and relied on by the peasantry for pastures, crops, wood, and foraging. The old term "enclosure" is today often used as a synonym for privatization, as when corporations take over property or processes that had before been public or communal.

As I passed by Greenville, I was on my way to visit my younger son, a musician who lives in St. Louis and whose income derives mainly from managing Mad Art.

It is a funky gallery, event space, and barbecue joint in a former police station owned by an ex-policeman. Mad Art still has the original jail cells, where tourists can have lunch during visits to the historic Soulard neighborhood or to the Anheuser-Busch brewery across the street. During my trip, Greenville prison and Mad Art bookended my musings about modes of enclosure. My son and his friend, the ex-policeman, have named the barbecue eatery in Mad Art "The Capitalist Pig." Their pulled pork sandwich is quite delicious. As for actual capitalist pigs, they have become far too powerful, and they are gaining ground—which still often means enclosing ground—at a great rate. As most Americans know, our democratic institutions are being bought up lock, stock, and barrel—that is, enclosed or privatized—by what Bernie Sanders calls "the billionaire class." It is no secret that, since World War II, the US has become a plutocracy. Witness the 2016 election of Donald Trump and his selections for his cabinet, also corporate billionaires.

Greenville is a federal prison, but the private prison industry is huge and growing. Further, private companies provide many of the services inside the Greenville "Correctional Institution" (just how much "correction" is occurring inside it is questionable). Because of the "prison-industrial complex" and the failed "war on drugs," the US, "land of the free," has the highest incarceration rate of any country in the world. Nearly 2.5 million people are currently locked up in places such as Greenville prison. More than half of those incarcerated are African Americans and Latinos, a manifestation of what Michelle Alexander calls "the new Jim Crow." Another manifestation is the recent media spectacle of the shootings of unarmed black men, boys, and sometimes women by the police, such as the murder of Michael Brown in Ferguson, Missouri, about five miles from Mad Art. The Black Lives Matter movement, protesting police brutality and the shootings of African Americans, is also protesting the officially authorized violence responsible for mass incarceration.

Just as it was once profitable to kidnap and enslave Africans, so it is profitable for private prison corporations to incarcerate as many prisoners as possible, no matter what their race may be. Caging people was and is big business. Prisons, of course, aren't the only institutions that are increasingly being privatized by corporations. So are educational institutions: as state legislatures underfund public schools, the charter school movement mushrooms.[1] Public universities such as the one where I taught for 38 years, Indiana University, have seen their support from state revenues dwindle from about 50 percent of their budgets in 1970 to around 15 percent or lower today. Privatizing city water systems represents only a fraction of the escalating "water wars" around the world, with large corporations draining entire lakes and aquifers to profit from them. Following the invasion of Iraq in 2003, private military outfits such as CACI, DynCorp, and Blackwater became collectively the largest occupying force after the U.S. military. Also, about 80 percent of the U.S. government's intelligence operations have been outsourced to private corporations such as Booz Allen Hamilton, the company that employed Edward Snowden. And on and on. Is there any business or activity or parcel of the world that cannot be privatized or enclosed by some corporation or other?

Enclosing the commons was the main version of "primitive accumulation," which Marx saw as the starting point for capitalist development. "The capital-relation," Marx wrote, emerges through "the process which divorces the worker from the ownership of the conditions of his own labour," or in other words which "frees" workers from the most basic means of subsistence, the land, and turns them into "wage-labourers" (*Capital* 1: 874). Once the peasantry had been cleared off the land, it became privately owned fields for crops or pastures, or sometimes deer parks for the pleasure of the wealthy. The early enclosure movement, a major development in the evolution of private property, and which often met with resistance such as Kett's Rebellion in Norfolk, England, in 1549, lasted for several centuries. Marx adds that "by about 1750 the [English] yeomanry had disappeared, and so, by the last decade of the eighteenth century, had the last trace of the common land of the agricultural labourer" (*Capital* 1: 883). But the enclosure of land did not end in 1750 in England or anywhere else. The rapacious desire for more land was a major factor in the formation of the European empires starting in the Renaissance. Early corporations such as the British East India Company spurred imperial expansion. And today corporations continue to buy up enormous parcels of land around the world.

If the first term in Marx's phrase "primitive accumulation" is interpreted to mean early, that is inaccurate: capitalist "accumulation by dispossession" is still going on, big time (Harvey, *The New Imperialism* 137–182). Look at the fights over the Keystone XL and Dakota Access pipelines, or over fracking, or over harvesting timber in the Hoosier National Forest near my hometown (Bloomington, Indiana), among countless instances. Or consider how the big agricultural corporations such as Cargill and Monsanto have been devouring small farms everywhere. According to Alexander Ross, "the land grabs that have taken place around the world since 2009 would encompass the entire Western United States" (*Grabbing Back* 20).

The main reasons for the current corporate attempts to acquire land are for large-scale agriculture and for resource extraction (oil and gas drilling, mining, forestry). In an article also entitled "Global Land Grab," Terry Allen reports that "some 2 billion people in the developing world depend on 500 million smallholder farms for their livelihoods. . . . But with spectacular speed, patchworks of plots that used to support local populations through subsistence farming and grazing are being amalgamated into massive industrial plantations" (15). The smallholders are being evicted, usually with very little or no compensation. So the old story of the enclosure of land continues. Just as during the earliest enclosures of land, so now, David Korten declares, millions of "small-scale producers—farmers and artisans—who once were the backbone of poor but stable communities are being uprooted and transformed into landless migrant laborers, separated from family and place" (*The Great Turning* 29). This is evident in many formerly flourishing country towns in the US and Canada that are now deserted, or nearly so. It is also evident on street corners in major American cities, where migrant workers—documented or not—wait patiently for someone to hire them for a day or perhaps a few days to do some gardening or painting or roofing. It is not hard to figure out why they have come to be uprooted and in desperate need of work.

Marx's treatment of primitive accumulation, David Harvey points out, "reveals a wide range of processes":

> These include the commodification and privatization of land and the forceful expulsion of peasant populations; the conversion of various forms of property rights (common, collective, state, etc.) into exclusive private property rights; [and] the suppression of rights to the commons . . .
>
> *(*The New Imperialism *145)*

Today, under the aegis of neoliberal economics, capitalism's goal is to privatize or enclose as much as possible, the entire planet and even beyond, if some amount of profit can be made by doing so.[2] In *Capitalism: A Ghost Story*, Arundhati Roy calls this the "era of the Privatization of Everything." She proceeds to excoriate corporations and the wealthy for grabbing up as much land as possible:

> All over the world, weak, corrupt local governments have helped Wall Street brokers, agribusiness corporations, and Chinese billionaires to amass huge tracts of land. (Of course this entails commandeering water too.) In India the land of millions of people is being acquired and handed over to private corporations . . .
>
> *(11–12)*

Roy recounts how the Indian government (which is supposedly a democracy), in collaboration with corporations and the very wealthy, is violently evicting entire communities to make way for gigantic industrial zones. As the poor are displaced from their homes and their land, she says, they are told it is all about economic growth and the jobs such growth will create. But "the connection between GDP growth and jobs is a myth" (12). In India, since independence, a new middle class has emerged along with a handful of billionaires, but the impoverishment of the vast majority keeps pace and then some with economic development.

Orthodox economics seldom addresses enclosure or "the dispossession of commoners as market forces seize control of common resources, often with the active collusion of government" (Bollier, *Think Like a Commoner* 40). In his first book on the topic, *Silent Theft*, David Bollier declares that "we are living in the midst of a massive business-led enclosure movement" (6). He notes that "the American commons," or what American citizens "collectively own," include "tangible assets such as public forests and minerals, intangible wealth such as copyrights and patents, critical infrastructure such as the Internet and government research, and cultural resources such as the broadcast airwaves and public spaces" (3). On many fronts, and for many reasons that add up to money, government at all levels has been willing to cede to corporate interests what had previously been within its purview, part of what Bollier calls our "commonwealth."

> Such enclosures of the commons are aided by a Washington officialdom increasingly captive to business and indifferent to ordinary citizens; a journalism profession that has grown soft now that it competes with entertainment and marketing; and the dominion of market culture over our civic identities.
>
> *(Bollier,* Silent Theft *3)*

Especially after the 2010 *Citizens United* decision by the Supreme Court, more and more Americans are waking up to the fact that we are now governed by corporations and plutocrats, serviced by the swarms of lobbyists who infest the corridors of power in Washington, and kowtowed to by our elected politicians (see Clements; Hartmann).

Much of the impetus behind privatization or the recent enclosure movement is supported by the widespread belief that government is generally wasteful and inefficient, if not altogether corrupt, while private businesses are much more efficient and cost-effective. This belief has been proven false many times over, and yet it remains the dominant view in many circles. Was the Enron pyramid scam an aberration, or was it typical of corporate practices? The banks and mortgage lenders whose criminal behavior tanked the economy in 2007–2008 revealed that Enron was not an aberration. The "too big to fail" banks were bailed out by the federal government using taxpayers' money. They have sometimes been fined millions of dollars for their misdeeds, as was Wells Fargo in 2016, but since 2008 no major banker or CEO has wound up in prison for thefts or scams amounting to billions of dollars. And of course, the more government agencies such as the EPA or HUD are underfunded, the less effective they become. We are asked by the powers that be to recognize ongoing privatization as progress, but it is difficult to see how wrecking the environment and reducing everyone's prosperity and access to public goods amounts to progress.

In the early going in Europe, the defenders of the enclosure movement viewed it as improving estates and modernizing agriculture—that is, as progress. Its opponents, however, recognized its human costs: many of the dispossessed peasants became landless farmworkers, frequently "rackrented" by their landlords, or else they migrated to towns and cities where, during the late 1700s and early 1800s, they often joined the ranks of the mushrooming industrial proletariat. "The dispossessed [peasant] tenant," writes Stephen Marglin:

> the meaning of his existence eroded as his economic, political, and social ties to the land and to his fellows eroded, became the modern wage worker, remaining on the land at the sufferance of his master. From there it was a short social and psychological step . . . into the 'reserve army' that constituted the labor force for England's industrialization.[3]
>
> *(87)*

Modern cages

Greenville prison and the jail cells in Mad Art point to the great contradiction between America "land of the free" and the stark fact of mass incarceration. And if enclosing or imprisoning 2.5 million people weren't bad enough, what about Abu-Ghraib, Guantanamo, and the "black sites" overseas to which the CIA has been "rendering" alleged terrorists so they can be thrown in dungeons and tortured? This is not the America kids learn about in school. Yet it seems all too characteristic of capitalist modernity and now postmodernity: prosperity for many, but poverty, hardship, and sometimes even torture for the vast majority. Long before Foucault analyzed the rise of "the carceral society," Max Weber famously warned that industrial capitalism was turning the modern world into "an iron cage":

> No one knows who will live in this cage in the future, or whether at the end of this tremendous development entirely new prophets will arise, or there will be a great rebirth of old ideas and ideals or, if neither, mechanized petrification, embellished with a sort of convulsive self-importance. For of the last stage of this cultural development, it might well be truly said: "Specialists without spirit, sensualists without heart; this nullity imagines that it has attained a level of civilization never before achieved."
>
> *(182)*

For Weber, the iron cage was a metaphor for the sorry "cultural development" capitalism was producing. Foucault, as if attempting to specify what exactly Weber's metaphor meant, claimed that the penitentiary was the institution most characteristic of modernity. And Giorgio Agamben has gone one better than Foucault, claiming that the concentration camp is the epitome of modernity.

The concertina wire that surrounds the prison at Greenville was invented and first used in South Africa during the apartheid era (Krell 173). Earlier during the second Anglo-Boer War (1899–1902), the British used barbed wire in constructing what have been called the first concentration camps, although the Spanish also employed them in Cuba at about the same time and the US followed suit during its invasion and colonization of the Philippines. But imprisoning large groups of people has a long history, predating capitalism by many centuries. And of course, it is not just a capitalist phenomenon: witness the Soviet Gulags. Perfecting incarceration is a distinctly modern phenomenon, however, that has involved many technological developments, including the invention of barbed wire in the 1870s.

Although it is only a minimum-security prison, it would not be easy to escape from Greenville. It isn't even easy to get into it or any other prison just to visit an inmate. After I returned home from my trip to St. Louis, I looked up Greenville Correctional Institution, and learned that it is one of many prisons where inmates manufacture such items as license plates and clothing for the U.S. military. Prison labor has been called "the new slavery" (Parenti, "Privatized Problems" 30). Prisoners may be eager to work, however, because they get paid and because it is less boring than rotting away in a cell. But a prisoner's pay is far below minimum wage (see Urbina).

Most prison time must be extremely boring. Perhaps that is why there are more movies about escaping from prison than about what it's like to be in prison.

Down by Law, Escape from Alcatraz, The Shawshank Redemption . . . jailbreaks are exciting and are all about freedom. The television series *Prison Break* received a Golden Globe Award nomination in 2005, and a year later won the People's Choice Award for favorite television drama. But there are also popular shows about life in prison—the HBO series *Oz*, for example, that dealt with conflicts between different groups of prisoners—Latinos, Muslims, the Aryan Brotherhood, and so forth—in a fictional prison ironically named after *The Wizard of Oz*, located somewhere near Attica with its infamous prison in upstate New York. Attica is where, in 1971, a riot took place during which 43 people were killed. MSNBC recently aired a series called *Lockup*, featuring interviews with actual prisoners—a sort of real reality show. Prison porn.

Some prisons or former prisons and jails are, like Mad Art, now tourist attractions. In Australia, which Europeans began settling in 1788 as a prison colony, several old prisons have been converted into historical landmarks and sources of genealogical information. The old prison at Port Arthur in Tasmania is especially scenic. If any of your ancestors were transported from England, Scotland, or Ireland to Australia as convicts, they may show up in one of the prison databases. Discussing "the cultural commodification of prisons" in the US, Paul Wright comments: "Chambers of commerce in Leavenworth, Kansas, and Cañon City, Colorado, compete with theme parks as tourist attractions, marketing their many prisons as must-see sites." He points out, however, that tours of prisons that are currently in use are not available:

> Instead, tourists can see prison museums and prisons that were closed due to their age. The Colorado Territorial Correctional Facility in Cañon City has a museum that displays prison memorabilia . . . and sells handicrafts made by today's prisoners. Around fifty thousand visitors pay the admission fee to visit the museum each year.
>
> *(102)*

Both prison porn in the mass media and prison tourism contribute to that all-time favorite theme in Western culture of crime and punishment, back at least to *Oedipus Rex*. That theme reduces complex social issues—class conflict, for example—to individual confrontations, with the typical but inaccurate moral that crime does not pay. This in turn allows for the comforting thought that there is nothing wrong with the societies in which crimes occur and are then (hopefully) punished. It's just that some people do bad things and deserve to be punished, including being locked up in places such as Greenville Correctional Institution.

Fencing the West

Further along on I-70 on my trip to St. Louis, passing by Cahokia Mounds historic site near Collinsville, Illinois, it occurs to me that the moment around 1893, when historian Frederick Jackson Turner announced that the western frontier had come to an end, was also the moment when much of the American West had become enclosed by barbed wire. In *Westward Expansion*, Ray Billington writes that for subduing the plains, a requisite was "efficient fencing material." According to Billington, "Struggling to keep milling steers from trampling new-planted corn, [farmers] demanded that cattlemen fence the range; ranchers answered with equal venom that farmers should protect their own fields" (600).

Joseph Glidden, a farmer from De Kalb, Illinois, is usually credited with inventing barbed wire in 1874. Soon he had a factory producing miles and miles of fencing. "Nearly 3,000,000 pounds of barbed wire fence were sold in 1876, 12,000,000 in 1877, 50,000,000 in 1879 and 80,000,000 in 1880," just six years after Glidden's invention (Billington 601). Once Glidden began to produce barbed wire, in only a couple of decades, its manufacture and sale were turning into a major, rapidly globalizing, capitalist industry.

The fencing of the American West with barbed wire and the enclosure movement in Europe starting in the late Middle Ages may seem to bear little resemblance to each other. One happened recently and rapidly, over just a few decades; the other progressed slowly, over several centuries. The recent one occurred under the aegis of capitalism; the other began as feudalism was evolving into mercantilism, which then fed into capitalism and the Industrial Revolution. But they were both versions of accumulation by dispossession. In the American West, the ranchers who could afford to fence large areas of land were similar to European aristocrats. The small-scale farmers who often also fenced their land were similar in social class terms to the peasantry. In both cases, the issue amounted to enclosing land, converting it into private property. And in both cases, the process of enclosure led to class conflict.

The fencing of the West was a continuation of the processes of conquest and settlement from the time of the first European colonies in the Americas. Native Americans had treated the territories they occupied as tribal or communal, not as private property. The closing of the frontier meant that the entire continent of North America was now dominated by the European invaders ("pioneers" or "settlers"), by private property, and by capitalism. Even the supposedly public places that came to be designated as national parks, forests, and wildlife preserves often excluded Native Americans from living and hunting there. The current attempt by Native Americans and their supporters to block the Dakota Access pipeline continues the long history of struggle against the seizure of their lands and sacred sites. Attacks by private security guards and the police have included the use of dogs, pepper spray, tear gas, rubber bullets, and razor wire fencing to keep protestors away from construction areas and machinery.

In his cultural and economic history of barbed wire, Reviel Netz writes: "Horse, steamboat, gun, railroad—as each tool of control over space reached the plains, a further step was made toward capitalism." With the replacement of bison by cattle and of Native Americans by ranchers and farmers, capitalism achieved domination of the West.[4] Most of the Western US became, in short, enclosed as someone's private property. Netz continues:

> The prehistoric bison hunt represented a precapitalist economy, with the killing limited by humans' precarious hold over their environment. The historic bison hunt by Indians represented the unstable interface of capitalist and precapitalist economies. With relatively little division of labor and thus a huge profit margin for the merchants, greed overcame reality. Extremely vulnerable in this exchange, becoming ever more dependent on American merchants, the Indians were driven to overkill and to ruin the basis for their way of life. At this point, with hardly a life left in the bison herd, Euro-American hunters, representatives of a more sophisticated capitalist system, came in to exploit what was for them merely a valuable, if dwindling, natural resource. The handling of cows, finally, represented a fully capitalist economy . . .
>
> *(15)*

The use of barbed wire to fence the American West was met with resistance, and not just by Native Americans. Fence-cutting "wars" broke out in Texas, New Mexico, and Wyoming in the 1880s. Large-scale ranchers began to fence their own and sometimes public land to enclose their herds and stop encroachments by small-scale farmers, rustlers, and squatters. According to Alan Krell, "the immediate cause of the destruction of fences in Texas was the harsh drought of 1883, which forced small landholders finally to recognize that streams and water-holes, once open to all, were now enclosed" (39). The big landowners usually did not have that problem, because their fences enclosed enough water for their cattle and horses.

In *Six and One-Half Years in Ranger Service*, Ira Aten gives an account of his role in combating fence-cutting, which sometimes destroyed many miles of fences. He planted bombs near places where they had frequently been cut. Mollie Morris's 1899 novel *The Wire-Cutters* is based on this violence over open versus enclosed land (Krell 39). *The Galveston Daily News* reported:

> Fence-cutting never would have become so great and destructive if it had not met with such popular sentiment . . . . It found its way into the fireside of every home, and the grievances of the lawless element of the communistic fence-cutters was [sic] held up in glowing colours.
>
> *(cited in Krell 43)*

There is some irony in applying the term "communistic" to Texas cowboys and small-scale farmers, who were the main saboteurs of fences. But the fence-cutters, in good populist fashion, had no trouble in identifying the fencing of the range with capitalism, and, though they probably did not use that term, the open plains with their "commons." "The Song of the Wire Cutters," published anonymously in the *Waco Examiner* in 1883, reads in part:

> What right has bloated capital
> To fence our prairies fair—
> We'll clip the insolent wire
> And make music in the air . . . .
>
> *(cited in Krell 157)*

As land was being fenced all over the West, Native Americans were being killed or corralled onto reservations, another form of enclosure not that much different from concentration camps.[5] The question of "Indian removal" in the early history of the United States was not just about "taming the savages," but was very much about gaining access to valuable land and resources. After passage of the Indian Removal Act of 1830, supported by President Andrew Jackson, the most infamous episode was the Cherokee "Trail of Tears" in 1838, but there were many such "trails." The Cherokees were one of the five "civilized tribes," along with the Seminoles, Chickasaws, Choctaws, and Creeks. Many Cherokees had become literate; they even produced a newspaper published in the Cherokee language. A few, like their principal chief John Ross, had become wealthy plantation and slave owners. Nevertheless, the Cherokees were forced to leave their ancestral lands and move west, Ross among them. The death toll among all of the uprooted tribes was huge; among the Cherokees, perhaps one-quarter of them died en route to the so-called Indian Territory west of the Mississippi. Although some escaped the roundup, those captured by the U.S. Army were imprisoned before they were force-marched for hundreds of miles, most of the survivors winding up on reservations in what is now Oklahoma. The discovery of gold on Cherokee land in Georgia made their removal virtually inevitable (Dunbar-Ortiz 111–113; Howe 356–371). Similar land-grabs occurred throughout the eighteenth and nineteenth centuries. In Indiana, the Potawatami "Trail of Death" cleared the way for my paternal great-grandfather, Washington Patrick, among other white settlers, to homestead in the 1830s on what had been Potawatami land.

Barbed wire plays an important role in Leslie Marmon Silko's novel *Ceremony*, about the Laguna-Pueblo people in the southwestern US. Apart from racial and cultural hostilities among the characters, one of the obstacles confronting the protagonist Tayo is quite literally barbed wire. During World War II, when Tayo and his brother Rocky are captured by the Japanese, they kill Rocky, after which Tayo winds up in a prison camp surrounded by "barbed wire enclosed in many more layers of barbed wire . . ." (49). Later, as Tayo searches for his grandfather's lost or stolen spotted cattle, he discovers them headed south, toward Mexico, on the other side of a line of fence stretching for huge distances through the desert:

> He rode miles across dry lake flats and over rocky *cerros* until he came to a high fence of heavy-gauge steel mesh with three strands of barbed wire across the top. It was a fence that could hold the spotted cattle. The white man, Floyd Lee, called it a wolf-proof fence; but he had poisoned and shot

all the wolves in the hills, and the people knew what the fence was for: a thousand dollars a mile to keep Indians and Mexicans out; a thousand dollars a mile to lock the mountain in steel wire, to make the land his.

(142)

Moreover, it isn't just Floyd Lee who has fenced the land: "Hundreds of miles of barbed-wire fence marked boundaries and kept the cattle and horses from wandering . . ." (142).

Toward the end of the novel, at an abandoned uranium mine also fenced in by barbed wire, Tayo witnesses the murder of his friend Harley by Emo, Pinkie, and Leroy. Before he dies, Harley is strung up on the fence and tortured, as if crucified. The "destroyers," including the drunken Indian veterans that have it in for Tayo because he is a "halfbreed" and who kill Harley instead, are destroying themselves, although the ultimate destroyer is the white man's A-bomb that the uranium was used to manufacture. As Silko implies, barbed wire has been an accomplice of the bomb and of human self-destruction. After the drunken vets have destroyed each other, the ancient ceremony Tayo has been gradually learning reaches fulfillment: he has rediscovered traditional ways that enable him to regain his sanity. Although tragic, *Ceremony* ends with the death of "witchery" at least locally. "Witchery" in general means modern life under capitalist domination.

Penitentiaries, Gulags, concentration camps, and reservations are obviously institutions for corralling large groups of people, fencing them off from the general population. Although these modes of enclosure are typically state institutions, they nevertheless serve capitalist interests, in the case of Indian reservations that aided and abetted the general enclosure of the Western US. The reservations were not exactly prisons, though their borders were typically patrolled by the U.S. Army. What happened if, as the expression has it, you "wandered off the reservation," as Tayo is doing in *Ceremony* when he cuts the fence to retrieve his grandfather's spotted cattle? Tayo gets away with it; but if a band of Indians left a reservation in the late 1800s, they were "presumed to be at war and therefore subject to military reprisal" (Berkhoffer 168). The antithesis to the story of the near-extermination of the Indians and the corralling of their remnants onto reservations is, of course, the myth of the free, white cowboy, riding the open range. So what if sometimes a cowboy gets drunk and shoots up a saloon, thus landing in jail? That just adds to the excitement.

The Great Wall of America

The great arch in St. Louis, overlooking the Mississippi River, marks the boundary between the Eastern United States and the West, that vast territory that had once belonged to Native Americans, and then for a short while, less than two decades, to an independent Mexico. Fencing the West continues today in part through the futile attempt to "secure" the U.S. border with Mexico to prevent the influx of Mexican and Central American immigrants. As the immigration crisis stews in

Congress, billions of American dollars and Mexican pesos are expended on the failed "war on drugs," fueling the private prison industry on this side of the Rio Grande, while billions more are spent in the absurd attempt to beef up the border patrol and erect the Great American Wall. Currently, President Trump is claiming he will build an impenetrable wall and make Mexico pay for it. The border is already "a militarized space," writes Antony Lowenstein, "where corporations, including arms manufacturers Raytheon, Lockheed Martin, and Boeing, as well as the leading Israeli arms company Elbit Systems, [have] earned billions of dollars trying to keep immigrants out" (194).

In *By the Lake of Sleeping Children*, Luis Alberto Urrea writes about German delegates to a conference on immigration who were taken to see a newly constructed part of the border wall, or rather fence, in San Diego. The Germans:

> peered through the fence at the Mexicans peering back at them. The hosts, various well-meaning Saviors of the American Way, thought the practical Germans would be impressed with the brilliant engineering of the fence. Imagine their alarm when the TV cameras went on and the German spokesman, visibly distressed, turned away from the border and said into the mike, "We tore down *our* wall," and walked away.
>
> *(14)*

Besides the billions that building the wall is costing American taxpayers, there are major environmental costs. There are also major costs in human lives and suffering. By no means has the Great American Wall and Fence (it is both) completely shut off the flow of the undocumented into the US, but it has made it more dangerous for them to cross the border in either direction.

According to Dave Shiflett, writing in *Bloomberg News*, "the Secure Fence Act of 2006 . . . created one of the most stunning boondoggles in US history." Shiflett continues:

> There's lots more holes than fence. The US-Mexican border stretches over 2,000 miles; the fence only runs along 700 of them. Part of the stretch through New Mexico, for instance, was built 6 feet into Mexican territory and had to be torn down and rebuilt at a cost of millions.

The fence has disrupted wildlife but has done little or nothing to slow drug trafficking or to prevent terrorism, which, contrary to some immigration opponents such as Tom Tancredo, does not enter the US from Mexico. "Footage from cameras posted along the fence show people scaling it with little trouble," Shiflett says; "in a truly hilarious scene [shown in a television documentary], a pickup truck roars up a ramp and flies over the barricade as if hellbent for Los Angeles in time for the cocktail hour."

Even if they can't be cut or forcefully breached, walls and fences can always be circumvented. When she was head of Homeland Security, Janet Napolitano declared, "Show me a fifty-foot wall and I'll show you a fifty-one-foot ladder." A portion of the Great American Wall extends into the ocean between Tijuana and San Diego, but not very far; it would not take much to sail around it and find landing sites to the north. In *Borderlands/La Frontera*, Gloria Anzaldúa writes:

> The sea cannot be fenced,
> *El mar* does not stop at borders.
> To show the white man what she thought of his arrogance,
> *Yemaya* blew that wire fence down.[6]
>
> *(3)*

And just how ludicrous and hypocritical is it for thousands of U.S. citizens to flock to Mexico on vacation or for business, easily crossing the border, while also depending on the cheap labor supplied by undocumented workers on their farms and in their homes and businesses to the north? When Alabama recently passed a strict-on-immigrants law and hundreds of Mexicans and Central Americans left that state, farmers raised a ruckus because they could not get their crops harvested.

Hundreds of U.S. businesses and industries have moved south of the border, into the *maquiladora* area, in such cities as Reynosa, Tijuana, and Ciudad Juárez—close enough to the border so the non-Mexican managers can still live north of it, crossing it legally and easily every morning to go to their places of work. Meanwhile illegal capitalist enterprises—drug cartels, human smuggling, sex trafficking, gunrunning—have flourished, along with, of course, the ever-mushrooming border patrol. The chief motive for U.S. businesses moving to Mexico and many other parts of the world has been "the race to the bottom" to find the cheapest laborers they can. Meanwhile, thousands of Mexicans travel north in search of work in the US. If they are undocumented, they may land in one of the many detention centers, often constructed and run by private prison corporations, where again there are millions to be made through caging people.

Mexicans on both sides of the border are getting screwed, just as Mexico itself was screwed after its defeat in the American-Mexican War of 1846–1848. The Treaty of Guadalupe signaled one of the biggest land enclosures in history, surrendering half of Mexico's territory that would become most of the Western US. It is no wonder that today "the prime distinguishing characteristic of the Mexican economy is inequality," writes John Gibler; "Mexico contains one of the greatest, most obscene, gulfs between its wealthiest and most destitute citizens of all the nations on the planet" (*Mexico Unconquered* 94). In regard to income inequality, however, the US is well on its way to catching up with its southern neighbor.[7]

As to the failed war on drugs, on both sides of the border many Mexicans and U.S. citizens profit mightily from narcotics trafficking. The Great American Wall is a wonderful aid to that trafficking. Though Mexicans also consume illegal drugs, most of the profits come from the epidemic of drug addiction north of the Rio Grande. "A study by the Mexican government found that the country's economy would shrink by 63 percent if the drug business were to disappear," Gibler writes in *To Die in Mexico*; "Mexico is the largest foreign supplier of marijuana and methamphetamines to the United States and is responsible for 70 to 90 percent of all the cocaine that enters the country" (55). The same study estimated that the U.S. economy "would shrink by 19 to 22 percent without the drug business" (310 n. 16). In short, precisely because of the war on drugs and the Great American Wall, both the narcotics trade and the prison-industrial complex are flourishing and proving to be indispensable factors in both nations' capitalist economies. And so, of course, is the manufacturing and sale of barbed wire.

After the Western frontier in the US shut down—that is, after most of the land west of the Mississippi had been enclosed by barbed wire or other means—there was still *el mar*, the Pacific Ocean, unfenceable, as Gloria Anzaldúa says. But with the U.S. involvement in Hawaii and then its invasion of the Philippines, the frontier—and the expansion of the American empire—moved offshore. It was during the war in the Philippines in the early 1900s, moreover, that the US imitated the Spaniards in Cuba and the British in the Anglo-Boer War by establishing its first concentration camps—first, that is, unless Indian reservations and slave barracoons are viewed as concentration camps. Some historians say that the invasion of the Philippines was the start of American imperialism, although others say the entire expansion westward after the Revolutionary War, pursuing Manifest Destiny, was empire-building. What else could that huge enclosure, the Louisiana Purchase, be called? Jefferson bought all that territory from Napoleon; nobody asked the Native Americans. And the Louisiana Purchase was followed a few decades later by the war with Mexico. Nobody asked either the Mexicans or the Native Americans for their approval.

From the 1500s to the present, capitalism and Western imperialism have wreaked havoc on much of the rest of the world, including, as Eqbal Ahmad puts it, "the genocidal destruction of grand civilizations," such as "the great Mayas, the Incas, Aztecs, and the Indian nations of North America." Of course, the Native American empires, such as the Greek and Roman ones, were forged through warfare and the dispossession of the conquered. History is largely a record of empires cannibalizing weaker societies, including older, weaker empires. As capitalism and Western imperialism developed in tandem from the Renaissance forward, both American hemispheres, much of Asia, most of Africa, and Australasia were enclosed by the European powers. "These were the centuries that witnessed the transformation, forced and bloody, of land and labor into commodities in the capitalist sense of the word," Eqbal points out; "Slavery was but one manifestation of this reality; the conversion of common land into individual estates, the wholesale dispossession of nations and peoples were the other manifestations" (cited in Bennis 10).

Enclosing land in Europe starting at least as far back as the 1300s was also not a peaceful process, but frequently led to peasant rebellions. The major English plantations or estates in Ireland beginning with the Tudors involved enormous, even genocidal violence against and retaliation from the dispossessed Irish over centuries. The English regarded their opponents as savages, "the wilde Irish," and treated them just as they were beginning to treat the natives of North America. Land enclosure in Britain produced masses of refugees, "a surplus population for colonial expansion" overseas as well as a "reserve army of labor" for industrialization (Ellen Meiksins Wood 86).[8] If agrarian capitalism meant improving the land—that is, increasing its productivity and profitability in the marketplace—it also meant the eviction and often extermination of very large populations of poor people. Especially during a famine, throwing peasants off the land that their families had farmed for generations was a murderous practice, one that supports the Irish nationalist charge that the Great Famine of 1845–1850 was a genocide (Brantlinger, *Dark Vanishings* 100–104).[9]

In the Americas, Australia, New Zealand, and parts of Asia and Africa, killing or chasing "the natives" off their land, as in the case of Indian removal east of the Mississippi, was obviously a genocidal practice. Even if the aboriginal inhabitants of a desirable territory were not directly slaughtered, depriving them of the places—their commons—that had sustained them for centuries through foraging, hunting, fishing, and farming inevitably and drastically reduced their populations. Not long after the First Fleet from England arrived in Australia in 1788, the entire continent was declared *terra nullius*, belonging to nobody, as if its Aboriginal inhabitants had never existed. In *The Destruction of Aboriginal Society*, C. D. Rowley speculated that, as the first Australians fled into the interior of the continent to escape the European invasion, "possibly more people died from the direct and indirect effects of starvation than from . . . newly introduced diseases or the use of the gun" (7).[10] But the use of the gun was also widespread.

Notes

1 The constitutions of all the states require that their governments provide public schools for everyone. Yet the appointment of Betsy DeVos as Secretary of Education by President Trump signals a full-scale attack by the federal government on public education. DeVos is a billionaire leader of the corporate movement to privatize public education.
2 In the run-up to the 2012 presidential election, Newt Gingrich proposed colonizing the moon. David Bollier reports that "the financial industry is now trying to create a futures market and derivative financial instruments for water, similar to those that exist for oil." Other natural resources are also being financialized, or in other words turned into objects of financial speculation, even though they may not yet come entirely into the possession of corporations (*Think Like a Commoner* 52).
3 Marglin cites the article by William Lazonick, "Karl Marx and Enclosure in England." Marglin also usefully qualifies what is meant by "the commons" in regard to the Middle Ages and after: "community-based agriculture did not mean a collectivism in which gangs of laborers plowed, harrowed, weeded, and harvested together. Much, perhaps most, of the actual work was done individually or in small groups. . . . land generally was not common property. Permanent 'commons' constituted a small part of village lands and were generally inferior lands that were not cultivated at all. In short, preenclosure agriculture was based in the community not because it was a kind of primitive communism but because it required a large measure of cooperation and mutuality" (81).
4 On the near-extinction of the bison (or buffalo) in relation to capitalism, see also Roxanne Dunbar-Ortiz, *An Indigenous Peoples' History of the United States* (142–143).
5 Dunbar-Ortiz has no hesitation in using "concentration camp" to describe the imprisonment of Native Americans even before the invention of barbed wire (138, 153).

6 Quoted with permission of Aunt Lute Books.
7 According to the most recent Gini coefficient numbers, the US ranks between Peru and Kenya in terms of income inequality.
8 At first, as Ellen Meiksins Wood explains in *Empire of Capital*, land enclosure in Europe involved changes in forms of tenancy from customary leases to "common law conceptions of exclusive private property. Leases no longer subject to the restrictions of rents fixed by custom were made responsive to the market" (76). The process was gradual, and did not always involve the violent eviction of peasants from their homes and land that they had previously understood was theirs by custom. But often the process was violent, "driving small producers off the land and excluding the community from [the] regulation of production" (77). The history of land enclosure in both Europe and the Americas reveals that changes in land possession and land use have typically been met with resistance, as in the Texas fence-cutting war.
9 In commenting on Marx's theory of "primitive accumulation," which is also the "accumulation by dispossession" of those who had previously owned or controlled land or other resources, David Harvey notes that Marx, however critical he may sound about the "expropriation of the people," was not nostalgic about a return to pre-capitalist times. For Marx, the way forward—progress—lay through capitalism, no matter what the consequences (Harvey, *The Enigma of Capital and the Crisis of Capitalism* 249).
10 In the Australian context, Doris Pilkington's book *Follow the Rabbit-Proof Fence* became famous after it was turned into a movie in 2002 that was shown around the world. In it, the fence supposedly encloses rabbits, but also serves as a guide for two of the three Aboriginal sisters, escaping from a prison-like boarding school, to find their way 800 miles back to their mother. In the early history of the European takeover of Australia, the first settlement at Botany Bay in 1788 was a prison colony, and others soon followed. In a sense, for several decades, the entire continent served as a prison (e.g., see Hughes). Fences were hardly necessary: the ocean and the outback served that purpose. Those convicts who escaped from the early prison camps may have found freedom, but life in the outback was not necessarily preferable to life in the camps. In Marcus Clarke's great crime novel *For the Term of His Natural Life* (1874), the tale of five convicts who escape from Macquarie Harbor in Tasmania is one of unmitigated savagery: they cannibalize each other in order to survive. Gabbet, the most savage convict of them all, is alone when he is recaptured, carrying an axe and a bag of human flesh.

2
URBAN SPACES

"Monstrous paradises . . . presume sulfurous antipodes."
— *Mike Davis and Daniel Bertrand Monk*

As the epigraph from Davis and Monk about heavens and hells suggests, urban spaces today exhibit the extremes of economic inequality, from mansions to slums. Thinking along similar lines about urbanization, Fredric Jameson starts his major book on postmodern culture this way: "Postmodernism is what you have when the modernization process is complete and nature is gone for good" (ix)—that is, when nature is completely enclosed, bought up by corporations, and turned into factory farms and megacities with their gigantic skyscrapers, parking lots, and landfills. Will the conquest and commodification of nature mean the end of the human species as well? There are many prognostications these days about the sixth or Anthropocene extinction, which could—mainly because of global warming—end all life on earth. But more about that bleak prospect in later chapters.

Jameson's diagnosis of the postmodern condition covers many cultural genres, but one he considers especially symptomatic both of modernity and of postmodernity is architecture. Its close connection to economic as well as esthetic factors makes it so.[1] If the skyscraper was emblematic of modernity, then buildings such as the Bonaventure Hotel in Los Angeles, Jameson contends, are emblematic of postmodernity. From the outside, its "glass skin" is impenetrable—you can't see into it because it reflects back to the observer only what is external to it: "the glass skin achieves a peculiar and placeless dissociation of the Bonaventure from its neighborhood." Inside it is a pleasure palace, rather like a people-friendly aquarium, especially for those staying there, catering to all of their needs and wants. The escalators and elevators, moreover, "account for much of the spectacle and excitement of the hotel interior" (42). Yet this example of "postmodern hyperspace" is disorienting in a variety of ways, Jameson muses, and therefore represents "the incapacity of our minds . . . to map the great global multinational and decentered communicational network in which we find ourselves caught as individual subjects" (44). Trump Tower may not be an obvious example of postmodern architecture, but insofar as it symbolizes a new "post-truth" era, it is perhaps ultra-postmodern. To cite another genre that Jameson emphasizes, the series of movies about *The Matrix* depict us all as enclosed in just such a disorienting, decentered communicational network.

"Postmodernist buildings," Jameson declares, "celebrate their insertion into the heterogeneous fabric of the commercial strip and the motel and fast-food landscape of the postsuperhighway American city" (61). Despite the "postsuperhighway" context of that remark, Jameson focuses mainly on the details and special effects of individual buildings. Focusing on cities themselves, however, whether Las Vegas or Detroit or Beijing, as Mike Davis does in *City of Quartz* and *Planet of Slums*, shifts the kaleidoscope. For one thing, a new building—whatever its architectural style, use, or context—is always surrounded by older buildings, at least in urban centers. It is as much the mixture of old and new, emphasized by Jonathan Raban in *Soft City*, that characterizes those centers (no matter how decentered they have become).

While the capital of my home state, Indianapolis, has been sprawling outwards in all directions in the last several decades, isolated buildings near the city limits have sprouted up in what were once corn or soybean fields. But then more buildings appeared around them, often with reflective, postmodern façades such as the Bonaventure Hotel. Where once were farms, now there are corporate headquarters frequently surrounded by new housing developments and shopping malls. In regard to decentering, it is now possible to live within the city limits and never have to go downtown: just go to the closest mall. Yet many people are moving out of the suburbs back into the city's center. In many cities, gentrification "is dispersing the urban poor into overcrowded suburban ranch houses," writes Barbara Ehrenreich, "while billionaires' horse farms displace the rural poor and middle class" (35).[2] Displacing them to where? Often back into urban centers, onto the streets and into homeless shelters.

Security or insecurity?

Other commentators besides Jameson have made architecture central to their ideas about postmodernism. I have in mind Robert Venturi (*Learning from Las Vegas*), Michael Sorkin (*Variations on a Theme Park*), and Nan Ellin (*Architecture of Fear*), among others. Venturi illustrates the "populism" Jameson finds in much postmodern architecture: the built environment should be fun and familiar rather than threatening in its assertion of mastery, and not at all concerned with originality. The garish neon signs and kitsch buildings, as with Caesar's Palace in Las Vegas, should be an architect's guide, much as Disney cartoons and Campbell's soup cans have provided models for postmodern artists Roy Lichtenstein and Andy Warhol.[3] The contributors to Nan Elin's anthology, however, stress a quite different aspect of present-day architecture: the widening social class and racial divisions in the US that have led to gated communities and a massive home security industry. Sorkin's essays stress both aspects of contemporary architectural developments—both the fun factor and the fear factor. By shutting out the neighborhood around it and creating a pleasure palace inside, the Bonaventure Hotel also illustrates both factors: the near-total separation of its interior from the decaying city around it, or in other words the separation between the haves and the have-nots of Los Angeles.

In that regard, the Bonaventure shares with another type of postmodern architecture, the gated community, its participation in what has been called "fortress America." There are major parts of the cities that I know best—Indianapolis, St. Louis, Chicago—that I have never visited. It isn't that those areas are closed off to me or anyone else, but they are neighborhoods occupied by the poorest inhabitants. In contrast, some of the areas where the richest reside are closed off unless you can identify yourself as a resident or a legitimate visitor. Many of the poorest city dwellers are, needless to say, African-Americans and Latinos. Today, their neighborhoods are not always within the inner city, because, as Ehrenreich indicates, some neighborhoods close to city centers have been gentrified while some suburbs have become new ghettos. So, for example, Ferguson, Missouri, where unarmed, black teenager Michael Brown was shot by white policeman Darren Wilson on August 9, 2014, is an incorporated area about five miles from downtown St. Louis and about six miles from Mad Art. Ferguson used to be mostly white, but is now mostly African American. Michael Brown's death was one of many recent police shootings of young black men demonstrating that racism is alive and well in America, and that has given rise to the Black Lives Matter movement.

That movement has inspired calls for "community policing" in many cities. One implication is that community needs to be restored not just by the police, but by the cities themselves. In their contribution to *Architecture of Fear*, Edward Blakely and Mary Gail Snyder argue that the "economic segregation" involved in gated and walled communities "undermines the very concept of civitas, organized community life" (85).[4] They add that "the American middle class is forting up," enclosing themselves in homes protected by security systems, by walls and fences, and sometimes by private guards. But "middle class" in their statement may be a misnomer, because that class, as many commentators have pointed out, is rapidly disappearing.

So where do the 1 percent live? They often own multiple homes, and typically their residences are both luxurious and thoroughly secure against intrusions from the outside. Besides Trump Tower, Trump's Mar-a-Lago estate in Palm Beach is exemplary: you can join the private club there for $200,000 a year. And if you don't belong or aren't invited, you will not get in. On the Internet, The *Pinnacle List* presents the top 10 most secure homes for 2014, including the Raptor Residence. It is:

> a palatial 18,500 sq. ft. luxury Hawaiian tropical estate owned by Michael Dell, the billionaire founder, chairman and CEO of Dell Inc. The luxurious 7 bedroom, 9.5 bathroom home is situated on a 189,704 sq. ft. oceanfront property in the private luxury residential gated community of Kukio on the Kona Coast of the Big Island in Hawaii.

Needless to say, you can't just go up to it, ring the doorbell, and expect Michael Dell to answer. Also making the top 10 list is the Safe House Estate, "a fortified mansion with extreme security on top of the Hollywood Hills":

> This five-story mansion with a dominant ridge-top location . . . has been called one of the safest homes ever built. Designed by world-renowned security expert, Al V. Corbi of SAFE-US, the home is a modern day fortress. It includes not just one panic room, but a fortified "safe core" that isolates an entire floor of the home, providing the owners with extreme security protection. Discreet protection measures envelope the estate providing privacy, security, and luxury, all within the confines of the 11,000 sq. ft. residence with a rooftop helicopter pad that enjoys one of the most prominent 360-degree citywide panoramic views of Los Angeles.
> *(Pinnacle List)*

It is hard to see how any dwelling on a ridge over the San Andreas fault could be "one of the safest homes ever built," but maybe when the shaking starts the helicopter perched on the roof provides the answer.

At the opposite end of the social class spectrum, there are the homeless (see Chapter 9 on "disposable people"), and also slums and housing projects. Some projects are surrounded by chain-link fences topped by barbed wire and are overseen by surveillance cameras. Some of them also have regular police or safety patrols within the buildings, but that is as much to control the residents as to prevent intruders from getting into them. In the HBO series *The Wire*, set largely in and around housing projects in Baltimore, the title doesn't refer to fencing material, but to the attempt by the cops to bug the drug dealers. While the neighborhoods and barrios where the poor live apparently need careful surveillance and policing, the neighborhoods, suburbs, and gated communities of the rich also need careful surveillance and policing, though obviously for different reasons.

In *Brave New Neighborhoods*, Margaret Kohn states that "almost ten percent of Americans reported that they live in communities that are surrounded by walls or fences, or where entrance is controlled by entry codes or security guard approval" (116). Kohn has in mind middle- to upper-class residents, not those who live in housing projects. The report on gated communities that Kohn cites was published in 2001; over a decade later, the signs of "fortress America" are everywhere. Especially since 9/11, both gun dealers and manufacturers and installers of home security devices are thriving.

In what might wrongly be considered the antithesis of prison porn (see Chapter 3), novels and movies about gated communities are often quite dystopian. Ideal places to live though these communities appear to be, many of the stories that are set in them feature protagonists who are struggling to escape. They never seem to be struggling to get into such communities. Are contemporary gated communities more like prisons than like happy valley, more like hell than like heaven? No doubt their developers, realtors, and perhaps many of their residents would say heaven. Again, however, a key motivation driving their construction and occupation is fear.[5]

"The security-driven logic of urban enclavization," writes Mike Davis in *City of Quartz*, "finds its most popular expression in the frenetic efforts of Los Angeles's affluent neighborhoods to insulate home values and lifestyles." He adds that "new luxury developments outside the city limits have often become fortress cities, complete with encompassing walls, restricted entry points with guard posts, overlapping private and public police services, and even privatized roadways. It is simply impossible for ordinary citizens to invade the 'cities' of Hidden Hills, Bradbury, Rancho Mirage or Rolling Hills without an invitation from a resident" (244).[6] As we shall see in the case of Hidden Hills, they are not as secure as they like to pretend. Within Los Angeles proper, "as part of a strategy of gentrification," the owners of one neighborhood:

> have decided to enclose the entire community in security fencing, cutting off to pedestrians one of the most vital public spaces along the "Miracle Mile." As a spokeswoman for the owners observed, "it's a trend in general to have enclosed communities."
>
> *(Davis,* City of Quartz *246)*

In 1992, when Davis published *City of Quartz*, there were already over 100 gated communities in the Los Angeles area. There are many more today.

Hidden Hills is featured in a 2012 article in *Forbes Magazine* entitled "America's Most Exclusive Gated Communities." Its author, Tanya Mohn, writes that Hidden Hills is an incorporated city containing about 700 homes, which sell for $3.5 million up to $13 million. Mohn quotes realtor Dana Olmes, who says: "There's a sense of normality," but it is hard to see anything normal about the lives of its rich and famous residents. "Once you get in there," Olmes adds, "you have no idea you are in L.A. I have clients who pick up their children on horseback." What's normal about that behavior? Or for that matter paying $13 million for a home in a community with only "a *sense* of normality," whatever that means, and not normality itself? "Buyers are not just buying a home. They're buying a lifestyle." And a very exclusive, abnormal lifestyle it is.

The official website for Hidden Hills states:

> Our 2,000 residents enjoy a city that has preserved a country way of life that has nearly vanished from the surrounding communities of Southern California. It boasts an authentic bucolic atmosphere as witnessed by the absence of sidewalks and street lights, the white three-rail fences, and bridle trails. Its beautiful and peaceful ambiance make it a treasured rural component of Los Angeles County and one example of small town Southern California living at its finest.

What is "authentic" about a fake "bucolic atmosphere"? And just how safe is it? Regarding security, the website's opening page announces a public safety meeting, a wildfire preparedness program, and a security service residents can purchase in addition to the one it already provides. Further along, under "crime statistics" for 2011, there were several thefts and two armed robberies, so Hidden Hills does not appear to be completely safe from intruders with bad intentions. Perhaps thieves are tempted to practice their craft there because of its "authentic bucolic atmosphere," or maybe just because of its heavy security—a challenge to any self-respecting burglar.

Not only in California, but everywhere in the world, writes Zygmunt Bauman:

> The elites have *chosen* isolation and pay for it lavishly and *willingly*. The rest of the population *finds itself* cut off and *forced* to pay the heavy cultural, psychological and political price of their new isolation. Those unable to make their separate living the matter of choice and to pay the costs of its security are on the receiving side of the contemporary equivalent of the early modern enclosures; they are purely and simply "fenced off" without having been asked their consent, barred access to yesterday's "commons," arrested, turned back and facing a short sharp shock when blundering into the off-limits regions . . .
>
> *(Globalization 21)*

And Jérome Bindé, thinking of the effects of privatization in general, speaks of "this padlocked garden where one would like to forget the snubs of real History" (cited in Ellin, "Shelter" 33). Perhaps there have always been gated communities and padlocked gardens, back to the Garden of Eden. Heaven has also, since time immemorial, been imagined as a gated community. Do St. Peter and the angels serve as security guards, keeping out the unrepentant and undeserving? It seems likely that hell is quite heavily guarded, too, only this time to prevent anyone from escaping.[7]

Are there any totally secure, crime-free gated communities? "The ambiguous and spotty successes and failures of gates and barricades as crime control measures," write Blakely and Snyder in *Fortress America*, "indicate that although people may feel safer, they probably are not significantly safer" (128). Green Valley, near Las Vegas, in the 1990s experienced a domestic murder, robberies, the crimes of a serial rapist, drug abuse among its school children, and pollution from a chemical plant in its vicinity (65). Whether they work or not, security measures such as fences and guards are always symptoms of insecurity and fear.

The security of all gated communities was called into question by the February 26, 2012 shooting of teenager Trayvon Martin by George Zimmerman, who was acting as an amateur guard for the Retreat at Twin Lakes community in Sanford, Florida. The unarmed Trayvon, who happened to be African American, was visiting his father and had been there several times in the past. He was not an intruder and posed no threat until Zimmerman confronted him. A commentary on the case in *The New York Times* declared that "gated communities churn a vicious cycle by attracting like-minded residents who seek shelter from outsiders and whose physical seclusion then worsens paranoid groupthink against outsiders" (Benjamin).

The futuristic and thoroughly dystopian gated communities—"burbclaves" such as "the Mews at Windsor Heights"—in Neil Stephenson's cyberpunk novel *Snow Crash* express the same sort of paranoid groupthink evident in actual instances, only magnified. The burbclaves, which are also "city-states," are guarded by private security firms such as MetaCop. They are "so insecure, that just about everything, like not mowing your lawn, or playing your stereo too loud, becomes a national security issue" (45). They are also the remnants of nations, which have been turned into "Franchise-Oriented Quasi-National Entities" (FOQNEs) that operate as gated communities. Besides outfits such as MetaCop, they have other cybernetic and cyborgian forms of security, presumably protecting them from violence and criminality, even though the Mafia has taken over pretty much everything, including the pizza business. Mr. Lee's Greater Hong Kong, for example, "the granddaddy of all FOQNEs," is guarded by "Rat Things," which are mutant pit bulls powered by nuclear batteries. These ferocious cyborgs move so quickly they have almost never been seen (89–98). Mr. Lee's Greater Hong Kong is itself "a private, wholly extraterritorial, sovereign, quasi-national entity not recognized by any other nationalities and in no way affiliated with the former Crown Colony of Hong Kong" (99). "Extraterritorial" means virtual or illusory and also, perhaps, outlandish. Among many other issues, Stephenson's sci-fi fantasy raises the spectre of "private, wholly extraterritorial" communities declaring their sovereignty or "quasi-national" autonomy from any larger community such as Hong Kong or, for that matter, the US.[8]

The quintessential actual secure community may be Celebration, Florida, a town of about 8,000 inhabitants enclosed within Disney World's gates and fences. Though a thoroughly corporate enterprise, Celebration bills itself as an all-American community, just as Disney World bills itself as an all-American amusement park. And as everyone knows, Disney World may be open to the public, but only to the paying public. Writing about Celebration and "countless other new developments," Margaret Kohn notes that they:

> sell consumers the dream of a place linked together by more than proximity and property values. The icons of the village center, town hall, and neighborhood pool are powerful marketing tools that trade upon a longing for public places. This longing is fueled by the sterile, ugly, commercial spaces outside the boundaries.
>
> *(131; see also Andrew Ross)*

Inside the boundaries is attractive commercial territory for those who can afford it; outside is just more commercial territory, only in a degraded but therefore perhaps more authentic or normal form.

The retro architecture of Celebration, including white picket fences, has reminded some observers of *The Stepford Wives* and also of *The Truman Show*. In both stories, everything seems too hunky-dory to be true. In both, paranoia creeps up on the protagonists, who discover they are living in artificial worlds. Inside their gated community, the Stepford wives may once have been human, but they have been turned into beautiful, docile robots by the men who live there. (The "Desperate Housewives" of television fame live in a gated community called "Fairview." Psychologically they may be robots, but they aren't docile.) The movie version of *The Truman Show* was filmed in Seaside, a privately owned (though not gated) community located in the Florida panhandle. "Seahaven" where Truman Burbank lives is, however, the illusory version of such a community, enclosed in a huge dome, supposedly somewhere in the Los Angeles area. Without his knowing it, Truman's entire life is being filmed as a reality TV show. Not coincidentally, his last name echoes Burbank, California, often called the media capital of the world. The actual town of Seaside is quite proud of its connection to the movie. Its official website announces that "The movie has had a lasting legacy. Location fees paid by Paramount pictures [have] helped to build the Seaside [charter] School. . . . For those who've never been here, the movie put Seaside on the map. The rest of us, of course, know it was already here"—already here, that is, since 1981, when its construction began, financed by entrepreneur and landowner Robert Davis. Does it seem eerie to the actual residents of Seaside that they live in a real place that has served as the illusion of a real place in a dystopian movie about a reality TV show that has enclosed its protagonist's real life in a gigantic dome?

Gated communities often contain a variety of amenities such as parks or swimming pools, so residents don't have to venture outside their boundaries in search of amusement. In some of them, they don't have to venture outside for any of their daily routines unless they choose to do so. Nevertheless, Ehrenreich notes the increasing evidence that today (2008), "the paranoid residential ideal represented by gated communities may be in serious trouble" (101). There are, first, studies that show that gated communities are not much more crime-free than non-gated ones. "The security guards often wave people on in, especially if they look like they're on a legitimate mission—such as the faux moving truck that entered a Fort Meyers gated community last spring and left with a houseful of furniture" (101). Second, gated communities have been just as prone to foreclosures as non-gated ones. Ehrenreich cites a story in the *Orlando Sentinel* about how many homeowners in one gated community, unable to keep up with their mortgage payments, "are taking off and leaving behind algae-filled swimming pools and knee-high weeds" (102). For a while at least, Florida had the highest foreclosure rate of any state in the US. Ehrenreich concludes that although residents of gated communities can keep out Mexicans, African Americans, or even teenagers, "there's no fence high enough to keep out the repo man" (102).

Armies of the poor

A much different but presumably secure kind of gated community from, say, Hidden Hills is a military base. Of course, it is government-funded rather than a privatized real estate enclosure. Because defense is the only area of government that most conservatives are willing to spend tax dollars on, military bases, one might assume, would be well-endowed places for the troops to inhabit—even if not equivalent to the commercial brand of gated communities, then at least decent and comfortable. As Ehrenreich points out, however, in a capitalist country "market forces ensure that a volunteer army will necessarily be an army of the poor." She cites Senator Harry Reid of Nevada, who "reports hearing from constituents that the army now includes applications for food stamps in its orientation packet for new recruits," and she goes on to state:

> The poverty of the mightiest military machine on earth is no secret to the many charities that have sprung up to help families on US military bases, like the church-based Feed the Children, which delivers free food and personal items to families at twelve bases. Before 9/11, trucks bearing free food from a variety of food pantries used to be able to drive right onto the bases. Now they have to stop outside the gates, making the spectacle of military poverty visible to any passersby. CBS has reported that a food bank near the Miramar Marine Air Station in the San Diego area serves five hundred military families a month.
>
> *(65)*

Is a gated community whose residents need food stamps more akin to a slum than to places like Hidden Hills and Celebration, Florida? Very few soldiers on U.S. military bases anywhere in the world will ever be able to buy a mansion in Hidden Hills or purchase a home in Celebration. And of course, the crime rate on military bases is not miniscule.

In February 2005 at Fort Bragg, North Carolina, an Army Special Forces trainee, Richard Corcoran, tried to kill his estranged wife, shot and wounded another soldier, and then committed suicide. "He joins a band of brothers," wrote Karen Houppert in a *Mother Jones* article on domestic violence on military bases; "Corcoran's is the 10th fatality in a slew of domestic violence homicides involving Fort Bragg soldiers since 2002; in one six-week spree four Army wives were murdered by their husbands or ex-husbands. Including nonfatal incidents, there were 832 victims of domestic violence between 2002 and 2004 at Fort Bragg alone, according to Army figures." And in an article for *Daily Finance* in 2009, entitled "High Crimes: Military Towns Are Among the Country's Most Dangerous," Bruce Watson wrote:

> Military bases and the neighborhoods surrounding them often seem like the ultimate refuge of middle-American values [N.B.: he does not say "middle-class American values"]. Run with military efficiency and discipline, the well-trimmed yards, cleanly-paved roads and orderly layouts convey an ideal image of life as it should be: safe, peaceful and friendly.

Watson goes on to cite the mass murder at Fort Hood in November 2009, in which 13 people were killed and 30 others wounded. He adds that "some of America's military towns have crime levels that place them among the country's most dangerous neighborhoods," although he concludes that most military towns and bases are relatively safe places to live.

If military bases aren't gated communities such as Hidden Hills, neither are they slums, although most of today's volunteer army in the US come from lower-income backgrounds. In that sense, "volunteer" does not exactly mean voluntary. Discounting military bases and also gated communities, far too many Americans now live in slums. They do so today often because of the collapse of the housing market in 2007–2008. That collapse was caused by banks and mortgage companies such as Fanny Mae and Freddy Mac defrauding thousands by getting them to sign up for subprime mortgages that they later discovered they could not afford.

When the crash came and many people were evicted from their homes, the *Wall Street Journal* and other conservative outlets tried to pin the blame not on the defrauders, but upon the ignorance and irresponsibility of the people who signed up for mortgages they could not pay for (Scheer 170–176). Being evicted from your home in the twenty-first century is not much different from being kicked out of your cottage and off the land during the earliest enclosure movements.

The bursting of the housing bubble has been a major cause of the increase of both poverty and homelessness since 2007, as well as the increase in foreclosures, slum clearance, and gentrification in inner cities all across the US. In terms of the living arrangements of ordinary people in the current world of globalizing capitalism, moreover, slums are everywhere on the rise. In *Planet of Slums*, Mike Davis writes:

> There are probably more than 200,000 slums on earth, ranging in population from a few hundred to more than a million people. The five great metropolises of South Asia (Karachi, Mumbai, Delhi, Kolkata, and Dhaka) alone contain about 15,000 distinct slum communities whose total population exceeds 20 million. "Megaslums" arise when shanty-towns and squatter communities merge in continuous belts of informal housing and poverty, usually on the urban periphery. Mexico City, for example, in 1992 had an estimated 6.6 million low-income people living contiguously in 348 square kilometers of informal housing. Most of the poor in Lima, likewise, live in three great peripheral *conos* radiating from the central city . . .
>
> *(26–27)*

Slums form many of the suburbs ringing Mexico City. "Informal housing" in them can be anything from shanties to more substantial but never completely built homes—never completed, because if finished the owners would have to pay property taxes on them. The dust from this gigantic ring of slums and the hundreds of taxis that ply back and forth between the suburbs and the city is a major cause of the air pollution that plagues the entire area. So bad is the air pollution in Mexico City that one of its mayors once advocated building a gigantic fan that would blow it in some other direction than the city proper. Where? Back over the slums?

"Throughout the Third World," writes Davis, the:

> frontier of free land for poor squatters has ended: the 'slums of hope' have been replaced by urban *latifundia* and crony capitalism. The constriction or closure of opportunities for non-market settlement at the edge, in turn, has immense repercussions for the stability of poor cities.
>
> (Planet of Slums 92)

The urban population mushrooms as rural land is bought up and enclosed in factory farms or in commercial and manufacturing complexes. As peasants are forced off the land into the cities, they move into "mega-slums" that have population densities "comparable to cattle feedlots: crowding more residents per acre into low-rise housing than were in famous congested districts such as the Lower East Side [of New York City] in the 1900s . . ." (92).

Davis stresses the obvious, that slums are notable for their filth, including human excrement. Commentaries on slums from Charles Dickens's *Oliver Twist* to the movie *Slumdog Millionaire*, featuring the slums of Mumbai, or Luis Alberto Urrea's nonfiction account *By the Lake of Sleeping Children*, about garbage dump pickers in Tijuana, more than emphasize this point. Once they have crowded into cities, the new arrivals are often driven to the dumps and landfills on the outskirts while efforts of urban renewal and gentrification go forward. Bodies piled on bodies, with little room to maneuver. Don DeLillo's novel *Underworld*, focusing on the theme of waste and its disposal, also stresses that we are what we throw away but nevertheless live increasingly enclosed within, trapped by our own garbage. One of the steps Brazilian authorities took to prepare for the 2014 FIFA World Cup was to bulldoze *favelas* in Rio, Sao Paulo, and other cities, forcing their residents to move elsewhere (typically to new slums farther removed from the urban centers). They did more of the same to prepare for the 2016 Olympics, from which various corporations made millions.

At least many slum-dwellers have homes, however tiny, filthy, or ramshackle they may be. That they are often residing on land that real estate investors may suddenly decide to enclose for some other use only leads to the repetition of "accumulation by dispossession" that was taking place during the earliest enclosures. The notion that slums are forms of real estate with little or no value is belied by the very large, noxious category of slum landlords, including subprime mortgage lenders. And decisions to engage in urban renewal and gentrification may suddenly elevate the value of land where slums are currently situated. The slum-dwellers may be valueless in the eyes of high-stakes capitalists, but not the land they occupy or even the slums themselves.[9]

Slums and ghettos are outcomes of poverty, yes, but to some extent also of the desire of those moving into them to live with people like themselves. Slums are, moreover, partly the creations of the realtors and landlords who gain from them. Various other business and industrial interests encourage their growth, not least to have workers and surplus labor living close to the factory gates. City, regional, and even federal governments often conspire in their creation. One way is through policing and another is through housing policies that enforce segregation. In his history of Hell's Kitchen on Manhattan's West Side, Joe Varga recounts how, beginning in the 1800s, city officials and the police criminalized that neighborhood, making it even more undesirable than it already was for middle-class residents, partly by enclosing it, or some areas of it anyway, in "frozen zones."

> The reality and perception of criminality led city officials to attempt to solidify the porous boundaries of the Middle West Side [Hell's Kitchen] through the creation of "frozen zones," areas in which either known criminals are arrested on site, or where crime is contained through a variety of both officially condoned practices and illegal ones, such as the collecting of bribes and graft. It was the particular spatial conditions created by these police zones that contributed to the formation of shifting identity groups within these areas, and thus the production of spatial difference.
>
> *(90)*

In the nineteenth century, partly because walking was their main form of transportation, workers tended to reside close to their workplaces. In southern cities in the US after emancipation, African Americans frequently lived near the white people they worked for as servants, blacksmiths, and many other occupations. As industrialization increased, particularly in the north, the new factories relied on waves of immigrants from Europe for their labor. But with World War I, the need to increase the workforce began to draw many African Americans to Chicago, Detroit, Pittsburgh, and other industrial cities. At the same time, Jim Crow legislation was enforcing segregation in housing and cities all across the US, leading to the formation of African American ghettos in all major U.S. cities both north and south. In their study of the partitioning of cities under the impact of globalization, Peter Marcuse and Robert van Kempen examine how urban areas are stratified by both class and race, with "citadels" or "exclusionary enclaves" at the top of the hierarchy and "ethnic enclaves" followed by racialized ghettos at the bottom. An ethnic enclave they view as a neighborhood, often close to city centers, where people of a specific ethnicity have more or less voluntarily settled—"Little Italies," for example. Ethnic enclaves, they contend, are "quite different from . . . the racial ghettos of the United States or the townships of apartheid South Africa" (18). They define a ghetto as "a spatially concentrated area used to separate involuntarily and to limit a particular racially, ethnically or religiously defined population group held to be, and treated as, inferior by the dominant society." They add that "a new urban ghetto is developing, under the polarizing impact of current economic changes; we call it the excluded ghetto. It [is] a ghetto in which race or ethnicity is combined with class in a spatially concentrated area whose residents are excluded from the economic life of the surrounding society, which does not profit significantly from its existence" (19).

Although Israel Zangwill in *Children of the Ghetto* declared that "the particular Ghetto that is the dark background upon which our own pictures will be cast is of voluntary formation" (13), he was thinking of the contrast between London and the ghettos in many European cities where Jews were forced to live. But ghettos both then and today are rarely if ever of "voluntary formation," a fact suggested by the use of the term as a verb: "to ghetto" or "to ghettoize" a group means to force it into segregated, restricted living quarters or even into some sort of imprisonment. The *OED* quotes the *London Times* for February 15, 1936 concerning Jews being "ghettoed under the racial legislation" of the Nazis.

If ghettos are defined as urban spaces where people of a certain race or religion are forcefully or legally enclosed, then it can be said that not all slums are ghettos. Slums are just neighborhoods where mainly poor people—whatever their race, nationality, or religion—are crammed into cheap, shoddy housing. But slums in many American cities are of course ghettos created by racial segregation as well as by poverty. After passage of the Chinese Exclusion Act of 1882, immigration from China into the US was drastically reduced, until that nefarious piece of legislation was repealed in 1943. Nevertheless, Chinatowns had begun to form in a number of cities, most famously in San Francisco, where for years city officials restricted the area in which the Chinese were permitted to reside. The Chinatown in San Francisco is today said to be the most densely populated and largest urban enclave of Chinese people outside of China and Taiwan.

Beginning around 1900, the creation of racially segregated enclaves by real estate companies, residence rules, and homeowners' covenants in white neighborhoods, as well as by city, state, and federal ordinances, became widespread. Kenneth Clark declared in 1965 that:

> the dark ghetto's invisible walls have been erected by the white society, by those who have power, both to confine those who have *no* power and to perpetuate their powerlessness. The dark ghettos are social, political, educational, and—above all—economic colonies. Their inhabitants are subject peoples, victims of the greed, cruelty, insensitivity, guilt, and fear of their masters.
>
> *(Clark 11)*

Quoting Clark in *American Apartheid*, Douglas Massey and Nancy Denton go on to assert that "racial segregation—and its characteristic institutional form, the black ghetto—are the key structural factors responsible for the perpetuation of black poverty in the United States" (9).

The Fair Housing Act of 1968 sought to end the ghettoization of blacks, but other forces continued to restrict where they could live. Those forces have been both overt and covert, both private and public. Despite attempts starting in the 1960s to desegregate schools, today schools are as segregated as ever. And that is largely because many poor African Americans are living in inner-city ghettos that are difficult to open up to greater racial and social class diversity. So-called urban renewal after World War II, supported by federal funding, took the form of slum clearance in many cities. "But in order to qualify for federal funding," write Massey and Denton, "local redevelopment authorities had to guarantee that an adequate supply of replacement housing would be made available to displaced families at rents within their means. To satisfy the latter provision, local planning agencies turned to public housing" (55). So there sprang up the "second ghettos" of "the projects" such as Cabrini-Green in Chicago. According to historian Arnold Hirsch, who uses the phrase "second ghetto," in prompting the growth of public housing in America's inner cities, the federal government "took an active hand not merely in reinforcing prevailing patterns of segregation, but in lending them a permanence never seen before" (cited in Massey and Denton 57).

Varga notes that class struggle, whether or not exacerbated by racial conflict, often works in "the microscales of area development, as residents push for a livable environment against the desires of developers to turn a profit." This is how "the battle for urban space" takes place (29). Zygmunt Bauman likewise contends: "Urban territory becomes the battlefield of continuous space war, sometimes erupting into the public spectacle of inner-city riots, ritual skirmishes with the police, the occasional forays of soccer crowds, but waged daily just beneath the surface of the public (publicized), official version of the routine urban order" (*Globalization* 22). In terms of residential spaces, the urbanized social classes have always been divided. But the United States is a democracy, where some version of equality is supposed to be the rule, though in fact increasing inequality is the rule. "We could let the nation continue to fall apart," Ehrenreich declares, "dividing ever more clearly into the gated communities on the one hand and trailer parks and tenements on the other" (19). And that is exactly what is happening.

Malls are for everyone (who can pay)

Contemporary cities still contain spaces, both public and privately owned, where the classes and races intermingle on a daily basis. Public parks are an obvious example, though in many cities these are being squeezed out of existence by private development. Shopping malls, which used to be primarily suburban, are now springing up in downtown areas, such as Circle City Mall in Indianapolis or the corporate makeover of Union Station in St. Louis. "The malling of America," which used to occur around the fringes of urban sprawl, is now ubiquitous (Kowinski). As the centers of towns and cities become hollowed out (think of Detroit's recent bankruptcy), suburbs and their new quasi-centers have sprung up, along with shopping malls and their gigantic, often fenced parking lots, occupying countless acres of what used to be farmland and, before there were farms, the common property of Native Americans. The designers of malls try to make them appealing, comfortable spaces of consumption, but they can be disorienting because of their size and mazelike complexity. In Don DeLillo's novel *White Noise*, an elderly brother and sister get lost in a mall and wander around in it for four days, eating scraps of food from trash cans, before they finally stumble upon an exit. "As in autochthonic Los Angeles, Hell and the Mall are never more than a freeway drive apart" (Davis and Monk 17). DeLillo suggests that sometimes they are the same place.

As commercial enclosures, though they are corporately owned and managed, malls have some of the characteristics of public spaces. They typically do not allow political demonstrations, union organizing, or religious proselytizing on their premises. The same is true, of course, of the big box stores such as Meiers, Lowes, and Walmart, often constructed in the same areas as multi-store malls. Walmart arrived in Bloomington, Indiana, at least 30 years ago, building its huge store and parking lot, along with a separate, equally huge Sam's Club, on the west side of the city. Recently, the corporation decided it needed an even larger store, so it abandoned its old site (except for Sam's Club) and moved about two miles further west, where it built a "super center." Reviews of the supercenter on the Yelp website are snarky. One reads: "If you like saving money and being surrounded by malodorous, angry cretins, Walmart is the place for you! Don't worry about the fact that you're helping to destroy the American economy: you're saving money!" And a second, equally snarky review says:

> Ok—given that everyone hates Walmart and they still seem to make billions because they price stuff so cheap, I still give this place a one [presumably out of ten]. The parking lot is an awful nightmare with magic deathly one-ways that never have enough signage. I get how to miss the occasional pedestrian (when so inclined to be nice), but a head-on car is one not easy to dodge. Then you get to the acres of undecorated earth-tone-tastic agony that people call "grocery shopping." The produce sucks . . . just don't get it. The boxed and canned goods are cheaper than anywhere, which is why people go. Yes . . . they also "have everything" from photographers to haircuts to vacation packages to oil changes to diapers . . . so the convenience is there. It's great for people who don't leave their house but once a month for the necessities . . .

Even though Walmart is supposed to appeal to all classes, the sarcasm in these reviews expresses social class snobbery extending even to the parking lot. At any rate, quite apart from undermining a huge chunk of locally owned business, Walmart has enclosed a huge chunk of ground that used to be farmland, converting it into its buildings and parking lots. After the new super center opened, the original Walmart building stood vacant for several years, but has now been leased by a Rural King outlet—perhaps good for the farmers who can no longer farm on the land now enclosed by Walmart.

No matter what a given society espouses—liberty, equality, and justice, for example—mutations in spatial arrangements, including architecture and patterns of residential and commercial development, are among the clearest expressions of its values. In the case of "fortress America," besides malls, gated communities, slums, and ghettos, so-called urban renewal, which does often include plans for lower-income housing and housing projects, is now increasingly about privatizing efforts that crowd out the poor through leasing or selling off land to corporate developers. After Hurricane Katrina, the four main housing projects in New Orleans were torn down even though they were deemed still livable. The plan was to replace them with mixed-income housing units. At least 3,000 poor, mainly black people were displaced, joining the thousands of others whose homes were flooded, many of them leaving the city altogether. Much the same happened in Chicago, where the last of the Cabrini-Green project buildings was demolished in 2011. The new housing that replaced the buildings there was also aimed at mixed-income residents. As in New Orleans, many of the 15,000 poor, mainly black residents lost out. If you were poor and black, you weren't invited back. And then there is the redevelopment of the area known as the Fillmore in San Francisco, which has caused the black population of that city to drop by roughly 70 percent between 1970 and 2013. Oakland activist Tiny Gray-Garcia says that the "poverty industry" in San Francisco is tantamount to the "genocide of poor people," and especially, of course, poor black people (cited in Meronek). In the land of the free and home of the brave, there are now far too many places where the public, or a large portion of it anyway, is no longer welcome. For the future, imagine a burbclave as large as the US guarded by drones, robocops, and digital "rat things" with a sign at the entrance: "No Trespassing." Woody Guthrie had a different idea:

> Was a high wall there that tried to stop me
> A sign was painted said: Private Property,
> But on the back side it didn't say nothing—
> This land was made for you and me.

Notes

1 Jameson writes that "it is in the realm of architecture ... that modifications in aesthetic production are most dramatically visible ..." (2). Victorian art and social critic John Ruskin went further, claiming that a nation's architecture reveals its moral condition. He contrasted medieval Gothic architecture, which he equated with the creative freedom of the workers or artisans who built Gothic cathedrals, to the drab, imitative commercial buildings the Victorians were erecting, which he equated with the capitalist enslavement of workers. According to Ruskin, the Renaissance began a decline from the spontaneity, creativity, and spirituality of Gothic designs toward the mechanical deadness of the modern world.
2 On gentrification, see Peter Moskowitz, *How to Kill a City*, and Matthew Desmond, *Evicted*.
3 No doubt with Venturi in mind, Jameson speaks of Las Vegas "within the rainbow-flavor landscape of its psychedelic corporate monuments" (97). But if its architecture is "psychedelic," it is not surrealist, or rather it is "surrealism without the subconscious" (Jameson 67). One of the key attributes of postmodern architecture is, according to Jameson, similar to the postmodern paintings of Warhol, exhibiting "a new kind of flatness or depthlessness, a new kind of superficiality in the most literal sense ..." (9). This is exhibited not only by the reflective façades of a building such as the Bonaventure Hotel, but also by the apparently

classless, one-dimensional sense anyone inside a postmodern edifice has that the only thing required of him or her is simply to consider buying whatever is for sale there. Outside the streets may be desolate, with very few parks or other public amenities and with panhandlers on every corner. Inside is a commercial wonderland for those who can afford to pay for the commodities and conveniences on offer.

4 Also in *Architecture of Fear*, editor Nan Ellin writes that the "impulse to privatize is epitomized by the growth of gated communities, residential developments with patrolled entryways and a clear separation from other neighborhoods, usually by a secure fence." She goes on to mention some other versions of "privatism" such as "the inward-turning shopping mall," and notes that "All of these places are patrolled by sophisticated security systems" (33–34).

5 The Car Barn, a condominium building near Capitol Hill in Washington, DC, is surrounded by 30-foot-high fences, far higher than the ones surrounding the White House. Once fear takes hold of a community or a nation, it tends to affect all aspects of life.

6 In "Building Paranoia," Steven Flusty also describes how individual homes in the Los Angeles area, whether or not they are in gated communities or "luxury laagers," have changed over the last several decades. His use of "laager" suggests apartheid. Most of them have security systems and burglar alarms installed in them. Many of them have walls and fences around them. And many are as much hidden from view from the outside as possible. Even inside gates and walls, many of the "laagers" no longer have public spaces where people are free to stroll at their leisure. "Public open space has come under assault as privatization has reacted opportunistically to public sector penury" (50). Flusty goes on to explain how, after passage of Proposition 13 that undermined property taxes, public funding in California and Los Angeles has plunged. Schools, libraries, parks, and other publicly funded entities are all giving way to various forms of enclosure or privatization.

7 In his contribution to *Architecture of Fear*, Peter Marcuse writes: "One may imagine that walls were not really needed within the Garden of Eden, just as clothes were not needed. But the Garden of Eden, if medieval paintings are to be believed, did have a wall around it; indeed, etymologically, a garden is an 'enclosed place,' and the word for 'garden' and the word for 'fence' or 'wall' are directly related in many languages (as, indeed, is 'town' with '*Zaun*,' the German word for 'fence')" (103).

8 Even in China, Mike Davis notes in *Planet of Slums*, "the gated community has been called the 'most significant development in recent urban planning and design'" (115). If you can afford it, you can live in "Orange County," for example, a gated community outside Beijing, perhaps not all that different from Greater Hong Kong in *Snow Crash*.

9 David Harvey comments: "The actual or attempted expulsion of low-income and vulnerable populations from high-value land and locations through gentrification, displacement, and sometimes violent clearances has been a long-standing practice within the history of capitalism. It unites those residents of Rio de Janeiro's favelas subject to evictions, the former occupants of self-built housing in Seoul, those moved through eminent domain procedures in the United States, and the shack-dwellers in South Africa" (*Seventeen Contradictions and the End of Capitalism* 99).

3
CAGING PEOPLE
From schools to prisons

"Today schools are but training grounds for prisons."

— *Mumia Abu-Jamal*

Mumia Abu-Jamal's statement stresses the contradictory links between the education system in the US and the prison-industrial complex. Schools should be "training grounds" to teach all students how to be law-abiding, productive citizens. But for many students, schools have the opposite effect.

Although there is nothing stylistically remarkable about Greenville Correctional Institution, current architectural developments include the prison boom that has accompanied mass incarceration in the US. According to Marc Mauer of the Sentencing Project, "While the philosophical and stated goals of the prison have fluctuated, the basic concept of imprisoning people in cages remains the central feature of the system," and has done so at least since the early 1800s. He adds that "it is a bit jarring . . . to speak of 'caging' human beings, since we normally prefer to use this term for animals and to conjure up fond feelings for our favorite zoo . . ." (4). True enough, although one thing that has changed since the 1800s is the role of corporations in the "prison-industrial complex." Today, prison corporations are eager to build and operate people cages or to privatize already existing facilities, and thus—supposedly—save state and federal governments lots of money. But it turns out they are less safe and more expensive than state and federal institutions.

Greenville prison, exemplifying "the architecture of fear," was constructed in 1994, during the height of the prison construction boom. That year, President Clinton signed into law the Violent Crime Control Act that greatly increased incarceration rates for minor drug offenses. Clinton has recently acknowledged that the Act damaged or destroyed many lives—not his own life, of course. The Greenville prison is about 50 miles east of St. Louis, just outside the small town of 7,000 mostly white citizens for which it is named. Located in the town is Greenville College, a Methodist school with approximately 1,600 students, slightly more than the number of inmates in the prison. Tuition and fees for an undergraduate are currently $33,376 per year to go to the college, which is about what it costs to keep a prisoner in the correctional facility.[1] Constructing prisons in or near rural towns such as Greenville has become a familiar result of the "war on crime" (or "war on drugs"—they are virtually identical) that began during Richard Nixon's presidency and increased in intensity during those of Ronald Reagan and Bill Clinton.

Introducing *Prison Profiteers*, Tara Herivel writes that starting in the 1970s, the United States "embarked upon an unparalleled experiment in industrialized mass imprisonment" (ix). In the early 1970s, there were approximately 300,000 inmates in U.S. prisons. That number increased to more than a million by 1990. At its peak in 2009, 2.5 million people were incarcerated in America. Combined with the numbers in immigration, military, and juvenile facilities and those under versions of probation and house arrest, the total was then at least 7 million (x). The prison population has declined slightly each year since 2009, but it is still much greater than 1.7 million, the approximate number of prisoners in the Soviet Gulag system in 1953, when Stalin died. The figures, which make the US, "land of the free," the world's leader in incarceration, cannot be explained by a skyrocketing crime rate: between 1980 and 2014, the general crime rate has been falling.[2] A partial explanation for the rise in mass incarceration is that corporations began to discover the many ways they could make crime pay by locking up as many people as possible.

The mass incarceration gold rush

In *Discipline and Punish*, Michel Foucault declared that post-revolutionary France was no longer a society of "spectacle," but rather a society of "surveillance" (217). Today, throughout Europe, North America, and the rest of the world, it is both. Legal punishment may now be largely hidden behind prison walls, so it would seem to be no longer part of the spectacle available to the public. But all of the processes of crime, policing, and punishment are available in fictional and sometimes documentary form, in the news, in movies, and on television. As mentioned in Chapter 1, prison porn is a major feature of today's mass media. Actual crimes and trials often become mass spectacles, exemplified both by the O. J. Simpson trial and by Fox Television's 2016 remake, *The People v. O. J. Simpson*. And consider the recent phenomenon of videos of police shootings of unarmed black men and boys in U.S. cities, perhaps a version of counter-surveillance. In mass culture, spectacle and surveillance merge, as we watch ourselves, our neighbors, the police, and the entire "punitive city" we inhabit as if we were simultaneously cops and robbers, victims and criminals, prosecution and defense. Mass culture is now a large-scale, phantasmagoric "selfie" as mug shot, a version of Jeremy Bentham's panopticon in which society is both warden and prisoner.[3] But if crime and punishment is mass culture's main theme, then it isn't society who stars in the show, but only individuals.

The hegemonic ideology of crime and punishment is reinforced by countless movies such as *Dead Man Walking* and *Straight Outta Compton*, and television programs such as *Law and Order* and *NCIS*. The corporate media reinforce the belief that the main thing wrong with society is individual criminality rather than any of its societal causes, such as poverty, racism, and the war on drugs. The solution is to catch the criminals and either shoot them or lock them up.[4] The general, obvious moral is that crime does not pay, even though everybody knows it often does, especially if the criminals belong to the 1 percent or are corporate "artificial persons" (that is, corporations). Crime most often does not pay for criminals who are poor and black or brown.

In 1968, presidential candidate Richard Nixon declared, "Doubling the conviction rate in this country would do more to cure crime in America than quadrupling the funds for . . . [the] war on poverty" (cited in Kilgore 28). It was Nixon who coined the phrase "war on drugs" to contrast with Lyndon Johnson's "war on poverty." A decade or two after Nixon was elected, the number of prisoners in the US had skyrocketed. With only 5 percent of the world's population, the US has 25 percent of its prisoners—land of the free, perhaps, but home of the caged. Over half of those in lockdown are either African Americans or Latinos, so the era of mass incarceration has also been the era of "the new Jim Crow" (Alexander; see also Pager).[5] Within the criminal justice system, and more specifically within prisons, racism is rampant.

Even though he could not say so publicly, President Nixon told his chief of staff, Eric Haldeman, that "the blacks" were the main problem confronting the US (Alexander 63; Kilgore 71–72). A key way of dealing with "the blacks" was to create the Drug Enforcement Agency in 1973, scrapping the war on poverty and waging war instead on crime and drugs—an unwinnable war that Nixon and Haldeman knew full well would be fought mainly in the inner cities and "dark ghettos" of the US. It was a way, too, for Nixon to implement the Republican Party's "southern strategy," encouraging white southern voters who had long been Democrats to switch to the other side.

"Convictions for drug offenses," writes Alexander, "are the single most important cause of the explosion of incarceration rates in the United States" (78). Particularly nefarious was the campaign against crack cocaine launched in 1985. "Almost overnight, the media was saturated with images of black 'crack whores,' 'crack dealers,' and 'crack babies'—images that seemed to confirm the worst negative racial stereotypes about impoverished inner city residents" (23). *Time Magazine* in 1986 named crack cocaine America's major social problem. *48 Hours on Crack Street*, aired by CBS in the same year, won the highest ratings for any news documentary over a five-year period (Elsner 18). Among black Americans, the conspiracy theory emerged that the CIA was behind the crack epidemic, engaging in a covert form of genocide. As Alexander points out, that theory was not entirely misplaced, in part because the CIA was supporting the Contras in Nicaragua who were smuggling drugs into the US (24). What is more, penalties for the sale or use of crack cocaine were 100 percent harsher than those for powder cocaine, a drug of choice in the white suburbs. Because a lot of drug trafficking in poor neighborhoods takes place on the streets instead of behind closed doors, the war on drugs has been a major factor in putting many poor people, including many African Americans and Latinos, behind bars (Clear 55). If you are doing drugs in the safety of your home in a gated community, you are not likely to get arrested.

Some of the worst effects of the war on drugs were reversed during Jimmy Carter's administration, but starting in the early 1980s, President Reagan ramped up that war. The Drug Policy Alliance reports that between 1980 and 1997, the incarceration figures for nonviolent drug offenses jumped from 50,000 to more than 400,000 (DPA). The Anti-Drug Abuse Act, passed in 1986 during the alleged crack epidemic, established mandatory sentences for selling and using narcotics. Two years later, the Omnibus Anti-Drug Act enacted mandatory sentences for merely possessing crack cocaine and raised the bar for drug conspiracy penalties. Someone guilty of being a conspirator—often merely associating with a person using or selling narcotics—could now receive as stiff a sentence as the dealer or user. Although the Fair Sentencing Act of 2010 significantly reduced the difference in penalties between types of cocaine and eliminated the five-year mandatory minimum sentence for simple possession of crack, the number of those arrested for drug offenses remains high.[6]

The war on drugs, which has cost billions of dollars and millions of lives, is still raging on the streets and in the ghettos of America, but also in many rural, mostly white communities such as Greenville. In 2015, the woman in charge of Indiana's drug enforcement bureau reported that my home state had set the record for arrests of people cooking and using methamphetamine; many of the arrests are made in small towns or out in the country rather than in inner-city neighborhoods. The war on drugs is, however, only partly to blame for the huge upswing in incarceration. Also to blame are the contradictory desires of state and local governments both to save money and to be "tough on crime," accompanied by the goal of private prison corporations to profit from putting as many people as possible behind bars.

In the corporate world, it is hardly news that crime pays. Mauer quotes the 1996 pitch to potential investors made by a representative of one prison corporation: "While arrests and convictions are steadily on the rise, profits are to be made—*profits from crime*. Get in on the ground floor of this booming industry now" (10). Further, it isn't just the prison corporations that are benefiting from mass incarceration. "More prisoners and prisons mean more and bigger contracts for a variety of private interests traditionally involved in incarceration," writes Phillip Wood, "especially construction companies and architectural firms that have built more than a thousand prisons in the last two decades" (18).[7] Many other businesses that provide prisons, whether publicly or privately run, with everything from food and laundry to addiction therapy and weapons, have profited greatly from the burgeoning prison-industrial complex. For example, "the law enforcement technology industry, which produces high-tech items like the latest stab-proof vests, helmets, stun guns, shields, batons, and chemical agents, is worth over $1 billion a year" (Elsner 29).

The criminal justice system in America employs more people than Walmart, Ford, and General Motors combined (Loury 5). Today, correctional corporations have discovered how to squeeze billions of dollars out of building new prisons, getting state governments to pay for them, so it is in the interest of both government and the corporations to lock up as many people as possible. Often the contracts with private prison operators include clauses that the government entities who are parties to them will pay the corporations if prison beds are not filled, a built-in incentive for law enforcement to get tough on crime, even though the crime rate is falling. Corporations have also discovered how to make money through prison labor, ignoring the fact that it is a version of slave labor. Thousands of prisoners are now producing goods and services in factories enclosed in barbed wire for corporations as varied as Boeing, Starbucks, and Nintendo, among many others (Wright 111). As Alan Elsner says, "there is big money to be made in prisons," but not by prisoners (206).

The biggest winners so far in the mass incarceration gold rush are Geo and CCA corporations. "No private stakeholder has had a larger interest in the growth of the American prison system than the world's largest prison company, the Corrections Corporation of America," writes Judith Greene:

> With a market capitalization of $2 billion [in 2006], CCA runs the nation's fifth-largest penal system: sixty-three correctional, detention, and juvenile facilities with a total design capacity of approximately seventy thousand beds in nineteen states and the District of Columbia.[8]
>
> *(11)*

For the diehard believers in "free enterprise," the more that incarceration can be farmed out to private businesses such as CCA, the better. As many studies have shown, however, privately run prisons cut lots of corners to increase their profits.[9]

The guards in private facilities are less well trained and paid than those in government prisons, and the health and safety records of the private ones are abysmal. Gang behavior, often with the collusion of guards and other prison staff, increases violence, sexual abuse, and drug addiction. In *Lockdown America*, Christian Parenti writes that "private prison growth" has slowed, in large measure because "recent events have unveiled private jailers as cheats, liars and liabilities . . ." (30). He adds that "the root cause of the financial crisis facing for-profit dungeon keepers is [their] appalling disregard for basic human rights" (31). Parenti offers as an example the escape of six prisoners in July 1998 from the Youngstown, Ohio Correctional Center, owned and operated by CCA:

> the Youngstown joint . . . was plagued with problems from the moment it opened in May, 1997. Poorly constructed, understaffed and immediately filled to capacity with both medium *and* maximum security convicts, the CCA prison became a chaotic gladiator's pit . . .. The fifteen months of operations preceding the escapes had seen forty-four assaults, sixteen stabbings (including one guard), and two murders.
>
> *(32)*

It was predictable that privatization of prisons would lead to some bad outcomes. The notion that for-profit corporations can run things better and more efficiently than government agencies is backwards. The corporations are out for profits, not efficiency, and certainly not the welfare of prisoners or the safety of prison guards. Parenti quotes Lance Corcoran of the California Corrections Peace Officers Association, who says that he and members of his association call private prisons "dungeons for dollars because their allegiance is to stockholders, not to the public" (35). In the introduction to *Capitalist Punishment*, the editors write that prison corporations "have not lived up to their promises":

> They have not saved governments substantial amounts of money, nor have [their prisons] proven to be more secure. Instead, they have contributed to an unacceptable level of neglect and violence against inmates and detainees, diminished rights for the guards and other employees . . . and are set to be a heavy burden for the public purse over many years . . . .
>
> *(15)*

Serving time in prison is not supposed to be fun. Nor, however, is it supposed to include being raped by other prisoners or staff, beaten by guards for the slightest provocation, driven mad by long-term solitary confinement, or killed by medical neglect. These are the fates of thousands of prisoners every year—men, women, and juveniles enclosed in steel cages that give Gitmo and Abu Ghraib a run for their money.

While Parenti, Coyle, and many others accuse the private prison corporations of greed because they take numerous shortcuts to increase their profits, Parenti emphasizes that the huge increase in incarceration since the 1970s can be explained by "society-wide class struggle." And in the US, class struggle also involves race war. The prison-industrial complex is:

> part of a larger circuitry of social control in which the poor are blamed for their own plight, class privilege is protected by force, and a portion of the population who cannot find work because of the market economy's metabolic need for unemployment, are managed by the state with violence and incarceration.
>
> *(Parenti 36)*

Michelle Alexander, Alan Elsner, Barbara Ehrenreich, and Marc Mauer agree.[10]

If prison corporations cut corners, so too does government by signing contracts with them. Why spend money on the health and welfare of felons? Saving money is the key reason why federal and state officials turn to the corporations. But the move toward privatization has exactly the opposite effect. One way that has happened is through efforts for state and federal officials to cut down on expenses for mental healthcare. Partly inspired by Ken Kesey's 1962 novel *One Flew Over the Cuckoo's Nest*, in 1963 the Community Mental Health Centers Act began the well-intentioned effort to deinstitutionalize mental hospitals, returning patients to communities where many of them were supposed to receive treatment at either existing or newly funded clinics. But Congress never came through with adequate funding for those clinics. The result has been that prisons, whether publicly or privately run, have become de facto mental hospitals, with predictably horrific results (Elsner 81–102).

So-called "supermax" facilities now exist to keep the most violent offenders in solitary confinement for years on end, with little or no attempt to rehabilitate them. Elsner writes that:

> in the 1990s, constructing supermax prisons became the hottest trend in corrections. They were sold to voters as places that would punish the most dangerous, incorrigible, violent, worthless and evil criminals in America by holding them in places that were both appropriately harsh and perfectly secure.
> *(154)*

There are today over 60 supermax facilities in the US. Elsner notes that after a supermax has been constructed in a state, its government comes "under enormous political pressure to fill it" (158). This is true of any prison, whether constructed by the federal government, a state, a prison corporation, or a public-private collaboration.

California leads the nation both in its overall prison population and in the number of prisoners in solitary confinement—about 11,000 men and women on any given day. At Pelican Bay, the state's first and most notorious supermax prison, the 1,500 occupants of the Security Housing Unit (SHU) and Administrative Housing Unit spend 22.5 hours a day alone in windowless cells measuring about 7 × 11 feet. The remaining 90 minutes are spent, also alone, in bare concrete exercise pens. With no phone calls allowed, and only the rare non-contact visit, these prisoners have no way to access the world outside their cells except via their "feeding slots." And their only interactions with fellow prisoners consists of shouting through steel mesh until the guards order them to shut up. More than 500 Pelican Bay prisoners have lived in the SHU in excess of a decade, nearly 80 have been there for more than two decades, and one prisoner recently marked his 40th year in solitary. Two-thirds of these prisoners are serving indeterminate stints "in the hole"—not because of any misbehavior, but because corrections staff labeled them gang members or "associates" (Ridgeway and Casella).

Meanwhile, the expansion of the prison-industrial complex has had a direct economic impact on many rural communities such as Greenville. In "Banking on the Prison Boom," Judith Greene observes:

> The explicit promotion of prisons as economic development was propelled during the 1980s by the "greed is good" flamboyance that epitomized much of the investment banking industry. The spirit of freewheeling speculation and junk-bond financing entered its zenith when hundreds of tiny rural

towns, desperate to stave off economic ruin triggered by mass capital flight overseas, reversed a long-standing tradition of "not in my backyard" and jumped into cutthroat competition to win the prison sweepstakes.

(13)

The 2007 PBS documentary *Prison Town, USA* shows what has happened to many small communities during the prison boom, when "a prison opened every 15 days." It portrays how Susanville in the California Sierras went from a town that "once thrived on logging, ranching and agriculture" to one dependent on "a new correctional economy [that] encompasses not only prisoners, guards and their families, but the whole community":

> Even today, the town offers a postcard image of small-town America under majestic peaks—if you keep the prisons out of the frame. Susanville, along with much of rural America, has seen its local agricultural economy go the way of the family farm. And like other communities that don't want to become ghost towns, Susanville decided to take a chance on the only industry that came calling—California's burgeoning prison system, hungry for space, new guards and low visibility.

(POV)

But the new, privately run prisons often do not benefit rural communities as much as anticipated. They frequently hire guards and other staff members from elsewhere and also contract with outside firms for services such as food and laundry (Kilgore 46).

The mostly white employees in the new prisons, frequently drawn from farming communities, confront every day the mostly black and brown inmates who come from far away, separated from their families and cities where they once lived. One effect has been to reinforce the racial prejudices of many rural, white Americans. "At least when officers and inmates are members of the same community," writes Elsner, "they have a common language. Each knows where the other is coming from. In these new rural prisons there is a total disconnect, aggravated by mutual fear and distrust" (57).

Further, in the past, some attention was paid in the criminal justice system to rehabilitation. With privatization, however, and the "get tough on crime" policies that have been the order of the day during the war on drugs, rehabilitation has given way to far more punitive methods of incarceration. Meanwhile, calls for the total abolition of prisons have been few and far between. In *Demand the Impossible!* Bill Ayers asks, "What if we stopped tinkering with the business of caging people and abolished the prisons altogether?" (21). An excellent question. But meanwhile, "Despite a sharp national decline in crime," writes Glenn Loury, "American criminal justice has become crueler and less caring than it has been at any other time in our modern history" (10). And with Donald Trump as President and Jeff Sessions as Attorney General, the business of caging people will only get worse.

Academic cages

The 2014 police shooting of unarmed black teenager Michael Brown in Ferguson, Missouri spurred the rise of the Black Lives Matter movement. The Justice Department report on Brown's death and its aftermath revealed that Ferguson's African American residents had for years been subjected to harassment by its almost entirely white police department. That is the situation in many other poor neighborhoods, often inhabited mainly by people of color, across the US. While those neighborhoods have been a major source of the burgeoning prison population, they are also locations inadequately served not only by the police, but by the schools located in them. It is easy to blame teachers and administrators for schools that are deemed to be "failing," but a main cause of their problems is underfunding. And as has often been noted, failing schools contribute directly to the cancerous growth of the prison-industrial complex.

Traditionally, schools and prisons have been viewed as antithetical. "He who opens a school door, closes a prison," as Victor Hugo put it. Good schools hopefully prevent their students from winding up in the justice system, teaching them how to get ahead in the world in positive, productive ways. But what about supposedly bad or "failing" schools, especially in neighborhoods deeply impacted by poverty, unemployment, and racism? In the US, so-called failing schools are located mainly in inner-city, low-income, racially segregated areas, and many of them are not all that different from detention centers. Besides having high fences around them to keep intruders out and students in, today schools often have metal detectors, surveillance cameras, and security guards such as the "school resource officer" at Spring Valley High School in Columbia, South Carolina, who was recently fired for physically throwing a black girl and the desk where she was sitting out of a classroom.

While it is easy to associate failing schools with inner-city neighborhoods, the mass murders and suicides at Columbine High School in 1999 occurred in a mostly white, middle-class suburb of Denver, and that has been the case with many other school shootings, including the one in 2012 at Sandy Hook Elementary School in Newtown, Connecticut, during which 20 first-graders and six employees were massacred. Nevertheless, in many school districts, because of "zero tolerance" disciplinary procedures, a student's misbehavior results automatically in a call to the police, even if there are already security guards working in his or her school. Instead of seeking ways to help errant students, too often teachers, principals, and police take punitive actions against them. One result is that many students do not see education as a pathway to success—just more of the same: bullying by other students, teachers, and the cops, and a future of racism, poverty, and injustice.

So-called "problem students" are frequently suspended and sometimes sent to "detention schools." In such prison-like schools, many of them privately run by such outfits as Community Education Partners, "it is rare to find a rigorous remedial curriculum and highly qualified teachers," and their results—or lack thereof—increase the number of kids who drop out of school as soon as they can.[11] "And a drop-out sentence for many students is tantamount to greasing the skids for entry into the juvenile or adult criminal justice system" (Fuentes 77). This is what has come to be known as the "school-to-prison pipeline." When the experts talk about that pipeline, they generally have "failing" schools in mind (Fuentes 9; see also Kim et al.; Mallett).

It does not matter how dedicated and hard-working the teachers and administrators in those schools may be. For a wide range of reasons, having little or nothing to do with teaching or the curriculum, students often come to class expecting to fail and to drop out. This is a key way in which the social classes in America are sorted into their current hierarchy of extreme inequality and racism. For far too many students, school is something to be resisted, rebelled against. As the old Pink Floyd song has it, "We don't need no education." The 1955 film *Blackboard Jungle* was followed by many others depicting teen rebelliousness both inside and beyond schools. The 1991 movie *Boyz n the Hood* depicts the struggles of African American teens in the Crenshaw ghetto of south Los Angeles to escape their homicidal gang culture and, in the case of one character, make it through high school into college. For most of the characters, life and death on the streets wins out over school.

Writing about Nathaniel Abraham, an African American boy who at age 11 accidentally shot a neighbor in Detroit and then was put on trial for second-degree murder as an adult, Mumia Abu-Jamal says: "more and more, a juvenile is just another commodity, a body to be caged . . . . Not a person in need, not a youth to be rescued, not a life to be transformed" (115). Fuentes similarly highlights "the entrenched interests—political and economic—that together have promoted and profited from the transformation of our schools into prisonlike institutions where children are treated like suspects" (9). And when juveniles recognize that is how the system is treating them, the outcomes are often both socially and personally catastrophic, as they are for most of the characters in *Boyz n the Hood*.

One summer when I was in college, I worked with African American teenagers at Baden Street Settlement House in Rochester, New York. Those were the good kids in the hood—many of the others had joined gangs and were out on the streets. But the good kids were themselves routinely getting kicked out of school for insubordination, fighting, setting fires in wastebaskets, and the like, leading to frequent suspensions. They were all asking the same question through their behavior: what good is school if it can't get you out of the ghetto, out of poverty, and out of racism into a brighter, more prosperous future? And no more than the settlement house was school, a frequent scapegoat in our society, to blame for their situation. Their school had not failed them, but the system had. And by "system," I mean capitalism exacerbated by racism, poverty, and class conflict.

Meanwhile, there are the supposedly successful, non-failing schools, many of them in the white suburbs, such as Columbine High. Here is what musician Malvina Reynolds long ago thought about them in her song "Little Boxes":

...And the people in the houses
All went to the university,
Where they were put in boxes
And they came out all the same,
And there's doctors and lawyers,
And business executives,
And they're all made out of ticky tacky
And they all look just the same.
And they all play on the golf course
And drink their martinis dry,
And they all have pretty children
And the children go to school,
And the children go to summer camp
And then to the university,
Where they are put in boxes
And they come out all the same.

Good schools, whether public or private, work to enclose students in the mind-boxes of conformity, so that "they come out all the same," unable or unwilling to question authority or the status quo. So-called failing schools also try to put their students into boxes of conformity, but the trouble is many of their students realize that conforming to the existing capitalist and racist system is not going to get them anywhere. The system has failed them, their friends, and their families, so why should they follow its rules? Perhaps the majority of Americans would not identify the system with capitalism, but that is its economic base, the machinery that encloses us all in boxes, both mental and physical, of many shapes and sizes, including both schools and prisons. On the *Democracy Now* broadcast for September 9, 2015, Robert Reich declared that "the system"—he also meant capitalism—"does not work for most people." That was an understatement.

The Vera Institute of Justice found that in 2012, the average national cost to keep a person in prison for a year was $31,286, almost exactly what it costs to go to Greenville College for a year. In contrast, the Department of Education reports that the average cost per student in the nation's public schools is about $12,000. So if schools really were the antidote to crime and prison, it would make sense to spend a lot more on education. But even the best schools cannot overcome the economic and social disadvantages into which many children—particularly black and brown children—are born. Meanwhile, just as it is in the prison industry, the pressure is on throughout the US to privatize public schools.

The first step toward privatizing schools was to mount a campaign that insisted there was a crisis in public education, one that had serious implications regarding America's global competitiveness and national security. It proved easy to scapegoat public education for poor results leading to high crime rates, widespread drug abuse, and overcrowded prisons. Rather than poverty, unemployment, and continued racial segregation, the main causes of the crisis in the public school system were supposedly ineffective teachers, principals, curricula, and parents. In 2001, the administration of President George W. Bush instituted "No Child Left Behind," starting a new national regimen of standardized testing in reading and mathematics, and also of teacher and school accountability. Under President Obama, that regimen has been ratcheted up by the "Race to the Top" program overseen by Secretary of Education Arne Duncan. The Secretary of Education in the Trump Administration, Betsy DeVos, is a champion of charter schools, home schooling, and school vouchers. She is pushing for the privatization of all public schools.

"Teaching to the test" is now the order of the day. As many teachers and parents have complained, standardized testing reduces the time spent in schools on such supposedly marginal subjects as history, music, and health and safety. It also militates against developing the critical faculties of students, keeping them from thinking on their own about, for example, the causes of poverty and crime (e.g., see Giroux). According to Diane Ravitch in *Reign of Error*:

> By the year 2014, all students were supposed to achieve proficiency on state tests. The states were required to monitor every school to see if every group was on track to reach proficiency. Any school that persistently failed to meet its annual target would be labeled a school in need of improvement (in the eyes of the media and thus the public, that means a "failing" school).
>
> *(21)*

Meanwhile, teachers' pay languished and state governments reduced spending in many areas, including public education.[12] Obviously, those schools and school districts that have been most severely underfunded are the ones most likely to fail, leading to such catastrophic results as the closing of 50 public schools in Chicago, a move supported by its Democratic mayor Rahm Emmanuel's eagerness to promote charter schools. Ravitch points out that:

> as 2014 approached, the majority of public schools in the nation had been declared failures, including some excellent, highly regarded schools . . . . In Massachusetts . . . the state with the nation's highest-performing students as judged by federal tests, 80 percent of the state's public schools were "failing" by [No Child Left Behind] standards in 2012.
>
> *(22)*

This absurd outcome has given a major boost to those corporations and individuals such as DeVos eager to privatize education at all levels. Yet state governments are obligated by their constitutions to create and maintain public school systems. Ravitch notes that "public schools were created by communities and states for a civic purpose. In the nineteenth century, they were often called 'common schools.' They were a project of the public commons, the community . . . to build and sustain democracy . . ." (239). Proponents of privatization such as DeVos, however, claim they want to further the cause of school choice, which they identify with freedom. They also claim they are attempting to counteract failing public schools by giving parents the ability to send their kids to better schools, including, of course, charter schools. But many studies have shown that while some charter schools achieve excellent results, on average they are no better than public schools. "To date, there is no evidence that charter schools provide better education than public schools when they enroll the same kinds of students" (Ravitch 352).[13] And there are plenty of studies demonstrating the obvious—that a key reason why schools fail is because they have been systematically underfunded. Charter schools and voucher programs contribute to underfunding by taking money away from public schools. They also take away many of the best students and teachers from those schools.

After Hurricane Katrina struck New Orleans in 2005, neoliberal economist Milton Friedman wrote that the destruction it caused presented a great "opportunity" to privatize that city's school system. This became, as Naomi Klein argues in *Shock Doctrine*, a blatant example of capitalism profiting from a disaster (410). Most of the public schools in New Orleans were closed after Katrina, many of them demolished, and several thousand teachers found themselves out of work. In their place came charter schools and the Recovery School District, "the first all-charter district in the nation," according to Colleen Kimmett. She reports that the new schools were run on a strict "no-excuses" basis, leading to high levels of expulsions. "Students at no-excuses charters described feeling like they were in prison or boot-camp" (19). Kimmett quotes Julian Vasquez Heilig, a professor of education at California State University in Sacramento: "You can say until you're blue in the face that this should be a national model, but this is one of the worst-performing districts in one of the worst-performing states" in the US (19).

Another recent report, this time by the Center for Media and Democracy, reveals that, between 2001 and 2013, 2,500 charter schools throughout the US either closed down or never actually opened, even though these schools, or promised schools, had received millions of dollars in taxpayer money. Nearly 288,000 schoolchildren in both primary and secondary systems had their educations disrupted. In 2011–2012, students in charter schools were well over twice as likely to have their educations disrupted by the shutting down of their schools than were those in public systems. When that happens, graduation rates fall perhaps by as much as 10 percent (Persson). Meanwhile, the corporations backing the failing charter schools are more than happy to rake in profits from their miseducational efforts.

In Indiana, the school voucher program, instituted by Republican governor and now Vice President Mike Pence and a Republican legislature, offers parents money to send their children to private schools, including religious ones. Despite violating the separation of church and state rule, this practice has been declared lawful by the state's supreme court. Meanwhile, "for tactical reasons conservatives have wrapped vouchers in the mantle of concern for poor African Americans and Latinos":

Indeed, voucher supporters are fond of calling school choice the new civil rights movement. This plays well not only with voters of color but also with liberal suburban whites who, while they may be leery of allowing significant numbers of minorities into their schools, nonetheless support the concept of equal rights for all.

(Miner)

So funding for public education shrinks. In Indiana, the property tax basis for supporting public education was eliminated several years ago, leading to budgetary crises in virtually all public school districts.

With the undermining of public schools in mind, Ravitch declares: "Privatization does not work well in providing public services. The need to cut costs and generate a profit for shareholders is inconsistent with the need to assure a reliable, dependable, and equitable public service" (351). As it is with prisons, so it is with schools. Are efforts to privatize public education contributing to the school-to-prison pipeline? Insofar as those efforts underfund and often shutter public schools in the poorest and most segregated neighborhoods in the country, they certainly do.

Notes

1 Costs per inmate rise depending partly on the security level of the prison. Greenville Correctional Institution is a "minimum-security" prison.
2 Much of the expansion of the prison population has nothing to do with an increase in the violent crime rate. It corresponds instead to an increase in the sorts of nonviolent crimes, mostly drug-related, that can lead to imprisonment. Coupled with increasingly harsh sentences—mandatory minimum sentences, truth in sentencing, and three-strike laws—America's jails and prisons are now overcrowded by inmates who have done little more than possess some "controlled substance" or even who have simply been in the company of someone who did (Clear 51–53).
3 Foucault treats Jeremy Bentham's design for an ideal prison, his panopticon, as a "dream building" characteristic of modernity. The panopticon is designed so that the warden could, from his central place of surveillance, see into all of the corridors and cells, simultaneously watching all of the prisoners, even though they could not see him. The warden did not even have to be watching to create the effect of surveillance and total power over the prisoners. Bentham's design has had many avatars. It is, Bentham declared, suitable for many purposes besides prisons, such as schools, barracks, factories, offices, and hospitals. These are among the institutions that constitute modern society and that Louis Althusser calls "ideological state apparatuses," enforced by "repressive state apparatuses"—the police, the military, the courts, jails and prisons. The general epic of capitalism, focused on crime and punishment, plays itself out panoptically in the media, through which we the masses become both watchers and the watched, the wardens and the inmates in all of the disciplinary mechanisms of society—in other words, in all of Althusser's ISAs and RSAs.
4 Some movies and television programs such as *The Wire* give more nuanced, sophisticated versions of this same old, same old story. *The Wire* presents poverty, racism, and the easy availability of guns and drugs as among the main causes of crime, while also emphasizing the symbiotic relationship between cops and drug dealers in Baltimore. According to David Simon, creator and director of *The Wire*, "We pretend to a war against narcotics, but in truth, we are simply brutalizing and dehumanizing an urban underclass that we no longer need as a labor supply .... *The Wire* [is] not a story about America, it's about

the America that got left behind . . . . The drug war is war on the underclass . . . . That's all it is. It has no other meaning" (cited in Žižek *The Year of Dreaming Dangerously* 93). The labor supply of unskilled, mostly black and brown people is no longer needed by large-scale industries, many of which have been outsourced, but private prison corporations can still make money by enclosing lots of those people in so-called correctional facilities.

5 "The prison population has changed from about 30 percent people of color in the 1970s to roughly 70 percent in 2012" (Kilgore 23). In the latter year, 40 percent of all prisoners in the US were African American and 22 percent were Hispanic. "More African American adults are under correctional control today—in prison or in jail, on probation or parole—than were enslaved in 1850, a decade before the Civil War began" (Alexander 200). Currently, one in three African American men can expect to do some prison or jail time.

6 According to the Drug Policy Alliance, "The presidency of Ronald Reagan marked the start of a long period of skyrocketing rates of incarceration, largely thanks to his unprecedented expansion of the drug war" (DPA). With the legalization of marijuana in Colorado, Washington, DC, and elsewhere that is now happening, and with the gradually declining national rate of incarceration over the last several years, the war on drugs, which has also been an undeclared war on people of color, may be gradually winding down. But there are still an unprecedented number of prisons, and people of color in those prisons, in the US.

7 Prisons are often built, moreover, on land that is undesirable for any other purpose, even on top of landfills. In "Coal and Unusual Punishment," John Washington writes about "toxic prisons."

8 The Corrections Corporation of America has recently been renamed CoreCivic.

9 Among other sources, there have been a number of recent articles about why the Justice Department is attempting to move away from using private prisons, such as "Justice Department Says It Will End Use of Private Prisons" by Matt Zapotosky and Chico Harlan in *The Washington Post* for August 18, 2016. With the election of Donald Trump, that will not happen during his presidency.

10 In *States of Emergency*, I discuss the top-down class warfare that has undermined the unions and much of the social safety net whose construction began with the New Deal under FDR. Among other observers, I quote Bill Moyers: "Our business and political class . . . declared class war [over] twenty years ago, and it was they who won. They're on top" (cited in Brantlinger 15).

11 On Community Education Partners, see Fuentes (80–89).

12 My home state, Indiana, is now facing a new crisis because of a severe shortage of certified teachers. Undergraduates are refusing to major in education because of low pay and also because of what they perceive as the mental stultification caused by the testing regime.

13 Ravitch notes that in several places, the performance of charter schools is worse than that of public schools. "Minnesota is the state with the longest history of charter schools." But studies in the Twin Cities have shown that charter schools there "consistently underperformed comparable public schools" (336).

4
THINKING INSIDE THE BOX

> In every cry of every Man,
> In every Infant's cry of fear,
> In every voice: in every ban,
> The mind-forg'd manacles I hear....
>
> — *William Blake, "London"*

What does "thinking outside the box" mean? It implies that thinking ordinarily occurs inside the box, whatever the box may be. And if there are Chinese boxes within boxes, finding an outside may be extraordinarily difficult or even impossible. Now suppose the boxes in question are either schools or prisons. Schools are among the "little boxes" that Malvina Reynolds' song refers to (see Chapter 3), though she might also have been thinking about prisons. In *The Great Turning*, David Korten writes about "prisons of the mind" (237–250), a metaphor William Blake would have understood. Anyway, every kid who rebels or intentionally breaks some rule in his or her school is to some extent thinking outside that "little box." And is there a prisoner anywhere who does not think beyond the steel cage that encloses him or her, wishing to be on the outside?

There are also much larger boxes to consider—an entire educational system, for example, or all of the assumptions, policies, laws, and procedures that have led to mass incarceration in the US. Beyond these macro-boxes there is the social totality "America," but also the current global disorder, or even all of history. And capitalism, of course—today's entire economic system. As its main current mental representation, neoliberal economics purports to explain that system. Supposedly, economics is a scientific discourse. Or is it just another mental prison, an ideological rationalization for capitalism—"the invisible hand" supposedly made visible—perhaps similar to believing that most social problems boil down to individual issues of crime and punishment? And in the US, it is next to impossible to separate issues of crime and punishment from race, an ideological box that, like capitalism, has affected—or infected—virtually all aspects of American history and culture.

What is ideology?

"A set of beliefs, values, and opinions that shapes the way a person or a group such as a social class thinks, acts, and understands the world," ideology is both epidemic and encyclopedic.[1] It refers to many or, depending on how it is defined, all of the boxes we think within. It is also typically used in a pejorative sense, to refer to "false consciousness"—racism, for example—while its antithesis, sometimes called "ideological critique" or just "critical thinking," means thinking outside its boxes.

Perhaps especially today, how is critical thinking about race or about economics even possible when "fences and tollgates are rising rapidly on the commons of the mind" (Rowe 71)? Of course, there have always been mental prisons, fences, and tollgates: ideological mystification of one sort or another did not originate with capitalism. But in a complex yet very real sense, racism did originate with capitalism. Before the late 1440s and 1500s, which saw the European discovery of the Americas and the beginnings of the slave trade, the simple observation that people from different parts of the world looked different from Europeans did not automatically give rise to pejorative judgments based on notions of race. But with the spawning of the European overseas empires, with slavery, and with genocidal wars against indigenous populations, versions of European or white supremacy arose. During the Enlightenment, racism began to receive supposedly scientific attention by natural historians, who constructed racial hierarchies with the white or "Caucasian" race at the apex and all of the other, darker races ranged in various degrees of inferiority or even degeneration below.[2]

Before Darwin, so-called scientific racism was supported by craniometry or skull measurement and similar procedures that have now been thoroughly debunked.[3] It was often asserted that the struggle between races was the main engine of history, and even that the races represented entirely different species. Darwin and his followers contended that there was only one human species, but also that the races had been separated for so long they had grown quite different from each other. Social Darwinism and the eugenics movement, also claiming the status of science, led into the twentieth century, the horrors of Nazism, and World War II. Today, biologists, geneticists, and anthropologists agree that the variations among populations commonly attributed to race mean little or nothing. The Genome Project has shown that, genetically speaking, every human being is at least 97 percent African in origin. And more or less observable differences such as skin color that supposedly demarcate human races bear no relationship to the mental or physical capacities of the individuals within those populations. Yet issues of race and racism itself are seemingly permanent mental prisons that, at least in the US, are difficult or impossible to escape.[4]

Strictly as an economic system, capitalism did not give rise to racism. But the creation of the major European empires and the rise of the slave trade during the period of emergent capitalism certainly did. Analyzing the origins of totalitarianism, Hannah Arendt declared: "Imperialism would have necessitated the invention of racism as the only possible 'explanation' and excuse for its deeds, even if no race-thinking had ever existed in the civilized world" (63–64).

What is more, if racism is a version of ideological mystification, one that was accorded the status of science for two and a half centuries, capitalism has been very effective at creating other versions of mystification, including neoliberal economics. It, too, purports to be scientific. And when a mental prison is widely held to be scientific, it becomes very difficult to think outside its "little box."

Fortunately, there have been other versions of economics—Marxism for one, of course, although neoliberal economics is more often contrasted by economists to Keynesianism. To many economists, whether neoliberal or Keynesian, Marxism supposedly does not count or can just be ignored. But there have been many other non-orthodox economists besides Marx and Keynes, including Elinor Ostrom (whether or not one chooses to identify her as an economist), back through Thorstein Veblen, J. A. Hobson, and Henry George to Robert Owen, St. Simon, and other early versions of socialist and utopian economists.

The history of the term ideology begins with the French Revolution of 1789, when a group of intellectuals calling themselves "ideologists" set about planning how best to educate the citizens of the new republic. In this initial version, ideology meant a science of ideas or of consciousness, just the opposite of mystification or false consciousness. Something similar can be discerned in Tom Paine's contention that up to his own revolutionary era all governments had been based on "force" and "fraud." By "force" he meant the conquerors who became the ruling classes—royalty and aristocrats. And by "fraud" he meant "priestcraft," which supported the conquerors by consoling and distracting the conquered from their subjugation. The priestly caste of all former societies, Paine thought, was responsible for creating and inculcating the ruling ideas imposed by the rulers. But the American and French Revolutions had ushered in the era of "government by reason"—that is, government by the collective rationality and deliberation of the citizens of the new republics of the United States and France. They could now all act as critical intellectuals, thinking outside the boxes of such orthodox ideas as the divine right of kings and the literal truth of the Bible.

Napoleon considered the French ideologists his enemies, so he used the term ideology in a pejorative sense, as false consciousness. That is how Marx and Engels used it in *The German Ideology* and elsewhere. Paine's "priestcraft" is echoed in Marx's assertion about religion as "the opium of the people." But In *Capital*, the key modern version of ideology is commodity fetishism. In general, for Marx and Engels, ideology came to mean ideas, beliefs, or just plain ignorance—as in their claim about "the idiocy of rural life" in *The Communist Manifesto*—that obscured the truth about capitalism and its processes of domination and subordination. The Italian Marxist Antonio Gramsci took their version of ideology a step farther through his treatment of "hegemony."

In every complex society, Marx and Engels contended, the various social classes with different interests and ideas are in continual struggle or class conflict, ranging from, say, nonviolent negotiations between trade unions and employers to outright civil wars. Gramsci's "hegemony" refers to the often-complicated processes by which a particular class—the bourgeoisie under capitalism, for example—achieves dominance over the other classes. That achievement, which does not necessarily entail violent coercion, involves the acceptance of domination by enough of the subordinated population to stabilize a social formation, even if only shakily and temporarily. As Terry Eagleton notes:

> hegemony is . . . a broader category than ideology: it includes ideology, but is not reducible to it. A ruling group or class may secure consent to its power by ideological means; but it may also do so by, say, altering the tax system in ways favorable to groups whose support it needs, or creating a layer of relatively affluent, and thus somewhat politically quiescent, workers.
>
> *(112)*

From Gramsci's perspective, ideology does not necessarily involve false consciousness or the acceptance of completely misleading ideas. It can take the form of common sense, which often constitutes public opinion. Gramsci calls common sense "the 'philosophy of non-philosophers,' or in other words the conception of the world which is uncritically absorbed by the various social and cultural environments in which the moral individuality of the average [person] is developed" (419). This "conception of the world" consists of the standard boxes we all find ourselves thinking within. As I noted in *Crusoe's Footprints*, "common sense is the ideological glue . . . that legitimizes and binds a social formation together by making its institutions and arrangements of power seem natural and wise" (96).

All complex societies develop institutions that help to maintain their stability, and hence their hegemonic class structures. Institutions, or what Louis Althusser refers to as "ISAs" ("ideological state apparatuses"), embed ideologies, so that they are not just the misconceptions of individuals. Churches, synagogues, and mosques, for example, express religious ideologies that have lasted for centuries, despite what individuals believe or don't believe. Similarly, racism shows up in segregated housing and neighborhoods, and capitalism is inextricable from corporations, the Federal Reserve System, the stock market, and the banks, no matter what individuals think of them. In the US, the ISAs that embed race and capitalism may be hegemonic, and yet criticism of and opposition to many aspects of both of them are widespread. But that opposition ordinarily gets scant attention in the corporate mass media, which treat capitalism as well as many versions of institutional racism as axiomatic.

To cite one more conception of ideology, Jürgen Habermas' theory of "communicative action" looks back to Max Weber's analysis of the patterns of "rationalization" evident in modernity. Weber, Habermas writes, "characterized cultural modernity as the separation of the substantive reason expressed in religion and metaphysics into three autonomous spheres. They are: science, morality, and art" (9). During the Enlightenment, each of these spheres began further to subdivide, leading to the divisions reflected in the academic disciplines, each staking its claim to reason and truth. Scientific discourse, moreover, has tended to dominate the other spheres, "colonizing" what Habermas calls the human "lifeworld." The sciences are ordinarily versions of "instrumental reason." The so-called science of neoliberal economics, for example, insists that its monetary, quantitative treatment of value can account for all values, while giving short shrift to moral and esthetic values. In striving to be scientific, the other social sciences also tend to neglect those aspects of human experience that cannot easily be weighed and measured. In sociology and political science, as well as in economics, statistical, positivist models of research are regarded more highly than qualitative models that involve participant observation, interviews, and narratives of life experiences.

Reason is supposedly antithetical to ideological mystification or false consciousness. And yet, as much as versions of complete mystification, versions of instrumental reason produce many of the distortions constitutive of Weber's "iron cage" of modernity. The technocratic, bureaucratic, corporatist treatment of employees as "human resources" is an obvious example of instrumental reason. Employees are viewed as commodified, replaceable parts in the machinery of a corporation or governmental agency. So, too, the instrumental approach to nature treats it as a bundle of resources to be dominated and exploited, too often with little or no thought as to whether they are finite or in some other ways difficult to replace. A mountaintop in West Virginia, for example, is just an impediment to the coal industry, with no consideration given to its environmental and esthetic values, or even its economic value, apart from coal.

Big box economics

Habermas shows why much of scientific reasoning, even though it is supposed to be antithetical to ideology, is in fact ideological. Neoliberal economics is an obvious example. In his *A Brief History of Neoliberalism*, David Harvey writes: "by 1990 or so most economics departments in the major research universities as well as the business schools were dominated by neoliberal modes of thought" (63). Today, the influence of neoliberalism may be waning, but no clear alternative has replaced it. By most of its academic practitioners, it is still viewed as scientific.

The version of economics presented on the mass media and in introductory college textbooks shows why it is not scientific. There are TV cable broadcasts devoted to "business news," and most national news programs include brief segments about the stock market, any unusual doings among major corporations (mergers, innovations, bankruptcies, outsourcings), and so-called job reports amounting to the official but misleading employment statistics.[5] Unless there is a large-scale strike going on or the movement of a major corporation to, say, Mexico, those statistics in turn are all that could be accurately described as labor news. The reporting about corporations ordinarily also doubles as free advertising.

The mass media of course simplify often highly complicated matters, but they do not report economic news in ways that would contradict what most academic economists preach.[6] From the media, or even from studying most of today's economists, the American public is likely to come away with these opinions, viewed as scientific or axiomatic: capitalism is the only economic system that works; economic "growth" equals progress (forget the environment and ecological sustainability); "free trade" is somehow identical to political and social freedom for individuals, not just for corporations; government regulations generally mean government interference; trade unions are also drags on business; private management is almost always preferable to government management; if left alone, markets are self-correcting; businesses produce and sell products in direct response to consumer demand; a job is a job is a job (be happy if you have one, even if it is a low-wage or just a temporary job); most workers get paid what they deserve, and so do most CEOs; the wealthy are job producers; raising the minimum wage will increase unemployment; some businesses, especially banks, are "too big to fail"; corporations are necessary arrangements guaranteeing prosperity for everyone; the main causes of poverty are dysfunctional families and poor people who lack initiative; the main causes of individual wealth are hard work and initiative; although 1 percent of Americans may be super-rich, the rest of us all belong to the great middle class (there is no reason to use the term "working class," let alone "proletariat"); there is more social mobility in America than in any other country in the world; we could all be entrepreneurs if we wanted to; and orthodox, neoliberal economics is a science, on a par with chemistry or biology.[7]

Most of these views can be found in the economic textbooks used in introductory courses in colleges and universities today (Brantlinger, *States of Emergency* 21–40; Keen). But both the mass media and the supposedly scientific textbooks convey either ideological mystification or what Habermas calls "distorted communication" (half-truths at best). Even if there are units at colleges and universities that attempt to teach critical thinking—cultural studies programs, for instance— these are minor players compared to economics departments and entire schools of business. In them, neoliberal economics reigns supreme.

As has often been pointed out since the economic crash of 2007–2008, however, many of the most influential economists in the US failed to predict it. Most notably, Alan Greenspan, who was at the time Chairman of the Federal Reserve, testified in Congress that he failed to "understand what went wrong in what he thought were self-governing markets." Perhaps if he had studied economic history, he would have realized that over the last several centuries, back to the South Seas and Mississippi Bubbles in the 1700s, markets have repeatedly failed. Rather than being governed by Adam Smith's Invisible Hand, always returning to equilibrium, they often go haywire and don't necessarily return to normal on their own. After the 2007–2008 crash, without the governmental stimulus package and the rescue of the American auto industry, the U.S. economy would not have come close to achieving even the slow recovery it has managed. Testifying before Congress, Greenspan admitted that he felt "very distressed" by having to acknowledge there was "a flaw" in his supposedly scientific understanding of the economy. "Those of us who have looked to the self-interest of lending institutions to protect shareholders' equity . . . are in a state of shocked disbelief," he confessed, adding: "This crisis has turned out to be much broader than anything I could have imagined" (cited in Žižek, *First as Tragedy, Then as Farce* 30).

In *A Failure of Capitalism*, Richard Posner noted "the disappointing performance of the economics profession" in failing to predict the 2007–2008 collapse, adding that "economists have become a lagging indicator of our economic troubles" (xiv, vii). And Nobel Prize winning economist Joseph Stiglitz has often declared that markets often and frequently fail. They may be "self-correcting," but that is because they produce "bubbles" that then burst, leading to economic hardship, and perhaps a modicum of humility on the part of those economists who place their faith in unregulated markets (e.g., see Stiglitz, *Globalization and Its Discontents* 12–18).[8] William Black similarly comments: "Economists have dominated the creation of public policies to prevent banking crises. Their track record has been abysmal." Their biggest mistake was believing that getting rid of government regulations and the oversight of banks and other financial institutions would produce major economic growth and widening prosperity. Black continues:

> They designed and implemented the disastrous deregulation that produced the US S&L debacle, they praised Japan's and East Asia's banking structures just before they collapsed, and they designed the IMF's crisis intervention strategy that intensified losses and human misery. They also designed and praised privatization programs in many transition economies that led to banking crises; they planned (and in some cases profited from) the catastrophic failure of "shock therapy" in Russia. The irony is that when financial experts were most confident in their consensus, they erred the most grievously.
>
> *(69)*

The claim that neoliberal economics is scientific is belied by N. Gregory Mankiw's *Principles of Economics*, the world's bestselling introductory economics textbook. In its fifth edition, students are spoon-fed misleading pabulum such as this: "Fortunately, criminal activity by corporate managers is rare" (486). This comes after a brief mention of the Enron and WorldCom scandals. But how "rare" are such scandals? Over the last decade, half of the major corporations headquartered in the US have been charged with criminal activities, and some of them have been charged several times over. Also from Mankiw's *Principles*, students can learn this tidbit of non-Euclidean geometry:

> When the government redistributes income from the rich to the poor, it reduces the reward for working hard; as a result, people work less and produce fewer goods and services. In other words, when the government tries to cut the economic pie into more equal slices, the pie gets smaller.
>
> *(5)*

It is hard to imagine that any intelligent person—and no doubt Mankiw is intelligent on many levels—could believe that such nonsense is scientific, beginning with the assumptions that rich people get that way by working hard and that most people will work less hard if they believe the poor are getting handouts. To state the obvious, many rich individuals acquire their wealth not by working hard, but through inheritance, well-informed or lucky investments, tax evasion, and so forth. And many individuals are poor because their parents were poor, not because they don't work hard.

Mankiw's stick-figure version of human nature (why people do or don't work hard) is based on *Homo economicus,* or the notion of the individual as a supposedly completely rational figure, behaving strictly according to what he or she judges to be of personal utility or benefit. Perhaps if Mankiw delved into the psychology books his students have in their backpacks, he would have come up with a more nuanced version of human nature.[9] Can you say that a suicide bomber who blows himself up along with dozens of others did not have his personal utility in mind? What is more, Mankiw's supposedly scientific assertion about slicing up pies is nonsense. Unless the government makes complete mincemeat of it, "the economic pie" does not get smaller when it "tries to cut" that pie "into more equal slices." The size of the pie, the gross national product, remains exactly the same. Raising the minimum wage to $10.10, as the Obama Administration proposed, or enacting a more progressive form of the income tax cannot have any great effect on the GNP.

Through the first half of the1800s, "political economy" was a standard phrase, suggesting that economics was not purely scientific. But, beginning with the theory of marginal utility in the 1870s, as capitalist economists started to use mathematics to make their subject supposedly more scientific, several things happened (e.g., see Gagnier). One was that marginal utility and price theory shifted class conflict to the back-burner. "In this new form of economics," writes Michael Perelman, "capitalists and workers alike no longer appeared as members of distinct classes, but as part of a homogeneous group of individuals. Whether the 'individual' is Wal-Mart selling toilet paper or a worker selling labor makes little difference" (25). From then on, for capitalist economics the main roles of its human actors were producers and consumers, sellers and buyers. Everyone became a thoroughly rational actor on the miraculously level playing field of the marketplace, able to judge the utility of any transactions he or she enters into: the customer is always right.

Among the many other errors most economists make is to believe that the best and perhaps only measure of progress is economic "growth." Growth of what? Growth of nuclear waste? Growth of carbon emissions? Growth of sweatshops? Aren't cancers growths? Continued economic growth in an overpopulated world with many finite, nonrenewable resources is an impossibility. Yet even as the middle class in the US slides into poverty while the very poor flounder in desperation and often homelessness, the question of economic growth dominates the news on the mass media. Americans want to believe in "the American dream," which insists that the US is the land of opportunity, where everyone can get ahead through hard work and thrift and a rise in the stock market means more wealth for everyone. The American dream will apparently not be realized without ever-increasing economic growth. The economic pundits may fret about unemployment, but supposedly anyone with enough gumption can start his or her own business; we are all potentially entrepreneurs. Among the so-called developed countries of the world, however, the US ranks near the bottom in terms of social mobility.

The much-touted triumph of capitalism and democracy over all opposition—"the end of history" announced by Francis Fukuyama in 1989—suggested that there was no longer any need to think seriously about alternatives to the status quo. With the failure of communism in Eastern Europe and the Soviet Union, all things were good and would only get better. Of course, there was still a lot of poverty in many parts of the world, but unimpeded capitalism, with its Invisible Hand spreading prosperity everywhere, would rectify that. And while there were still quite a few undemocratic regimes in places such as China, Cuba, Chad, and Turkmenistan, democracy would eventually win out over tyranny. Fukuyama can perhaps be forgiven for the optimism that gave rise to his mistake. Of course, history did not end back then, and it is not about to end any time soon, except maybe through global warming, a nuclear catastrophe, machines superseding us, an alien invasion, or a large asteroid slamming into the earth.

The mass media today

All of the conceptions of ideology that I have just mentioned, ranging from religious mystification to instrumental reason and neoliberal economics, purport to be versions of historical materialism—that is to say, they are antithetical to versions of nonhistorical essentialism and idealism, including the patently false assumption that the status quo is the natural outcome of inevitable forces beyond human control. But Marx, Gramsci, Althusser, and Habermas did not pay enough attention to the actual media of communications. That is true as well of N. Gregory Mankiw. In this regard, they were not materialist enough, and neither is Mankiw. But among the various quite literal boxes that influence what is commonly called public opinion and sometimes called ideology, the most effective in determining how most people view the world are their television sets, so-called smartphones, and computers.

Marshall McLuhan's famous assertion in 1963 that "the medium is the message" is partly correct, and is of major importance in considering mental prisons or enclosures—that is, in considering how ideology works today. Equally important is who controls the media, including owners, but also those who produce the ruling ideas that meet with the approval of the owning and ruling class. And the mass media today are ICAs, not Althusser's ISAs—that is to say, they are ideological corporate apparatuses. From the late 1950s through the 1980s, moreover, the most powerful mass medium was undoubtedly television. Today, it may have been surpassed by the Internet, but television is still immensely powerful. On average, Americans spend at least five hours every day watching television. How many Americans are there who could say, if they were honest about it, "I let Fox News do my thinking for me?" Currently, Fox News has more viewers than CNN and MSNBC combined.

In the US, when there were at first only three major television networks—ABC, CBS, and NBC—media analysts worried that their domination of the airwaves was antidemocratic. No matter what their political affiliations, the dependence of the three networks on advertising revenue meant that their general ideological pitch was pro-capitalist and unquestioningly patriotic. They all had news programs sometimes featuring such renowned journalists as Edward R. Murrow, but it was a rare moment when they aired anything critical about capitalism or, for that matter, about American foreign policy. News on PBS, the Public Broadcasting Service established in 1967, was more in-depth, but only somewhat more critical than news on the three commercial networks. Today, with much less public money to support it, PBS now also airs advertising and its news broadcasts are more in line with those on the commercial networks. Witness, for example, the disappearance of *Bill Moyers' Journal* from PBS in 2010.

With the growth of cable television in the 1970s and 1980s, the medium seemed to be opening up to alternative views and the predilections of viewers in a much more democratic way than when there were only the three commercial networks. In relation to ideology, however, nothing changed. While greatly expanding the number of channels viewers could watch, cable television has contributed little if anything to American democracy. This has been in part an effect of information overload, the same problem that prevents the Internet from directly contributing to democratic enlightenment.[10] Through the basic television service that I subscribe to, I have access to over 100 channels. Many of them are channels devoted entirely to sports; fewer feature news broadcasts (one is the inevitable Fox News), and those that do so differ very little from each other. A couple of the sports channels I get feature guns, promoting—guess what?—gun sales and the NRA. The cable news sources supposedly more liberal than Fox, CNN, and MSNBC, have recently grown less liberal and enlightening. There can be no doubt that the rapt attention they paid to Donald Trump from the primaries through the 2016 election helped get him elevated to the presidency.[11] Today, they continue to give him rapt attention, if not exactly homage.

The news programs on the commercial networks are all highly repetitive. And they avoid some of the most urgent issues of the day such as global warming. An editorial in *The Nation*, published a month after the 2016 election, states: "not one question about climate change was posed in any of the presidential debates. The media gave more airtime to the size of Trump's hands than to the scope of his climate delusion."[12] Sheldon Wolin adds that the media, whether deliberately or not, squeeze out whatever seems controversial or somehow opposed to the interests of their corporate advertisers:

> The result is an essentially monochromatic media. In-house commentators identify the problem and its parameters, creating a box that dissenters struggle vainly to elude. The critic who insists on changing the context is dismissed as irrelevant, extremist, "the Left"—or ignored altogether.
>
> *(35)*

On all the corporate channels, moreover, whether focused on sports or news or entertainment, approximately one-quarter of the time is devoted to advertising—commodity fetishism in your face. Along with the countless commercials showing smiling individuals who are ultra-happy because they are using this or that magical toothpaste or deodorant or cure for "ED," there is the relentless implicit message that capitalism spells abundance and is therefore the best of all possible economic systems. Moreover (the message continues), the happiness of everyone consists in continued economic "growth," even though capitalism is using up nonrenewable resources at an alarming and accelerating rate. Meanwhile, Big Oil and its lobbyists have worked hard to keep the facts about global warming a secret, no doubt on the premise that ignorance is bliss. So what if glaciers and islands and entire species of animals and plants are disappearing?

The airwaves are supposed to be part of the modern-day commons, belonging to the public, but the mass media in the United States are now owned and controlled by a handful of powerful corporations, and the number of these has been shrinking. The recent ruling against net neutrality by the FCC means that the Internet will soon follow the privatization or enclosure of radio and television. In 1983, 50 corporations controlled most of the mass media. In 2012, that number had dwindled to six corporations controlling 90 percent of the media: Comcast, NewsCorp, Disney, ViaCom, Time Warner, and CBS (Lutz). Along with the frequent blurring of advertising and news on all the major channels, television news does little to encourage critical thinking about anything. The mental box called "the news" comes in bits and bytes, almost always in the present tense. A news story is rarely contextualized, failing to give it any sort of background, much less an adequate history that would help to explain why a particular bit or byte has occurred. Newsworthy events just seem to happen, out of the blue, something like secular, quotidian miracles—just like the surprising election of Donald Trump. News is always new, isn't it? Only these miracles are frequently bad ones: mass murders, disasters, wars, accidents, and the election of Donald Trump. Moreover, they are treated as equivalents: a mass shooting, a tornado, a scandal, an election . . . all grist for the media's simpleminded and simplifying mill (for anyone who cares to pay attention). This is one reason why, as even television journalists report, we are now in a "post-truth" era.

Supposedly objective reporting often takes the form of presenting both sides to any controversy as though both sides have equal merit. Sometimes there are many sides or perhaps even no discernible opposing side to a story. But news anchors and pundits typically pretend that there are two sides anyway, a yin-yang version of what they present as truth or at least as accuracy in reporting. Journalistic objectivity means you do not take sides, which also means as a reporter you apparently have no opinions. Was it right or wrong for the US to invade Iraq in 2003? You can't say, because you are supposedly an objective reporter. As another example, there is today no major controversy among the scientific community about global warming. And yet the mass media regularly air the views of climate science deniers who claim that the scientists haven't reached a consensus or that "I'm not a scientist."

Or else the media don't talk about climate change at all. Republican Todd Young, newly elected Senator from Indiana, recently asserted that he is not a climate science denier, he is only an "agnostic"—a pretty big word for a Hoosier politician. I could almost be proud of Young for using that word, if taking such a position weren't so imbecilic. And not long ago, Senator James Inhofe of Oklahoma, speaking in the Senate, held up a snowball to prove that it was cold outside—hence, that the climate could not be warming. Somebody should have told Inhofe that if he waited a few moments, the snowball would melt, thus proving that global warming was occurring right there in the Senate. Incredibly, after the 2014 midterm election, Inhofe was named Chair of the Senate Environment and Public Works Committee. Perhaps he should be praised for thinking outside the box of science, but not for thinking hard enough about what happens to snowballs when they melt. Of course, Inhofe's snowball demo made national news. The melting of the snowball did not, because news never waits around very long.

After decades of warnings from the scientists that global warming is happening and is now reaching catastrophic limits, that topic has at least begun to receive some notice on television. On weather forecasts on local stations, however, it is still hardly ever mentioned. Out of sight, out of mind. Other stories about the environment—the rapid depletion of many fisheries, or the latest oil spill, or the pollution added to the soil through fertilizers and pesticides—are underreported, if reported at all. And environmentalists themselves are frequently represented as tree-huggers or half-crazed activists, left-wingers, sometimes even as terrorists, though that term is usually reserved for Islamic jihadists.

There is also the frequent phenomenon of completely unbalanced reporting, as in the case of the U.S. bombing campaign against ISIS in Iraq and Syria. A recent report by Fairness and Accuracy in Reporting (FAIR) shows that there was almost no dissension about the bombing on the corporate media:

> In total, 205 sources appeared on the programs discussing military options in Syria and Iraq. Just six of these guests, or 3 percent, voiced opposition to US military intervention. There were 125 guests (61 percent) who spoke in favor of US war. On the high-profile Sunday talk shows, 89 guests were invited to talk about the war. But just one, *Nation* editor Katrina vanden Heuvel, could be coded as an anti-war guest.

On television news programs, everything seems to change from day to day, yet nothing changes. Meanwhile, buy the advertised products to ensure you can get an erection or to own and drive the latest luxury vehicle. Brand X will do you a world of good; the other brands won't, even though everyone knows they are virtually identical. Do viewers pay more attention to the news or to the commercials? Not everyone watches news programs anyhow. They may keep their television sets on 24/7, but the sets are more likely to be tuned in to sports or sitcoms or crime shows than to the news. And viewers don't always pay close attention to whatever the program that's on may be, perhaps partly because news programs cover the same stories several times a day. The repetition is, no doubt, reassuring: even when there's an earthquake or a terrorist bombing, life goes on as it always has and presumably always will. Crime is a constant that never pays in the end (unlike in real life). The family that laughs together stays together. And so forth and so on in the endless production of mind candy. Marx lamented the idiocy of rural life; now we can add the idiocy of television and perhaps Internet life. But it isn't the idiocy of the consumers of mass culture that is the problem; it is instead the idiocy of the cultural products themselves—that is, both the commodities such as television programs and the ads that support them.

Are the masses to blame for the culture they consume? Do they demand the programming the television networks and Hollywood produce for them? Not exactly. They don't write the scripts of the shows that they watch or of the commercials supporting those shows. Nor do they choose what is presented to them as "the news." In reconsidering "the culture industry," Theodor Adorno declared that "the consciousness of the consumers . . . is split between the prescribed fun which is supplied to them . . . and a not particularly well-hidden doubt about its blessings." On the part of many consumers, that doubt involves a sort of self-critical cynicism: *soap operas are silly, of course, but I watch them anyway* . . . . Adorno continues:

> The phrase, the world wants to be deceived, has become truer than had ever been intended. People are not only, as the saying goes, falling for the swindle; if it guarantees them even the most fleeting gratification they desire a deception which is nonetheless transparent to them. They force their eyes shut and voice approval, in a kind of self-loathing, for what is meted out to them, knowing fully the purpose for which it is manufactured.
>
> *(103)*

And the main purpose of a television show such as a soap opera is to hold its viewers' attention long enough to get them to consider buying the products advertised while it is on. Adorno notes as well that:

> the concoctions of the culture industry are neither guides for a blissful life, nor a new art of moral responsibility, but rather exhortations to toe the line, behind which stand the most powerful interests. The consensus which it propagates strengthens blind, opaque authority.
>
> *(105)*

I would translate "blind, opaque authority" as blind acceptance of the capitalist status quo: this is just how the world works and how it should work. Most people most of the time, no matter how intelligent and well informed they may be, want to toe the line in the sense of accepting the status quo as natural or normal.

The news is usually bad news anyway, so why should anyone pay attention to it? Just as the number of corporations involved in television broadcasting is shrinking, so too is the number of independent print newspapers:

> Hundreds of weekly and daily newspapers went out of business between 2007 and 2011. According to one industry survey, 300 newspapers folded in 2009 . . . and another 150 went under in 2010. Broadcast news scaled back operations. The number of working journalists plummeted. Foreign news bureaus shuttered at the most rapid rate in history. Washington D.C. bureaus shut down and downsized just as rapidly, leaving vast sectors of the federal government uncovered.
>
> (McChesney and Nichols, The Death and Life of American Journalism 11)

Meanwhile, most Americans don't read newspapers. According to a Pew Research Center poll conducted in 2012, only 23 percent of respondents say they read a print newspaper every day, a decline of 18 percent from a decade ago. Are they reading books? Forty-one percent say they have not read a book in the past year. Besides, reading a book is no guarantee that the reader is gaining any new information, critical or otherwise. And as to movies, these days they are frequently crime stories or action-adventure films in which the characters seem to exist—although not necessarily for long—in a hail of gunfire. Then there are video games for the young at heart, in which there is even more gunfire, among many other forms of violence. So this is what much of contemporary American culture has turned into: let's shoot or be shot, sponsored by the NRA.

Accompanying these developments has been the "war on terror," initiated by the invasions of Afghanistan and Iraq after 9/11. Declared to be a potentially endless war by Vice President Dick Cheney, it of course has had many ideological and political consequences, ranging from Islamophobia to the creation of a "surveillance state" that threatens an end to individual privacy.[13] It is an enormous distraction from other crises and dangers, including climate change and general environmental degradation. At the same time, it has been a bonanza for many corporations engaged in such activities as producing military hardware and private security services. With 9/11, Antony Lowenstein notes, "the war on terror gold rush" began, bringing "untold riches to corporations keen to profit from fear" (11). Among those corporations is Halliburton, where Dick Cheney was CEO before becoming Vice President. So-called national security, bolstered by patriotism, now comes before all else. Both al-Qaeda and ISIS know very well how to distract the Western public. But there are many other distractions at least equal to them today on corporate television, such as football games and the Super Bowl. Besides those immediately impacted by it, if Hurricane Katrina had occurred during the Super Bowl, would anyone besides the drowned and drowning have noticed?

Notes

1 This definition comes from Encarta's World English Dictionary (Microsoft).
2 The idea of the darker races as degenerate was supposedly based on the Bible. Presumably, Adam and Eve were white and near-perfect specimens, closest to God. After the Flood, Noah's sons dispersed into various parts of the world, where their offspring degenerated, growing darker and less perfect. Africans were supposedly the descendants of Ham.

3   See, for example, Stephen J. Gould, *The Mismeasure of Man*.
4   In *Race and Reality*, Guy Harrison writes: "Imagine six gigantic boxes in which we can place all the people in the world. Let's sort out everyone into six groups: 'Asians,' 'blacks,' 'whites,' 'Latinos,' 'Native Americans,' and 'Pacific Islanders.' But wait, there is something very unusual about our boxes. They don't do a very good job of keeping the different kinds of people apart, because these bizarre containers don't have tops, bottoms, or sides. We know the boxes are there because we say they are there, so we keep sorting people into them. But the fact is, nobody can really see or feel the sides, tops, or bottoms of them. Meanwhile, millions of people keep moving from box to box, pretty much as they please. You might be wondering what significance these boxes have if we can't see them and they are unable to contain the people we put into them. Do these boxes really exist, or is there some sort of 'emperor's new clothes' scenario going on? This is what biological races are: boxes without tops, bottoms, or sides—inadequate, to say the least" (33).
5   The official employment statistics are misleading because they do not include those who have dropped out of the job market altogether and because they do not calculate the extent to which high-wage, permanent jobs have been replaced by low-wage, temporary jobs.
6   Many of the books and articles I cite throughout *Barbed Wire* are critical of neoliberal economics. See, for instance, Mosche Adler, *Economics for the Rest of Us*; David Harvey, *A Brief History of Neoliberalism*; Steve Keen, *Debunking Economics*; and David Kotz, *The Rise and Fall of Neoliberal Capitalism*.
7   Constructing a similar list of the so-called scientific findings of neoliberal economics, Bill Ayers writes: "All of this accepted wisdom is just a collection of clichés—nothing more than gobbledygook and pure bullshit" (62).
8   In "Why Myths of the 'Free Market' Survive," John Buell writes that the idea of a "free market" is absurd, especially when it is used to imply that economic freedom and political freedom are identical or nearly so. One of the leading exponents of that falsehood was neoliberal economist Milton Friedman, who also declared that "there is no free lunch." Just so, like free lunch, free markets exist only in la-la land. In economic terms, all "free" means in relation to markets is unregulated by government "interference."
9   "The psychology invoked by economists," writes George Brockway, "has . . . borne little relationship to that studied by psychologists" (17). James Galbraith points out that "modern behavioral economics has begun—but only begun—to notice" the many ways humans behave inconsistently, often with little or no regard to economic self-interest. Together with the myth of the market as a perfect machine, for the orthodox economist "economic man is a machine to whom whimsy and evolution are unknown" (22). And Stephen Marglin writes that so far, behavioral economics has not done enough to challenge any of the basic assumptions of orthodox economics (5). Besides psychology, mainstream economists seem weak in what C. Wright Mills called "the sociological imagination."
10 It has become commonplace to wax euphoric over the democratic or even revolutionary potential of the Internet. In *Viral Spiral*, for example, David Bollier declares that the Internet "commons," created by tech-savvy "commoners," "is a new paradigm for creating value and organizing a community of shared interest." It is "a viable alternative to markets that have grown stodgy, manipulative, and coercive." However, he does not go farther and declare that it is an alternative to capitalism, although he adds that the "commons is a means by which individuals can band together with like-minded souls and express a sovereignty of their own" (4). What he means by "sovereignty" is perhaps not very much. I will say more about the digital "commons" in Chapter 8.
11 In the run-up to the November 2016 election, the supposedly more liberal cable news outlets, CNN and MSNBC, gave huge amounts of attention to the words and deeds of Donald Trump and to the daily fluctuation in the election polls that provided a lot of free advertising for Trump and a lot of misinformation about public opinion. The both explicit and implicit attention they paid to Hillary Clinton's supposedly scandalous e-mails was also outrageous.

12 "Trump's Irreversible Threat." Though occasionally a mainstream media pundit would mention that Trump has been accused of sometimes "stiffing" his employees, rarely if ever did any of them point out that he has been sued several thousand times by the workers and businesses he hired because he refused to pay them what he had promised. Nor did they say much if anything about Trump's ties to the mafia. Yet because he was said to eschew political correctness and to "speak his mind," the media often suggested that he was deemed more trustworthy than Secretary Clinton—at least according to the untrustworthy polls that asked respondents how trustworthy they considered the candidates.

13 What was Cheney hopeful about? There is so much money to be made through the war on terror for corporations such as Halliburton. And think of the veering to the hard right that war has introduced into American and global politics.

5

CORPORATIONS AS GREED MACHINES

A corporation died and went to the heaven of dead corporations. It was met at the Oily Gates by St. Petrol, Inc., who asked how successful it had been. "Oh," said the dead corporation, "I was very successful. I scammed the public, cooked the books, outsourced production to Kyrgystan, and laid off as many workers as possible. I completely fucked up the environment—a mere externality. Exercising my free speech rights, I bought as many politicians as I could and spent millions on lobbying and advertising. On the stock exchange my value skyrocketed. I earned hundreds of millions for my management, who mismanaged just about everything. So they got huge bonuses and golden parachutes. Soon I was producing nothing but toxic investment vehicles and mortgage frauds, leading to my bankruptcy. And here I am." "And you call that being successful?" St. Petrol replied. "Why? What would you call it?" asked the dead corporation. "In my opinion," said St. Petrol, "for a corporation that is being super-successful. Come right in. The Godfather of All Corporations is expecting you." When the dead corporation stepped through the Oily Gates, the temperature shot through the roof because of celestial—or rather infernal—warming. Everything was in flames . . .[1]

History

Between tragedy and farce, irony is history's modus operandi. It is hugely ironic that the US, which originated in a rebellion partly against a British corporation's monopoly of the tea trade, is now mostly enclosed—or run, at least indirectly—by corporations.[2] At the time of the Boston Tea Party, the East India Company was the largest transnational corporation in existence. Through war as well as trade, it had surpassed its main rivals, the Dutch and French East India Companies. Among its many other effects, it threatened to wipe out tea merchants based in the colonies. But of course, its biggest impact was the establishment of the British Raj in India. Several of the other early corporations chartered by the British government, such as the Hudson

Bay Company, were also imperializing ventures. The Royal African Company dating from 1660 was the main British player in the slave trade until 1752, when it was replaced by the African Company of Merchants that lasted until 1821. Such corporations were both mercantilist monopolies and empire builders.

Until the latter half of the 1500s, most European businesses were either individually owned and managed or else they were partnerships involving just a few people. The corporate form, typically with a small number of directors, allowed many people to invest in large-scale ventures both at home and abroad. In Britain, the Company of the Mines Royal originated in 1564 as a "joint-stock company," an early name for a corporation. A year later, the Company of Mineral and Battery Works was formed, followed in the early 1600s by several utilities, including the New River Company that supplied fresh water to London.

By the late 1600s, as the number of corporations in Britain multiplied rapidly, so did corruption and fraudulent enterprises. In *The Corporation*, Joel Bakan explains how, around 1700, "stockbrokers, known as 'jobbers,' prowled the infamous coffee shops of London's Exchange Alley . . . in search of credulous investors to whom they could sell shares in bogus companies":

> Such companies flourished briefly, nourished by speculation, and then quickly collapsed. Ninety-three of them traded between 1690 and 1695. By 1698, only twenty were left. In 1696 the commissioners of trade for England reported that the corporate form had been "wholly perverted" by the sale of company stock "to ignorant men, drawn in by the reputation, falsely raised and artfully spread, concerning the thriving state of [the] stock."

(6)

Starting in 1711, the promoters of the South Sea Company perpetrated a gigantic fraud on its unwitting investors. It promised to open trade throughout Spain's South American colonies—an impossibility, given the enmity between England and Spain. Investors would reap "'fabulous profits' and mountains of gold and silver in exchange for common British exports, such as Cheshire cheese, sealing wax, and pickles" (Bakan 7). While the Company did participate in the slave trade to the West Indies, its bogus promises led to "fabulous" overinvestment. At one point, as Adam Smith notes in *The Wealth of Nations*, its stocks were valued at over three times the total worth of the Bank of England (II: 264). And in his history of the financial revolution in Britain, P. G. M. Dickson writes that investors grabbed up South Sea stocks "with a blind enthusiasm reminiscent of the Gaderene swine" (133; see also Carswell).

> Thus the deluded Bankrupt raves,
> Puts all upon a desp'rate Bett,
> Then plunges in the *Southern* Waves,
> Dipt over head and Ears—in Debt.

So wrote Jonathan Swift in his poem "The Bubble."

When the South Sea Company's bubble burst in 1720, the widespread financial ruin and the scandal that followed led Parliament to try to regulate corporations more rigorously than before. It passed the Royal Exchange and London Assurance Act—also known as the Bubble Act—in the same year. Smith understood why corporations were necessary for some large-scale enterprises, but he also opined that the directors of them, "being managers rather of other people's money than of their own, it cannot well be expected, that they should watch over it with the same anxious vigilance with which the partners in a private" enterprise pay attention to theirs (II: 264–265). From the outset of their history, corporations were risky businesses, and quite a few of them were frauds.

Most of the "founding fathers" of the US opposed corporations, which they viewed—rightly—as threats to freedom. They understood that corporations, besides sometimes being in the business of empire-building, were institutional machines fueled by greed. Those who stood to benefit most from them—"the moneyed interest"—did not care about the public interest, except to maintain peace and order while they profited. In 1816, Thomas Jefferson wrote: "I hope we shall crush in its birth the aristocracy of our moneyed corporations which dare already to challenge our government in a trial of strength, and bid defiance to the laws of our country" (cited in Hartmann 103). And James Madison declared that "the power of corporations ought to be limited . . . . The growing wealth acquired by them never fails to be a source of abuse" (cited in Kahn and Minnich 30).

Besides fraud and corruption, corporate avarice was expressed through forms of enclosure, taking possession of whatever might yield a profit, including land, enslaved Africans, and the opium trade. In the early going, although they were chartered by governments, corporations were fairly easy to tell apart from those governments. Nevertheless, John Locke, who was an influential formulator of the concept of the private ownership of land, was principal author of the early constitution for the Lords Proprietors of the Carolinas. This document recognized the Lords Proprietors as the owners of territory extending from what is today North Carolina to Florida. Besides land ownership, it also recognized their right to own "negro slaves." A key formulator of modern political liberalism, Locke, in his *Two Treatises of Government*, declared that throughout much of the non-European world, "there are still great tracts of ground to be found, which the inhabitants thereof" do not cultivate, Native Americans among them (139). (In fact, Native Americans practiced many forms of agriculture.) "The Indians," Locke argued, cannot therefore be said to own the lands that are essentially "waste" until Europeans come to settle and cultivate them. Locke's conception of landed property as thoroughly individualistic, dependent on the labor (cultivation) the owner invests in it, was repeated by later commentators such as legal authority William Blackstone. In Europe and much of the rest of the world, ideas about land ownership were, if not communal as among Native Americans, qualified by notions of obligation to families, communities, lords of the manor, or national or imperial governments. But in colonial North America, once Native Americans were excluded from ownership of the land, identifying the individuals who settled on it and cultivated it as its exclusive owners appeared to make sense (see Linklater 79–85).

Nowadays, corporations and governments are often so intertwined they can be hard to distinguish from one another. Take the defense industries in the US, which the Pentagon supports with billions of dollars in taxpayers' money, often by issuing no-bid contracts for services and products that might be much cheaper if competition were involved (e.g., see St. Clair). Further, the revolving door between federal agencies and lobbying firms representing corporate interests spins at a dizzying rate. The number of registered lobbyists in Washington, DC in 2014 stood at 12,281, though the actual figure may be closer to 100,000. Lobbying firms are said to earn about $9 billion a year.[3] The amount of money corporations and their heads such as the Koch brothers spend on elections is equally staggering. For the 2016 presidential election, the Kochs alone planned to spend nearly $1 billion (what they actually spent is unclear).

Originally chartered to be just a trading operation, the East India Company led, as noted, to the creation of a major feature of the British Empire, "the Jewel in the Crown," the Raj. While still a trading enterprise with a handful of small outposts in India, "John Company" did not need to enclose much land. But it began to develop an army made up of British officers and Indian troops or sepoys, which gradually conquered most of the subcontinent by war, diplomatic maneuvering, and financial bullying and chicanery. It settled on India because the Dutch East India Company had already established dominance in "the spice islands," including much of what is today Indonesia. In both cases, there was little to distinguish between their corporate activities and imperialism.

As it came to control more and more land, the East India Company privatized it by removing it from the possession of native rulers and setting up the class of *zamindars* or landowners, who collected rent and turned over a major portion of the proceeds to the Company (Wolpert 48–49). By the end of the 1700s, the rapacity of the so-called nabobs such as Robert Clive—Englishmen who enriched themselves by fair means or foul in India—was notorious, and led to the seven-year-long Warren Hastings trial for corruption at the end of the 1700s (Hastings had been Governor General of Bengal). The Company also acted with increasing independence from Britain. The corporations that, like the East India Company, have gone global are often beyond effective control by the nations where they are officially headquartered. Today, the representatives of transnational corporations are busily helping to forge trade agreements such as NAFTA and the TPP, and establishing and running new institutions such as the World Trade Organization that can override national laws and regulations.

Despite the objections to corporations expressed by Jefferson and Madison, during the early years of the US, the corporate form proved indispensable for binding the states together. The first treasurer of the US, Alexander Hamilton, saw the need for a national bank, a mint, and a centralized taxation system. The Bank of North America, a corporation chartered in 1781, was the first attempt to establish a central economic authority. It was followed by the First Bank of the US, chartered by Congress in 1791, and then after its charter expired, the Second Bank of the US in 1816. The federal government owned 20 percent of its publicly traded stock, while the rest belonged to private investors, so it is a good early example of a corporation with major public responsibilities answerable to the government, and yet also a vehicle for private investment. In that regard, it was similar to the East India Company and many other early corporations.

Under the conservative direction of Nicholas Biddle, the Second Bank seemed to many to be too restrictive with credit and a drag on the ability of the states to pursue their own economic policies. When its charter came up for renewal in 1832, it was approved by Congress, but vetoed by President Andew Jackson, who saw the Bank as overriding states' rights. This was the culmination of the "Bank War" of the early 1830s, but it was by no means the end of efforts to standardize money and credit and stabilize the economy at the national level.

Meanwhile in the first half of the 1800s in the US, there were other large-scale enterprises that demanded corporate organization for financing. Among these enterprises were the first railroads. The Baltimore and Ohio railroad, incorporated in 1827, began operations three years later. For the next three decades, the railroad boom, accompanied by the electric telegraph from the 1850s, eventually spanned the continent; along with barbed wire, all three proved vital in "taming the West." But taxation disputes at the state and even county levels raised legal issues, leading to the Supreme Court decision in 1886 that seemed to affirm that corporations were legal "persons," with the same rights as individual citizens. This unfortunate decision became the basis for the infamous *Citizens United* decision of 2010 (Clements; Hartmann).

The 1886 case pitted the Southern Pacific Railroad against Santa Clara County in California. The railroad's lawyers contended that it did not need to pay taxes to the county for land it traversed because, as a corporation, it had the same legal rights as persons under the Fourteenth Amendment. The Court ruled, in part, that the county's claim for back taxes was a "nullity," because it had improperly included fences in its assessment. Chief Justice Morrison Remick Waite also declared that, in his opinion, the Fourteenth Amendment, "which forbids a state to deny to any person within its jurisdiction the equal protection of the laws," applied to corporations. But it was a court reporter who interpreted the ruling to mean that "corporations are persons . . ." (cited in Hartmann 23). The reporter's interpretation was not part of the official Supreme Court ruling. Nevertheless, it was crucial to the 2010 ruling, which, as Jeffrey Clements declares, "is the biggest and most radical . . . decision in a regular series of recent Supreme Court decisions in favor of corporations" (xi). The 2010 decision has cleared the way for corporations to spend as much as they want on election campaigns:

> In *Citizens United*, the Supreme Court overturned decades of precedent, reversed a century of legislative effort to keep corporate money from corrupting democracy, and upended the American ideal that we are a government of people rather than a government of corporate wealth. The decision . . . symbolizes how far off the track we have fallen from ideal of the American Republic, governed by the people.
>
> *(Clements xi)*

The result is just what Jefferson and Madison feared, that the "moneyed interest" has won out over democracy, turning the US into a plutocracy.

Goldfingers: or, just how good is greed anyway?

"Greed is good," says Gordon Gekko, protagonist of the 1987 Oliver Stone movie *Wall Street*. Has the US returned to the age of the robber barons? Or has it surpassed that age many times over—surpassed, that is, in a negative sense? Is ours now "the age of greed," as the title of a recent book by Jeff Madrick has it? Charles Derber also speaks of "our new age of greed," involving "the culture of greed, materialism, and manic consumerism that the new corporate order has bred" (5, 7). Further, Phyllis Bennis writes that "Enron became the poster company for profiteering and cronyism, and Enronitis is the new code word for corporate greed" (37). And the subtitle of Ariana Huffington's *Pigs at the Trough* is self-explanatory: *How Corporate Greed and Political Corruption Are Undermining America*.

In Stone's movie, Gekko might be quoting Ayn Rand's *Atlas Shrugged*, a near-sacred screed for Republican House Speaker Paul Ryan and a number of other right-wing politicians.[4] The full quotation in the movie is:

> Greed, for lack of a better word, is good. Greed is right. Greed works. Greed clarifies, cuts through, and captures, the essence of the evolutionary spirit. Greed, in all of its forms; greed for life, for money, for love, knowledge, has marked the upward surge of mankind and greed, you mark my words, will not only save Teldar Paper, but that other malfunctioning corporation called the USA.

The last phrase suggests both that the US is today virtually a corporation and that greed is the ultimate form of patriotism, which from a neoliberal or free market standpoint makes perfect sense—that is, if you believe that, devouring the planet, the ultimate version of enclosure, makes perfect sense.

Gekko's behavior, both legal and illegal, illustrates some of the ways that investment practices, as a major aspect of the capitalist system, can be accurately called greedy. In Stone's movie and its 2010 sequel, *Wall Street: Money Never Sleeps*, Gekko gets rich partly through corporate raiding and insider trading. He is arrested and convicted of multiple securities violations. After his prison term, he continues amassing wealth through investing a trust fund meant for his daughter in a hedge fund and through short-selling municipal bonds. Each of his investment practices illustrates how the stock market, and not just Gordon Gekko the individual, is avaricious. Insider trading is illegal if the trader takes advantage of information about an investment opportunity that has not yet been made public. But once the information enters the public domain, insider trading is generally legal, though the trade has to be reported to the Securities and Exchange Commission. Corporate raiding, also a legal practice, involves the hostile takeover of a company by purchasing enough shares in its stock to force it in directions its management may not have wanted to go, such as downsizing its workforce, replacing its management, or declaring bankruptcy. The aim is not to improve the company or add anything to the economy, but to maximize the profits of the raider. And the practice of short-selling municipal bonds or any other asset involves selling something that the seller has borrowed, in the belief that its price is going down. Once that happens, the seller buys it back at the lower price and pockets the remainder as profit (see Michael Lewis, *The Big Short*). In all of these instances, and indeed in many other Wall Street practices, the concern is not about what any business or corporation is producing—its social utility—but only about the money that can be made in what amounts to gaming the system.[5]

In "The Greed Fallacy," published toward the end of 2008, Arthur MacEwan writes:

> Various people explain the current financial crisis as a result of "greed." There is, however, no indication of a change in the degree or extent of greed on Wall Street (or anywhere else) in the last several years. Greed is a constant. If greed were the cause of the financial crisis, we would be in financial crisis pretty much all the time.
>
> *(58)*

Slavoj Žižek also contends that "talk of greed" is an ideological smokescreen. While commenting on the Occupy Wall Street movement, Žižek writes:

> Let us then prohibit talk of greed. Public figures from the Pope downwards bombard us with injunctions to resist the culture of excessive greed and consumption, but this spectacle of cheap moralization is an ideological operation if there ever was one.
>
> *(The Year of Dreaming Dangerously 78)*

According to both MacEwan and Žižek, to rail against greed does not get at what is problematic about capitalism as a system.

Marx does not mention greed in *Capital*, although it is implicit in everything he says about the exploitation of labor through the extraction of surplus value. But in the *Grundrisse*, he writes: "Money is therefore not only the object but the fountainhead of greed. The mania for possessions is possible without money; but greed itself is the product of a definite social development, not *natural*, as opposed to *historical*" (222). That is to say, greed is the result of the emergence of money as the supreme measure of value and the commodity that can represent all other commodities. According to this logic, greed is not simply a sin or some private, personal inclination, but neither is it the result of capitalism, because there have been many non-capitalist societies that employ money. Nevertheless, Marx goes on to say that "monetary greed, or mania for wealth, necessarily brings with it the decline and fall of the ancient communities . . . ." Once greed dominates, "this presupposes the full development of exchange values, hence a corresponding organization of society" (223)—that is, capitalism. The substitution of exchange values for earlier, traditional, communal values represents the general transition from *Gemeinschaft* to *Gesellschaft*, to use Ferdinand Tönnies' terms, including the emergence of the capitalist market society, in which everything has its price and in which all individuals and institutions are forced or at least encouraged to vie for money. They are forced or encouraged, in other words, to accept Gordon Gekko's mantra that "greed is good." The "organization of society" around "exchange values" has now reached what appears to be its apogee in present-day, corporate, globalized capitalism. From this standpoint, greed and capitalism are inseparable.

The *Citizens United* ruling by the Supreme Court, moreover, affirmed that corporations are persons and that the money they or their owners pour into elections is speech. If that absurd ruling were any reflection of reality, then it would be perfectly logical to attribute moral failings—or the virtue of greed, as Ayn Rand and Gordon Gekko insist—to corporations. And even if corporations aren't persons, they often take on the personas of their CEOs, as Purnima Bose argues in the case of GE's Jack Welch (18–63). Of course, not all people are greedy, or greedy all the time, or greedy to the same extent as other people, so perhaps in that respect people differ from corporations. It is also possible for a CEO to be charitable, moral, and the opposite of a greedy individual. To be an effective corporate manager, however, he or she must be greedy on behalf of the corporation and its shareholders.

Bakan notes that the *Multinational Monitor* listed 42 "major legal breaches" by GE in the 1990s (75). In *The Great American Stickup*, Robert Scheer also comments on GE's role in the mortgage bubble that led to the stock market crash in 2007–2008. GE "could be the textbook example of how short-term greed can serve executives while destroying a company's future" (Scheer 44). And Jerry Mander points out that GE "made $14.2 billion in profits in 2010, of which $5.1 billion came from the United States . . . but [it] paid no taxes at all" (205). Hundreds of corporations today offshore not just jobs, but billions of dollars to tax havens in Panama, Bermuda, Cyprus, and elsewhere.

During the Great Depression of the 1930s, GE established a credit branch, GE Capital, that for five decades provided credit at reasonable rates, enabling people to purchase GE appliances:

> In the 1980s . . . with GE being run by legendary high roller Jack Welsh [*sic*], the company put growth above all else. GE Capital rapidly expanded its loan business into areas where it had scant knowledge, including credit card and property loans.
>
> *(Scheer 44–45)*

When the economy tanked in 2008, GE was pulled out of the ditch by a $100 billion bailout from the federal government. Scheer quotes *The Economist* for March 19, 2009: until the crash, "GE Capital flourished as a member of the 'shadow banking' system of firms that offered myriad financial products without having to bear the regulatory burdens of banks." The crash proved that both the banks and corporations like GE engaging in "bank-like activities" would need "much stricter oversight" (cited in Scheer 45).

The former workers at the GE plant in Bloomington, Indiana know all about GE's greedy and sometimes criminal behavior. Despite several promises that it would not do so, since 2009 GE has downsized its Bloomington facility, laying off most of a workforce of 3,200 at its peak who earned an average of $24 an hour plus benefits, and relocating to Mexico where the new workers receive $2 an hour without benefits. Currently, GE is going to reduce or eliminate the pensions of Bloomington workers, many of whom were forced to retire early because the plant was closing. No wonder its former Hoosier employees refer to GE as "GrEed" (Bose 53, 56). This is, of course, just one example out of thousands of corporations behaving avariciously.

If corporate "persons" are inevitably greedy, it is perhaps only natural that their executives also behave greedily. In regard to CEO compensation, Sam Pizzigati reports that Yahoo "has succeeded royally at what our contemporary corporations do best: enrich executives":

> Yahoo's current CEO, former Google honcho Marissa Mayer, came on board at the company in 2012, the company's fourth CEO in four years. She replaced Scott Thompson, who stood to make $26 million his first year, but only lasted four months. Thompson's predecessor, Carol Bartz, signed on for $32 million. She followed Yahoo founder Jerry Yang, who put in a brief stint after his hand-picked successor Terry Semel flamed out, but not before collecting an astounding $489.6 million for a half-dozen years in the Yahoo chief executive suite.

Pizzigati goes on to note that Mayer hired a former colleague at Google who "didn't quite work out," so she "had to give him the heave-ho. His severance package: $58 million for 15 months of executive labor." Yahoo's shareholders were apparently critical of such executive pay extravagances, so Mayer hired H. Lee Scott, a former Walmart CEO, who before leaving Walmart received in his last year there $30.2 million, "over 1,500 times average Walmart worker pay" (Pizzigati). The Yahoo example could be multiplied many times over.

In regard to Walmart, currently the largest corporation in the world, it is well known that the Waltons, its major owners, are the wealthiest family in the US, to the tune of at least $90 billion. They have been called the greediest family in America. Can or should the Waltons behave differently? In moral terms, certainly. But in terms of the supposed rationality of the capitalist system and those who act according to its rules, certainly not. Walmart is famous for its bad labor practices, squeezing its workers in many ways. Walmart Watch has often commented on the many ways that corporation's greed affects local communities. The website for Making Change at Walmart reports:

Although the company will often cite higher numbers, the average Walmart Associate makes just $8.81 per hour according to a study published by Bloomberg News. An employee who works Walmart's definition of full-time (34 hours per week) makes just $15,500 per year. That means hundreds of thousands of people who work full-time at Walmart still live below the poverty line.[6]

The many, many Walmart workers who are not allowed to work full-time (40 hours a week) are among those applying for food stamps and other government aid, just to make ends meet. To borrow Ralph Nader's phrase, this is "corporate welfare" with a vengeance. Walmart costs American taxpayers at least $1 billion because its employees have to rely on public assistance. At least until the passage of the Affordable Care Act, to get health insurance workers at Walmart had to pay the corporation for it, taking a large chunk out of their already non-living wages. Also well known is the fact that Walmart opposes all attempts by its workers to unionize. Demonstrations all over the country against Walmart's bad labor practices were held on Black Friday, November 28, 2014, but seem to have had little impact.

"Turnover rates of workers [are] unusually high at Walmart and worker abuse [is] a virtual managerial requirement," writes Jeff Madrick, who continues:

> Over the years, there were many allegations of [harsh] and sometimes illegal practices. Workers were locked in stores at night, underage workers were regularly hired, workers were forced to work more hours than Walmart reported and were paid for, and illegal workers were hired below minimum wage (though they are legally entitled to the minimum wage).
> *(148)*

Walmart used to claim that what it sold was made in America, but now much of what it sells is made in China, where the abuse of workers is rampant. In regard to Walmart's policy of underpaying its employees, Barbara Ehrenreich notes that many of them can't even afford to shop at Walmart: "The sad truth is that people earning Walmart-level wages tend to favor the fashions available at the Salvation Army. Nor do they have much use for Walmart's other departments . . ." (57).

Financialization

"Enron has collapsed," Vijay Prashad declares; "But the Enron stage of capitalism, that Second Enclosure Movement, moves onward at full throttle" (10). And full throttle means an increasing emphasis on financialization rather than on the production of goods and services. The essence of financialization is the creation of investment vehicles whose sole aim is to make more money for the investors, not by producing anything of substantial value, but by profiting from other people's and institutions' financial difficulties—that is, from their debts. Writing in 2001, James Petras and Henry Veltmeyer state that for every dollar "circulating in the real economy, $25–50 circulates in the world of pure finance . . . . Less than five percent of circulating capital has any productive function whatsoever" (15).

Greed may be a constant in corporate behavior, but its role has mushroomed as financial markets have become dominant throughout the world, overtaking industrial production and real commodities markets.[7] As David Harvey notes, the leading economic gurus in both the US and throughout the world have supported this development: "Neoliberalization has meant . . . the financialization of everything" (*A Brief History of Neoliberalism* 42).[8] In 1952, total financial assets in the US represented approximately 400 percent of GDP. In 2000, the percentage had grown to about 900 percent. So for every dollar invested in the production and sale of real commodities, $900 were invested in such items as derivatives and credit default swaps (Henwood 191).

Beginning in the 1970s, financialization has become dominant not just in the US, but in the global economy. Its biggest benefits go to high-end investors such as banks, hedge funds, and their managers, in part because they can diversify their holdings and can therefore afford (up to a point) to take risks, especially with other people's money, expecting that if a specific investment registers a loss, other investments will likely pay off. The economic collapse of 2007–2008 came largely through "the widespread use of complicated and opaque securities, known as derivatives, in a deregulated, interconnected, and global financial system," as Marty Wolfson explains. Mortgages were packaged together as derivatives called "mortgage-backed securities," which formed a pyramid based mainly on the individual holders of single mortgages. Many mortgages were issued to homebuyers whom the lenders knew were likely to be unable to keep up their payments. So the subprime mortgage bubble began to grow until it burst toward the end of 2007. The major financial institutions, including those such as Fannie May and Freddie Mac that were supposedly under government control, thought they were safe because they developed such items as collateralized debt obligations and credit default swaps that only inflated the bubble. These are types of insurance backed by other lending institutions. But if the institutions toward the end of the chain are unable to meet their obligations, "the protection against loss is illusory" (Wolfson 136).

Derivatives markets did not amount to much in the 1980s. But by 2011, their "notional sum" globally was somewhere around $700 trillion "for over-the-counter and probably a similar sum for exchange-traded derivatives" (Lapavitsas 22). According to Costas Lapavitsas, international banking institutions are the main driving force behind the derivatives markets, in which nothing of value is added to societies or to the lives of individuals around the globe, except for those institutions and individuals profiting from them. Derivative markets are just money multiplying money, or rather debt piled on debt. Lapavitsas claims that for regulation of international capital flows, interest rates, exchange rates, and the operations of banks to be effective, they would need to be accompanied by increasing public ownership of major aspects of the economy, including financial institutions such as banks. He concludes that "confronting financialization" will involve "reasserting the importance of public housing, health, education, pensions, and consumption . . . ." There needs to be a new emphasis on "the notion of a public right to access basic goods and services. The expanded rule of money over the livelihood of households and individuals would thus be reversed" (349). He is, in other words, arguing in favor of some version of democratic socialism and against the current dominion of unrestrained capitalism.

Yet because of the austerity measures imposed by the European Union on Lapavitsas' home country, Greece, starting in 2010, that nation has been forced to undertake "the biggest fire-sale in the history of state-owned assets" (Lowenstein 97). The corporate enclosure of much of Greece's publicly owned property and public services is supposed to overcome its indebtedness to the rest of Europe, but instead has been having the opposite effect. Greek poverty and unemployment are now at all-time highs. Austerity and privatization have also stoked the rise of the Golden Dawn, a neo-Nazi political party that has been making life miserable for immigrants. The same economic factors—and not just immigration itself—are at work in the rise of authoritarian and anti-immigrant movements elsewhere in Europe and the US.

In contrast to Lapavitsas, and despite calling his book *Infectious Greed: How Deceit and Risk Corrupted the Financial Markets*, Frank Partnoy does not think that much is wrong with the world of high finance, because:

> Participants in the financial markets are rational economic actors: they violate legal rules not because they are evil people, but because it makes economic good sense for them to do so. If the gain from cooking the books is substantial, and the probability of punishment is zero, the rational strategy is cook, cook, cook.
>
> *(409)*

Whether or not corporations can be understood as having the same moral weaknesses as persons, the behavior particularly of the financial sector over the last several decades has been reprehensible. That is the main theme of *Infectious Greed*, though Partnoy clearly admires many of the financial high rollers whose "rational" shenanigans and crimes he recounts. He clearly agrees with Gordon Gekko that "greed is good."

"Greed" is the term Partnoy chooses to cover the entire story of corporate capitalism from Enron to the 2007–2008 debacle. Besides the well-known cases of fraud and corruption such as Bernard Madoff's scam that have made the headlines, Partnoy notes that most financial trading has been going on in private, out of the public spotlight. American Andy Krieger's currency swaps, for example, using New Zealand dollars or "kiwis" unbeknownst to the New Zealand government, almost bankrupted that nation. Introducing his book, Partnoy declares that "any appearance of control in financial markets is only an illusion, not a grounded reality." Further, the markets "came to the brink of collapse several times" before they crashed in 2007–2008, "with the meltdowns related to Enron and Long Term

Capital Management being prominent examples" of behavior that was widespread. "Today, the risk of system-wide collapse remains greater than ever before. The truth is that the markets are still spinning out of control" (3). But Partnoy's general message is that, because the system encourages greedy, even criminal, behavior, the smart set should go right ahead and take advantage of it.

It is also frequently profitable as well as greedy to bet on business failure rather than success. Charles Ferguson points out that as the bubble leading to the 2007–2008 crash ballooned, the incentives to bet against its continued expansion grew:

> Without question, thousands of Wall Street loan buyers, securitizers, traders, salespeople, and executives knew perfectly well that it would end in tears, but they were making a fortune while it lasted, with no individual ability to stop the bubble and very little to lose when it ended.
>
> *(124)*

So make hay—or money—while the sun shines, because it will soon set. Greed, in other words, is built into the system, in such a way that many individuals and institutions such as hedge funds were making millions when the crash came and even after it came.

It is true that the greed of individuals can't be blamed for the 2007–2008 crash, because it was a system failure. Of course, there were swarms of greedy CEOs, bankers, hedge fund managers, and Wall Street investors ready to take advantage of the crisis. In their financial wheelings and dealings, well described by Partnoy, Scheer, Stiglitz, Lapavitsas, Ferguson, and many others, they simply took advantage of what the system encouraged them to do. Those same individuals—the 1 percent in Occupy Wall Street lingo—have been making out like bandits all through the great "recession" or even "depression," while many of the 99 percent have been left in various economic ditches, collectively known as poverty.[9] And very few of the bandits have gone to jail. Stiglitz points out that:

> greed may be an inherent part of human nature, but that doesn't mean there is nothing we can do to temper the consequences of unscrupulous bankers who would exploit the poor and engage in anticompetitive practices. We can and should regulate banks, forbid predatory lending, make them accountable for their fraudulent practices, and punish them for abuses of monopoly power.
>
> *(The Price of Inequality 122)*

A more accurate metaphor for a corporation than "person," as in the *Citizens United* ruling, may be "vampire." Among the many synonyms or near-synonyms for greed, voracity is one that suggests vampirism. Marx declared that capital "is dead labour which, vampire-like, lives only by sucking living labour, and lives the more, the more labour it sucks" (*Capital* 1: 342). And Jim Hightower calls Jack Welch, CEO of GE, "the Count Dracula of the corporate world" (cited in Bose 51).

Certainly even the best-behaved corporation is closer to being some sort of inhuman monster than being a normal human. In Frank Norris's *The Octopus*, concerning the battle between the railroads and the courts in the 1880s, Dyke the engineer concludes that he:

> had been merely the object of a colossal trick, a sordid injustice, a victim of the insatiate greed of the monster, caught and choked by one of those millions of tentacles suddenly reaching up from below, from out the dark beneath his feet, coiling around his throat, throttling him, strangling him, sucking his blood.
>
> *(681)*

Dyke's nightmarish thought that the monster is not only a gigantic octopus, but also a vampire, echoes Marx and many others on the voracious activities both of capitalists and of corporations. According to the proponents of free market capitalism, however, the profit motive is simply what oils the wheels of the economic machine. For them, Bernard Mandeville's thesis in *Fable of the Bees* (1705) is axiomatic: the pursuit of self-interest produces the public good. In contrast, writing about the 2007–2008 crash, Joseph Stiglitz declares: "clearly, the pursuit of self-interest—greed—did not lead to societal well-being . . ." (*Freefall* 281).

Notes

1 "The global economic system is rewarding corporations and their executives with generous profits and benefits packages for contracting out their production to sweatshops paying substandard wages, for clear-cutting primal forests, for introducing labor-saving technologies that displace tens of thousands of employees, for dumping toxic wastes, and for shaping political agendas to advance corporate interests over human interests" (David Korten, *When Corporations Rule the World* 118). Compare the behavior of Citigroup as described by Jeffrey Clements in *Corporations Are Not People* (129–130).
2 The 2016 election of Donald Trump and his choice of a number of billionaire corporate heads for his cabinet, such as Rex Tillerson of ExxonMobil to be Secretary of State, is symptomatic of how far the American government has been taken over by corporations.
3 Not all lobbyists represent corporations, but most of them do. For the statistics, see Lee Fang, "Where Have All the Lobbyists Gone?" In *Seventeen Contradictions and the End of Capitalism*, David Harvey further explains: "Government planning at a variety of scales (macroeconomic, urban, regional and local) takes centre stage sometimes in competition with but more often in partnership with private and corporate activities. A large segment of capital accumulation then passes through the state in ways that are not necessarily directed to profit-maximizing but to social and geopolitical ends. Even in states most devoted to the principles of privatisation and neoliberalisation the military-industrial complex is set apart from the rest of the economy as a lucrative trough at which private subcontracted interests feed freely" (63).
4 Jonathan Hoenig agrees with Gekko, titling his 1999 book about the wonders of "free" markets *Greed Is Good: The Capitalist Pig Guide to Investing*. He had earlier titled the finance journal he produced *The Capitalist Pig*, presumably without pejorative connotations. There are a couple of other books using "greed is good" as their titles (see Thomas Frank 141).

5 Because they are virtually monopolies, or at least oligopolies, it is not possible to square enormous outfits such as GE or ExxonMobil with the Adam Smith model of free enterprise based on competition among equals in the marketplace. But the Smithian ideal is still presented in introductory textbooks on economics such as Mankiw's *Principles* as the scientific truth of how capitalist economies function. In the fifth edition of his tome, Mankiw pays almost no attention to the differences between small business and transnational corporations. He recognizes that "perfect competition" is not the same as "monopoly control," but this "is a matter of degree," and therefore "we will not go far wrong assuming that firms operate in competitive markets, even if that is not precisely the case" (340). This falsification allows him to say very little about how corporations often behave quite badly, even destructively. In relation to corporations, the "Invisible Hand" supposedly governing their behavior was voodoo economics from the beginning.

6 In recent business news reports, Walmart has just raised the pay of many (but not all) of its hourly employees to $10, still not enough to be considered a living wage.

7 By "real commodities," I am of course referring to material goods and services rather than to the manipulation and repackaging of debts such as subprime mortgages.

8 Economist Doug Henwood of the *Left Business Observer* agrees: "the new economy" involves "the financialization of everything" (*After the New Economy* 191). And see Joseph Stiglitz, *Freefall* (13).

9 Steven Mnuchin, Donald Trump's Secretary of the Treasury, has been accused of running a fraudulent mortgage factory when he was CEO of OneWest. In one instance, it foreclosed on a 90-year-old widow because of a 27-cent payment error.

6
GLOBALIZATION AND EMPIRE

> "In the cabaret of globalization, the state shows itself as a table dancer that strips off everything until it is left with only the minimum indispensable garments: the repressive force."
> — *Subcomandante Marcos*

Given the increasing power of transnational corporations (TNCs), to some observers, such as Subcomandante Marcos, the term "globalization" suggests the capitalist enclosure of the entire planet. To others, however, it suggests breaking down barriers through "free trade" and through cultural exchanges that promise ultimately to unify the world in peace and harmony. From the neoliberal perspective, the latter prospect would bring to an end the long history of imperialism, during which more powerful polities have conquered and dominated weaker ones, often enslaving their populations, exterminating them, or both. According to neoliberalism, corporations are progressive engines of globalization-as-democracy rather than engines of enclosure and empire: "Corporations are seen as virtuous as well as dynamic agents of progressive change," writes Ronaldo Munck; "Globalization will, according to this view, lead to a decline of inequality and poverty worldwide as the market works its magic" (2). Munck points out, however, that exactly the opposite has happened: worldwide poverty and inequality have increased dramatically since the 1970s.[1]

Discourse about globalization can make it sound benign—the world is becoming a "global village," as Marshall McLuhan announced in the 1960s. But he also claimed that that village was "retribalizing," which hardly sounds benign. The processes of globalization bring people and cultures closer together (think of the ease and speed with which anyone today who can afford a ticket can fly around the world). But the same processes also weaken the power and sovereignty of nation-states, causing the rise of often virulent forms of nationalism, expressing a longing for the stability and secure identity nations are still deemed to provide.[2] Instead of declining, hostilities, wars, and even genocides continue, and may even be increasing. The "war on terror," which was ramping up well before 9/11, has been declared, by former Vice President Dick Cheney among others, to be potentially endless. Meanwhile, American imperialism marches on.

History also marches on, of course

Is there any difference between globalization and imperialism? The former is often viewed as a quite recent phenomenon, but in the modern era the two have the same origin, during the Renaissance "age of discovery." Only with the first European voyages down the west coast of Africa and to the Americas did both globalization and the Western conquest of much of the non-Western world become possible. From the 1500s to the mid-1900s, Spain, Portugal, the Netherlands, Britain, France, and ultimately Germany and Italy "globalized" by force much of the rest of the world. Those who see globalization as quite recent stress the fact that direct rule by the European and American powers has ended, with many former colonies since World War II becoming more or less independent nation-states. But indirect rule by economic clout and by the threat, at least, of military force continues. For the most part, so-called "postcolonial" scholars such as Edward Said see today's version of globalization as imperialism on steroids. And the American invasions of Afghanistan and Iraq make it obvious that Western imperialism has not ended.

While those invasions were occurring, members of the Bush II regime asserted that America was not and had never been an imperializing power. Asked on April 28, 2003 by Al Jazeera television if it worried him that the invasion of Iraq "might create the impression that the United States is becoming an imperial . . . power," Secretary of Defense Donald Rumsfeld replied:

> We've never been a colonial power. We don't take our force[s] and . . . try to take other people's real estate or . . . resources, their oil. That's just not what the United States does. . . . That's not how democracies behave.

So, too, Secretary of State Colin Powell: "We have never been imperialists." And the "commander guy," Bush II: "America has never been an empire."

Conservative historian Niall Ferguson quotes Rumsfeld, Powell, and Bush at the beginning of *Colossus*, and expresses surprise that three of America's most powerful politicians deny that America is an imperializing power. A defender of British imperialism, Ferguson thinks that it is a mistake for American imperialists not to stand up for their own interventions and wars in the Middle East and elsewhere.[3] Whether Rumsfeld, Powell, and Bush believed their statements or not, denying that the US has ever had or been an empire is based on an extreme version of American exceptionalism. The US can't be an imperialist nation because "we" are a peaceful, freedom-loving democracy, which is why "they" hate us so much.

Besides Ferguson and postcolonial scholars such as Said, among the many authors that have addressed American imperialism since 9/11 are Benjamin Barber (*Fear's Empire*), Roger Burbach and Jim Tarbell (*Imperial Overstretch*), Greg Grandin (*Empire's Workshop*), Robert Jensen (*Citizens of the Empire*), Chalmers Johnson (*The Sorrows of Empire*), John Judis (*The Folly of Empire*), Gabriel Kolko (*World in Crisis*), Michael Mann (*Incoherent Empire*), John Newhouse (*Imperial America: The Bush Assault on the World Order*), and Michael Parenti (*Against Empire*). Unlike Ferguson, these authors are all highly critical of American diplomatic meddling and military interventions in the Middle East and elsewhere. They all suggest that imperialism may spell the end of the American way of life, although America has always been an imperializing power (e.g., see Peter Onuf, *Jefferson's Emipre*). Kolko, for one, writes:

> Capitalism is in a growing crisis and the century of American domination is ending—perhaps it has ended already. Even in the absence of any viable opposition, American capitalism is tending to commit suicide—it is taking other nations with it.
>
> *(3)*

Whether or not America along with "American domination" is committing suicide, it arose out of a rebellion against British imperialism, so to some it has seemed reasonable to view its history as inherently anti-imperial. "We" have always been in favor of liberation and democracy everywhere. When the US invades another country, the government almost always declares its aim is to liberate that country from some version of tyranny. Further, there has also been some degree of controversy about whether the US became an imperializing power only with the Spanish-American War and the acquisition of Spain's overseas possessions at the end of the 1800s.[4] Today, most historians agree that the westward expansion of the US, including the Louisiana Purchase and its war against Mexico in the late 1840s, which led to the takeover of most of its western states, was a version of empire-building.[5] It certainly contributed to globalization, defined as extending the reach of capitalist "development" into new territories.

Rather than emphasizing military force, in *Imperialism in the Twenty-First Century*, John Smith contends that imperialism involves the capitalist "super-exploitation" of labor and of natural resources by TNCs. His analysis does not treat empire as first and foremost involving military conquest. In partial contrast to Smith, Jan Nederveen Pieterse in *Globalization or Empire?* distinguishes between imperialism and economic neoliberalism, yet sees them "twinning" in contemporary circumstances: "The core of empire is the national security state and the military-industrial complex; neoliberalism is about business, financial operations, and marketing . . . ." Yet "neoliberal empire," an apparent oxymoron, "is an attempt to merge the America whose business is business with the America whose business is war . . ." (Pieterse 45).

Smith does not insist on making distinctions between types of globalization or of capitalism, or between globalization and imperialism. He focuses instead, as the TNCs globalize, on the weakness of labor protections in places such as Bangladeshi sweatshops. "Super-exploitation" can mean, among other things, the increasing devaluation and precarity of labor.[6] Pieterse, who makes such distinctions, nevertheless recognizes that America has always engaged in both business and war, or in both capitalism and imperialist expansion and domination—they are not identical, but they are inseparable. Both Smith and Pieterse understand globalization as capitalism exceeding national boundaries, and both stress that it is a continuation of imperialism whose main beneficiaries are "a new international capitalist class" (Petras and Veltmeyer 12).[7]

In *The New Imperialism*, David Harvey also insists that "the territorial and capitalist logics of power" are "distinct from each other" (29). But the capitalist side of the equation nevertheless often involves territorial enclosures, if not through colonization, then through, for example, specially carved-out industrial and export zones. Today, TNCs are purchasing huge areas of land in Africa and elsewhere, in part as hedges against future difficulties (see Alexander Ross). In *Empire of Capital*, moreover, Ellen Meiksins Wood writes that early "agrarian capitalism, which was gradually enveloping the English countryside," involved "new principles of imperial expansion":

> The history of early agrarian capitalism—the process of domestic "colonization", the removal of land from the "waste", its "improvement", enclosure and new conceptions of property rights—was reproduced in the theory and practice of empire.
>
> *(78)*

At least before World War II, the major European empires were the largest versions of territorial enclosure yet devised. But contemporary globalization via the TNCs can be interpreted as capitalism's attempt to enclose virtually everything.

Along with the major European empires came colonization—invasion and settlement by Europeans—typically resisted by indigenous populations.[8] The slave trade and plantation slavery in the Americas flourished as major offshoots of early modern imperialism. Like the peasantry in Europe, many indigenous populations were evicted from land desired by the colonizers, a process that frequently involved genocidal exterminations. In both North and South America, Native Americans, if not totally vanquished, were soon relegated to the status of a "vanishing race." Wood notes that in North America, the British at first followed the pattern of their conquest and settlement of Ireland. But their "expropriation of indigenous peoples" on the other side of the Atlantic "was even more complete." Eventually, their aim was the complete removal (or extermination) of Native Americans. "There were to be no indigenous landlords, tenants or even labourers; and transplantation became genocide" (90). For two centuries, many observers believed that so-called "primitive" or "savage races" everywhere were doomed to extinction as the "white race" advanced, enclosing land along the way.[9]

While the formal empires that developed through trade, war, colonization, genocide, and slavery were finally giving way in the twentieth century to decolonization, the new, supposedly independent nation-states were still largely dependent on the economic power of the West and of Western corporations. The rebellions and euphoric pronouncements of independence that accompanied decolonization frequently led to disillusionment because of economic dependency, a major theme in Kwame Nkrumah's writings and speeches. "The result of neo-colonialism is that foreign capital is used for the exploitation rather than for the development of the less developed parts of the world," he declared in 1965; "Investment under neo-colonialism increases rather than decreases the gap between the rich and poor countries of the world" (21).

Besides continued economic dependency and exploitation, the Western powers continue to interfere with the internal affairs of the supposedly newly independent states, as the US has repeatedly done in Latin America.[10] Often the interference has involved gunboat diplomacy and outright invasions, and often, too, it has directly benefited American corporations, as when in 1954 the CIA toppled democratically elected Jacob Arbenz in Guatemala. Arbenz had attempted to retake (while paying for) uncultivated land technically owned by the United Fruit Company. He planned to distribute that land to impoverished peasants. Its recent invasions of Afghanistan and Iraq have destabilized the entire Middle East, but the US is not about to colonize either of those countries, at least not in the sense of planting settlements there, any more than it planned to colonize Guatemala. Nevertheless, its invasions demonstrate that the so-called "new imperialism" is little different from the old variety.

In the 1990s, Western commentators such as Thomas Friedman (*The Lexus and the Olive Tree*) and Francis Fukuyama (*The End of History and the Last Man*) made it sound as though globalization was something entirely new and liberating for the entire world. Friedman even suggested that when a McDonald's franchise opened in a country, it would be at peace with the world. (Clearly he did not have the US in mind.) That was just as absurd as Fukuyama's claim that, largely because of the fall of the communist regimes in Eastern Europe and the Soviet Union, history had come to an end. For both Friedman and Fukuyama, from the 1990s on, capitalist globalization would be a matter of ever-expanding freedom and prosperity for everyone.[11] Even in that decade, however, well before 9/11 demonstrated that history was not about to end, others were not nearly so sanguine. In *Against Empire*, for instance, Christian Parenti interpreted globalization as I am doing, as the continuation of Western imperialism:

> The "global economy" is another name for imperialism, and imperialism is a transnational form of capitalism. The essence of capitalism is to turn nature into commodities and commodities into capital. The live green earth is transformed into dead, gold bricks, with luxury items for the few and toxic slag heaps for the many. The glittering mansion overlooks a vast sprawl of shanty towns, wherein a desperate, demoralized humanity is kept in line with drugs, television, and armed force.
>
> *(208)*

Sixteen years earlier, in *The Postmodern Condition*, Jean-François Lyotard also offered an "end of history" thesis, but unlike Fukuyama's his was hardly an optimistic one. He contended that the postmodern era was marked by "incredulity toward metanarratives," including all ideologies that dealt with universal history and emancipation. He did not view the lack of any major opposition to globalizing capitalism as a triumph. As he put it, "The rise of independence struggles after the Second World War and the recognition of new national names seem to indicate a strengthening of local legitimacies and the disappearance of any prospect of universal emancipation" (322).

If Fukuyama and Friedman had been on the lookout for history in the 1990s, they might have noticed the genocidal conflicts going on in the former Yugoslavia or in other parts of the world such as Rwanda and Indonesia. And of course, they paid no attention to the role that capitalist corporations played in those conflicts, because corporations were, they thought, part of the solution rather than part of the problem. Nor did they pay much attention to the growing turmoil in the Middle East and increasing incidents of terrorism arising out of that turmoil. In that decade, those were just a few of the signs that history was failing to end by reaching a capitalist-liberal nirvana. Capitalist globalization continued to extend its reach by "super-exploitation" in the poorest countries of the world and by the old imperialist method of military domination. We—meaning the human species—just could not let go of history, aka exploitation, war, and genocide.

Lyotard contended that "the immense economic-financial battles now being waged by the multinational companies and banks" to dominate the global market offered "no cosmopolitan prospects": "The world market is not creating a universal history in modernity's sense of that term. Cultural differences are . . . being promoted as touristic and cultural commodities at every point on the scale" (322–323).

Those cultural differences are not just commodities, however—they are a main source of the animosities that have led to genocides in Bosnia, Guatemala, Rwanda, the Congo, the Sudan, Indonesia, Myanmar, and parts of the Middle East. As the sovereignty of all nation-states weakens under the impact of corporate globalization, a sort of hysteria builds around icons of national identity, which in turn often enflames hatred of others. Meanwhile, capitalism, according to Lyotard, was "doing nothing to reduce the inequality of wealth in the world, and is in fact increasing it" (323). As a major aspect of "the postmodern condition," McLuhan's "global village" is being "retribalized" with a vengeance.

Today, the world is engaged in a potentially endless war on terror, begun not by terrorists, but by the US. Even al-Qaeda might have been brought to heel by international police action rather than by "shock and awe" warfare. And just why did the US launch its war on terror? Was it because terrorism after 9/11 was so terrifically threatening to Americans? No. It was launched mainly in the interests of Big Oil. Represented by President Bush and Vice President Cheney, Big Oil managed to take over both the U.S. civilian government and the U.S. military, and, through lots of cajoling, bribes, and outright lies, managed also to get the military to invade Iraq in 2003. As has often been pointed out, there was no connection between Sadam Hussein and the 9/11 terrorist attack on the World Trade Center and the Pentagon. But toppling Sadam, the Bushites believed (even though they denied that was their goal), would open the high road to Iraq's state-owned oil fields for American and British corporations to enclose.

Recently, Donald Trump, 45th president of the US, has asserted that "we" should have seized "their" oil to begin with, apparently not realizing that has already happened. During a CNN special broadcast in 2013, Antonia Juhasz pointed out that:

> Before the 2003 invasion, Iraq's domestic oil industry was fully nationalized and closed to Western oil companies. A decade of war later, it is largely privatized and utterly dominated by foreign firms. From ExxonMobil and Chevron to BP and Shell, the West's largest oil companies have set up shop in Iraq. So have a slew of American oil service companies, including Halliburton, the Texas-based firm Dick Cheney ran before becoming George W. Bush's running mate in 2000.
>
> *("Why the War in Iraq Was Fought for Big Oil")*

Juhasz also quotes a number of government officials who, unlike Cheney and Bush, acknowledge that the invasion of Iraq was all about oil: "Of course it's about oil; we can't really deny that," declared General John Abizaid, who was in charge of military operations in Iraq in 2007. The former Secretary of Defense Chuck Hagel asserted, also in 2007, "People say we're not fighting for oil. Of course we are." And in his memoir, Alan Greenspan stated: "I am saddened that it is politically inconvenient to acknowledge what everyone knows: the Iraq war is largely about oil." According to Juhasz, currently 80 percent of Iraq's oil production is being exported by the private corporations that pump it out of the ground, while Iraqis are mired in poverty and in the pervasive violence that has devastated their country (besides Juhasz, see Everest).

The destruction visited on Iraq and Afghanistan by U.S. and NATO forces was aided and abetted by the many corporations, including private security companies such as Blackwater and DynCorps, which collectively constituted the second largest military power in both countries after the US. Meanwhile, billions of dollars of taxpayers' money have been embezzled, lost, and squandered by corporations contracted to rebuild Iraq and Afghanistan's infrastructures. In *Disaster Capitalism*, Antony Lowenstein reports that a bipartisan U.S. Commission on Wartime Contracting in 2011 indicated that:

> between $31 billion and $61 billion worth of Pentagon projects ... had amounted to nothing due to fraud and waste. In the same year, the Center for Public Integrity concluded that the Pentagon's no-bid contract system had exploded from $50 billion in 2003 to $140 billion in 2011.
>
> *(37)*

Fraud and corruption aside, Lowenstein demonstrates how the outsourcing and privatization of war has become big business, in which greed—"vulture capitalism"—feeds upon the new killing fields of the world.

The burning of fossil fuels is the main cause of global warming. The CEOs and boosters of the corporations profiting from the extraction, refining, and sales of those fuels are also among the main deniers that global warming is happening. That is the stance of Rex Tillerson, Secretary of State in the Trump Administration and former CEO of ExxonMobil. In an October 2015 report for *Ecowatch*, Bill McKibben noted that as early as 1978, scientists working for Exxon told its chief managers that climate change was "caused by man and would raise global temperatures by 2–3C this century [2015], which was pretty much spot-on." By the 1990s, further research proved beyond doubt that catastrophe is looming. Exxon lied about the findings of its own scientists and proceeded to stake out leases in the Arctic, which they knew would soon be free of ice for much longer than in the past, thus enabling exploration and drilling for oil. Exxon also:

> helped organize campaigns designed to instill doubt, borrowing tactics and personnel from the tobacco industry's similar fight. They funded 'institutes' devoted to outright climate [change] denial. And at the highest levels they did all they could to spread their lies.

McKibben calls this behavior by the "largest oil company on Earth" an "unparalleled evil." Exxon:

> helped organize the most consequential lie in human history and kept that lie going past the point where we can protect the poles, prevent the acidification of the oceans or slow sea level rise enough to save the most vulnerable regions and cultures. Businesses misbehave all the time, but . . . [no] corporation has ever done anything this big and this bad.

McKibben's conclusion is dismal:

> this company had the singular capacity to change the course of world history for the better and instead it changed that course for the infinitely worse. In its greed Exxon helped—more than any other institution—to kill our planet.

Flows

Writing about the emergence of capitalism, Gilles Deleuze and Félix Guattari claim that the transition from feudalism to modernity is "defined by a simple decoding of flows, and they are always compensated by residual forces or transformations of the State." Furthermore, "these flows . . . carry the seeds of a new life":

> Decoded flows—but who will give a name to this new desire? Flows of property that is sold, flows of money that circulates, flows of production and means of production making ready in the shadows, flows of workers becoming deterritorialized: the encounter of all these flows will be necessary . . . in order for capitalism to be born . . . .

They add that "the only universal history is the history of contingency" (223–224).

The anti-Oedipal analysis of "universal history" offered by Deleuze and Guattari, with its emphasis on flows and contingency, is symptomatic of our era of capitalist globalization. Overtopped by the flows of the TNCs, the walls and fences of today's nation-states can no longer contain them.[12] The hero—or antihero, rather—of their analysis of the "schizzes-flows" of history (xxi) emerges as "the nomad," pursuing his or her random "lines of flight" away from all forms of enclosure. "The State" persists in attempting to control nomadism, however; it erects borders, walls and fences, even prisons to stop the flows of people, money, property . . . .

In their 2000 book *Empire*, Michael Hardt and Antonio Negri similarly write: "The creative forces of the multitude that sustain Empire are also capable of autonomously constructing a counter-Empire, an alternative political organization of global flows and exchanges" (xv). Perhaps. But their assertion implies that "Empire," like "the State" for Deleuze and Guattari, is somehow antithetical to "global flows and exchanges." That is hardly the case.[13] Both nation-states and empires, rather than preventing, promote "flows" of certain types (money, commodities) and also promote "nomadism" by certain classes of individuals (CEOs, tourists, members of the military). Yet "flows" seem antithetical to "enclosures."

Both nation-states and the territorial empires of the past are being superseded by what appears to be "an alternative political organization of global flows and exchanges." Or maybe it should be called an alternative economic organization, because its political control or management is negligible. It, instead, increasingly appears to be rule or misrule by TNCs. Besides the increasing domination of TNCs, globalization's "most striking feature," according to Arjun Appadurai, "is the runaway quality of global finance, which appears remarkably independent of traditional constraints of information transfer, national regulation, industrial productivity, or 'real' wealth in any particular society, country, or region" (13). Through the flows of financialization, it is as though capitalism has been transformed into a Boeing 747 without a pilot. The people who come closest to controlling it are a handful of billionaires such as Bill Gates, Carlos Slim, and the Koch brothers playing its high-stakes game, though none of them is in control of it either. As noted in Chapter 5, if the world's GDP is close to $63 trillion, that is less than one-tenth of the value of the global derivatives market, currently estimated at some $700 trillion.

Experts on globalization often talk about flows if not floods: the flows of financial transaction, the flows of commodities, the flows of people. In *Zombie Capitalism*, Chris Harman writes that by 2007, "international trade flows were 30 times greater than in 1950, while output was only eight times greater. Foreign direct investment shot up: flows of it rising from $37 billion in 1982 to $1,200 billion in 2006 . . ." (255). He adds that when globalization became a term of choice in the 1990s, combined with neoliberal economic orthodoxy, it appeared to represent "a whole new phase of capitalism—for enthusiasts a phase very different to any previously." The enthusiasts believed that "the world should be organised according to the free flows of capital, without any intervention by governments . . ." (257).

The "free flows of capital," however, are anything but free, in several senses. "The pattern was not one of capital flowing effortlessly over a homogeneous worldwide landscape," Harman points out. For one thing, "it was 'lumpy'"—that is to say, its effects benefited some regions, nations, and individuals, and not others (263). Much of the "lumpiness" was caused by the artificial and often-detrimental national boundaries the Western empires had imposed. Also contributing to that "lumpiness," notes David Bollier, "Private interests are increasingly committing 'boundary violations' as they erect barbed-wire fences on resources that are publicly owned and on terrain where no private fences should exist" (*Silent Theft* 48).[14]

If global financial flows seem generally unimpeded, something like "free trade" taken to the nth degree, the flows of people around the world are hardly unimpeded. Wealthy, cosmopolitan travelers and tourists go where they like and when they please.[15] But immigrants and refugees do not. If caught, illegal immigrants may be deported or thrown into prison ("detention centers"). Refugees by the millions are crowded into camps behind barbed-wire fences where they may feel lucky to get food, water, and a tent over their heads.

So there are at least two types of nomads, one free and the other coerced, one pursuing whatever lines of flight he or she wishes, and the other struggling to escape poverty, war, famine, persecution.[16]

In *Capitalism: A Structural Genocide*, Garry Leech cites Marx on primitive accumulation and the "expropriation of the agricultural producer, of the peasant, from the soil," as "the basis of the whole [capitalist] process." It is through capitalist "accumulation by dispossession" that a "reserve army of labor" is produced. This "surplus population" in the twenty-first century, Leech continues, consists of millions of individuals who scrape by in the informal economy, often on less than a dollar a day. Capital does not lack potential laborers, whose vast numbers keep wages low (41). Driven from the land by the general process of corporate enclosure and into the world's major urban conglomerations, typically they cannot find full-time, well-paying jobs, so the jobs they do find (if any) leave them impoverished. This leads to what John Smith calls "super-exploitation."

The global apartheid that now divides populations both within and among all nations between the haves and the have-nots seems destined to result not only in what Mike Davis has called a "planet of slums," but in a "lifeboat world," a nightmare future imagined by Garrett Hardin, who also authored the tragically influential essay entitled "The Tragedy of the Commons" (see Chapter 8). An overpopulated world where the vast majority are poor, Hardin argues, will force upon the rich and powerful a "lifeboat ethics"—he should have called it a non-ethics—in which they can survive only by letting the rest drown.

(In this nightmare, the flows of globalization seem to have inundated everything.) Sounding like the Rev. Thomas Malthus, Hardin asks if "everyone on earth [has] an equal right to an equal share of its resources?" He thinks not:

> If we divide the world crudely into rich nations and poor nations, two thirds of them are desperately poor, and only one third comparatively rich, with the United States the wealthiest of all. Metaphorically each rich nation can be seen as a lifeboat full of comparatively rich people. In the ocean outside each lifeboat swim the poor of the world, who would like to get in, or at least to share some of the wealth.

Hardin asks what the wealthy passengers in the global lifeboat should do? If "we" attempt to rescue "the poor of the world," the result, he claims, will be disastrous for everyone:

> We have several options: we may be tempted to try to live by the Christian ideal of being "our brother's keeper," or by the Marxist ideal of "to each according to his needs." Since the needs of all in the water are the same, and since they can all be seen as "our brothers," we could take them all into our boat.... The boat swamps, everyone drowns. Complete justice, complete catastrophe.

This, he asserts, is another example of "the tragedy of the commons": sharing the world's wealth will have ruinous consequences (Hardin, "Lifeboat Ethics"). But what is the "lifeboat ethics" suggested by Arundhati Roy in *An Ordinary Person's Guide to Empire*? Roy writes that as "we continue sailing on our Titanic ... it tilts slowly into the darkened sea":

> The deckhands panic. Those with cheaper tickets have begun to be washed away. But in the banquet halls, the music plays on. The only signs of trouble are slightly slanting waiters, the kabobs and canapés sliding to one side of their silver trays, the somewhat exaggerated sloshing of the wine in the crystal wineglasses. The rich are comforted by the knowledge that the lifeboats on the deck are reserved for club-class passengers. The tragedy is that they are probably right.
>
> *(20–21)*

Perhaps it is Garret Hardin's tragedy that he believes "the rich" are incapable of helping the rest of the world before we all go down together.

Clearly, "free market," globalizing capitalism has failed to float all boats. While it was supposed to be spreading prosperity throughout the world, that hasn't happened (Bello 27). In many impoverished countries, the structural adjustment programs or SAPs imposed by the IMF have led to the severe contraction of social spending on such items as education and public health, leaving them floundering in debt and much worse off than before. Nevertheless, the economic recoveries of Germany and Japan after World War II, with massive help from the US and other governments, suggest what can be done.

In his 1999 study of globalization, sociologist Zygmunt Bauman also points out that rather than bringing the benefits of free market capitalism to everyone in the world, neoliberal policies, as enforced by the IMF, World Bank, and WTO, have increased prosperity for some while also increasing poverty for millions of others. The latest phase of globalization reminds Bauman of earlier times:

> The new freedom of capital is reminiscent of that of the absentee landlords of yore, notorious for their much resented neglect of the needs of the populations which fed them. Creaming off the "surplus product" was the sole interest the absentee landlords held in the existence of the land they owned.
> *(Globalization 10)*

It wasn't the peasants who ruined the commons, but the landlords who enclosed the commons and evicted the peasants that caused much of the poverty and economic tragedy of the past. The same is true today. Mexican and Central American peasants are desperately trying to get across the border into the US largely because giant agricultural corporations, after the passage of NAFTA, have flooded their countries' markets with corn and other crops that used to be their chief means of economic support.

Contra Garrett Hardin, the poorest inhabitants of the world aren't about to drown quietly in the economic flows engulfing them while "we" rich are safe in "our" lifeboats. Just as the early land enclosures in Europe led to peasant rebellions, so today's globalization through neoliberalism and the TNCs meets opposition in many forms of resistance such as the Landless Workers Movement in Brazil, Via Campesina, the Zapatista uprising in Mexico, and Occupy Wall Street. According to Maia Ramnath:

> Grassroots mobilizations that focus on manifestations of transnational corporate capitalism, engaged in the unmasked act of accumulation by dispossession, also function as implicit indictments of the neoliberalized state. So land acquisition struggles can easily be seen as continuing resistance to colonization, or at any rate to the economic processes included historically within the colonial package. This is what enclosure of the commons looks like.
> *(234)*

Or rather, this is what resistance to enclosure and colonization looks like.

For the poorest nations and people of the world, the economic largesse of globalization does not flow their way. The richest, most powerful nations have the ability to change course by, for example, debt forgiveness for the poorest nations, but so far they have lacked the political will to do so. A recent example is what has been happening in the European Union, where neoliberal economic orthodoxy has led to the imposition of austerity measures on Greece, Spain, and other debtor nations, plunging them even farther into debt and poverty, and potentially driving them out of the EU altogether, onto the other side of the global apartheid fence. Meanwhile, globalizing capitalism flows on.

The global sweatshop

"As the river of goods flows to the rich country markets," Robert Ross comments in *Slaves to Fashion*, "the globalization of the rag [garment] trade erodes standards in older industrial countries, creating sweatshops in New York and Los Angeles and weighing down the hope of advance in Nicaragua and Mexico" (124). On a hopeful note, Ross says that "in the long run this tide may create ... more lasting and positive social effects," though his quite thorough study of "poverty and abuse in the new sweatshops" suggests just the opposite. He continues with his tidal metaphor: "The tide of imports that eroded the American garment workers' hard-fought gains is a signal of the creation of a truly worldwide pool of industrial labor" (124). While it is conceivable that this global "pool" of labor may one day become organized and win higher wages and better working conditions, Ross recounts in great detail the many obstacles preventing that development. That the term "sweatshop," originating in the mid-1800s, continues to be applicable to labor conditions today suggests that, if there has been any progress in the sphere of industry, it isn't on the side of labor.

Writing about "the global sweatshop" in *Sweatshop Warriors*, Miriam Ching Yoon Louie contends that "sweating workers through subcontracting has emerged as standard operating procedure in industries across the board," and not just in the garment industry (5). Meanwhile, global financial flows continue their vertiginous electronic dance, in which billions of dollars change hands instantaneously. Those flows appear to be independent of any substantial reality, including the global sweatshop in which much of today's consumer goods are produced. Corporate globalization has freed up both financial services and many industries to pursue unregulated or poorly regulated investments and also the cheapest labor they can find anywhere on the planet.

The 2000 Millennium Declaration promised to eradicate "extreme poverty" everywhere in the world by 2015. It is now 2017, and even the World Bank acknowledges that extreme poverty has increased rather than diminished in most parts of the world. According to Jim Hightower, in the US, "a cabal of corporate and political elites (including Presidents Clinton, Bush II, and Obama) has stealthfully negotiated international trade deals during the past two-plus decades that have fabricated, piece by piece, what now amounts to *a privatized world government*" ("New Trade Pacts" 1). Besides NAFTA, CAFTA, and other trade deals, this "privatized world government" includes the IMF, World Bank, and the WTO. "It's a secretive, autocratic, plutocratic, bureaucratic government of, by, and for multinational corporations" (1). It was in reaction to this version of globalization that the Battle of Seattle took place in 1999 and that the World Social Forum began its annual meetings in Porto Alegre, Brazil, in the following year.

"The domestic face of globalization," writes Louie, "has become increasingly obvious since the Reagan administration began by busting the air traffic controllers union, trashing the poor, and once again making the United States safe for the Robber Barons" (6). She demonstrates that since the 1980s, the dominance of neoliberal economics—aka Reaganomics—has involved the imposition of the sweatshop production model on a global scale. That is also John Smith's contention, using the Bangladeshi garment industry as an example, in *Imperialism in the Twenty-First Century*. While the consumer side of the new global economy allows the rich to go where they wish, purchase what they want, and enjoy whatever they please, the production side is an altogether different phenomenon. Most workers in today's global sweatshop are not much better off than slaves.

Sweatshops are not new, however, just as land enclosures are not new. In volume 3 of *Capital*, Marx included a section on "Work in Enclosed Spaces in General" (*Capital* 3: 185). He contended that businesses often economize by limiting what they spend on space, including such items as doors, windows, and ventilation. To that list could be added restrooms, cafeterias, first-aid stations, and the like. If workers can be crowded together in a shop or a factory, so much the better for the bottom line. Marx's three main examples are mines, factories, and tailors' establishments. The third item is most commonly identified with sweatshops, although just about any workplace that crams employees together in unsafe spaces, pays them badly, and overworks them deserves to be so labeled, especially if it violates labor laws. The global sweatshop produces clothing but also many other commodities such as cellphones and computers. Nike Corporation is infamous for the sweatshop conditions in which its shoes are manufactured. In a Chinese factory turning out iPads for Apple Corporation, management put up nets around the building to prevent overstressed, underpaid workers from committing suicide by jumping out of windows.

Clothing was and still is frequently made and paid for through piecework: a worker has to sew or help to sew X many articles of clothing within a certain period to get paid, and if the quota isn't met, the pay diminishes or disappears altogether. In the past, sweated piecework could be done by individual tailors or seamstresses working in their homes. It soon proved more cost-effective for both the middlemen and the capitalists on top of the garment industry hierarchy to gather the pieceworkers together in one place, where the middleman or some more immediate overseer could enforce the hours and pace of work.

There are many crowded, dangerous workplaces with no proper ventilation (let alone air conditioning) and sometimes not even windows to jump out of, where the workers labor for long hours with low pay and no benefits. So far, as in Marx, this description could apply to mines and factories. But because of the origin of the terms "sweating" and "sweated labor," because of recent scandals and accidents in garment factories, and also because of the activities of the No Sweat movement on North American college campuses, sweatshops today are most frequently associated with garment-making. Supposedly typical are garment factories in non-Western countries, although there are plenty of sweatshops throughout the US and Europe. Most of the workers in such factories are girls or women (they have "nimble fingers," and besides they are thought to be less likely than men to organize and protest against low pay and bad working conditions—in short, they are easier than men to exploit both economically and sexually by their male overseers). The terms "sweating" and "sweated labor," however, originated in Britain between 1830 and 1850, and did not at first refer to workplaces, but to versions of "piecework."

Wages for piecework, Marx explained, "form the basis for a hierarchically organized system of exploitation and oppression":

> . . . piece-wages make it easier for parasites to interpose themselves between the capitalist and the wage-labourer, thus giving rise to the "subletting of labour." The profits of these middlemen come entirely from the difference between the price of labour which the capitalist pays, and the part of that price they actually allow the worker to receive. In England, this system is called, characteristically, the "sweating system."
>
> (Capital 1: 695)

Just as in the case of plantation slavery, it was typically the middlemen or overseers who made the workers literally sweat. Marx adds:

> A *sweater* is someone who undertakes to deliver a certain quantity of work at normal prices to an entrepreneur, but who then has it carried out for a lower price by others. The difference, which goes to make up his profit, is *sweated out* of the workers who actually perform the labour . . .
>
> (Capital 1: 1071)

Sewing garments seems like relatively safe and certainly sedentary work. But in *The Condition of the Working Class in England*, Friedrich Engels declared that "it is precisely the workers engaged in the manufacture of those articles intended for the personal adornment of middle-class ladies whose health is most seriously threatened by the nature of their employment." The establishments engaged in making hats and dresses:

> employ many young girls—there are said to be 15,000 in all—who have their meals and sleep on the premises. Since most of them are country girls they are held in a state of complete servitude by their employers. During the London season, which lasts for about four months every year, even the well-conducted establishments work fifteen hours a day.

Sometimes the young women are forced to work even longer, getting only a couple of hours of sleep. "The only limit to their labour is the physical impossibility of holding a needle any longer" (237). Engels adds that "these unfortunate girls have been driven by their modern slave drivers—the threat of dismissal takes the place of the whip—to work such long and unbroken periods . . . as a strong man could not be expected to perform" (237).[17]

The tenements in New York City explored by Jacob Riis in *How the Other Half Lives* were often locations of sweatshops. They typically employed recent immigrants, frequently entire families of them. Thus housed, the sweaters, sometimes the heads of immigrant families, were able to evade the restrictions that, by 1890, had been placed on child labor and other aspects of work in factories (101–114). Whether in Britain or the US, it is from the development of workshops in such places as tenements that the term "sweatshop" and its modern definition originate. Today, that term is applied to industries that bring hundreds or even thousands of low-wage workers together in conditions often worse than in tenement sweatshops.

In 1995, an exposé about sweatshop slavery in Los Angeles opened many eyes. Thai con men had lured impoverished young women by promising them good jobs sewing garments in the US. When they arrived in LA, the Thai women were basically kidnapped and locked away in an apartment building in El Monte, a suburb not far from LA. Talk about caging people! They were held captive by armed guards. According to David Shipler's account, "They ate, slept, and worked behind razor wire and windows covered with plywood. For seventeen or eighteen hours a day, they were forced to sew and assemble clothing for major American manufacturers . . . ." Besides the guards, they were threatened with retaliation if they tried to escape. They were told that their families back in Thailand might be murdered, and that they themselves would be recaptured and beaten. They were also threatened with being turned over to the Immigration and Naturalization Service and deported (80–81).

Scandals more recent than the one in El Monte have given sweatshops glaring, worldwide notoriety. An outfit called Ali Enterprises in Karachi, Pakistan had been visited by two inspectors working for the nonprofit Social Accountability International. SAI is supposed to check up on workplace safety and health, wages, hours of work, and whether there is any child labor going on, among other issues. One problem is that much of the financing of SAI comes from the corporations involved in the garment trade themselves. The inspectors gave Ali Enterprises their approval in nine different areas. Not long after their inspection, on September 12, 2012, a fire broke out, and hundreds of workers found themselves trapped inside the building, which had only one exit. There were bars on the windows on its lower floors, presumably to prevent thieves from breaking in but also to prevent workers from sneaking out. The fire resulted in "one of the worst industrial disasters in history—one that killed nearly twice as many workers as the landmark Triangle Shirtwaist factory fire of 1911 in New York." In the Karachi tragedy, there were 289 deaths and over 600 injuries. As happened during the Triangle Shirtwaist catastrophe, many workers leapt to their deaths from the unbarred upper-floor windows.

The Wikipedia article on the Karachi disaster states that it was:

> a huge embarrassment to the factory monitoring system, in which many Western garment and electronics companies rely on auditing groups to provide a coveted seal of approval to their low-cost suppliers in the developing world. . . . For international rights campaigners, the fact that the factory had been certified by a respected Western organization made clear the failings of a controversial 15-year-old industry initiative.

According to Scott Nova, who heads the Worker Rights Consortium (WRC), "The whole system is flawed. This demonstrates, more clearly than ever, that corporate-funded monitoring systems like S.A.I. cannot and will not protect workers" (Wikipedia). SAI admitted that it had subcontracted its inspection to RINA Group, an Italian outfit. It claimed that it would start a review of its own accountability. Should an accountability outfit funded by corporations review its own accountability? Do sharks review sharks?

The owners of Ali Enterprises disappeared from Karachi shortly after the fire, but were caught and wound up in court in Pakistan. Their bank accounts had been frozen, their passports canceled, and they faced criminal proceedings. Quite apart from the criminality of the owners, a government investigation revealed gross negligence and corruption on the part of the Pakistani regulatory bureaucracy. At least that aspect of the investigatory process demonstrated that part of the Pakistani government is not corrupt. Nevertheless, most of those who profit from and even those who directly own and manage sweatshops never face criminal proceedings.

In 2012, and again in 2013, textile factories in Dhaka, Bangladesh were also in the headlines because of major accidents. Within a 20-year span, those factories sprang into existence, soon employing more than a million workers in and around Dhaka, the vast majority of them women. On November 24, 2012, fire broke out in the Tazreen Fashion factory in the suburbs of Dhaka. The confirmed death toll was 117, while over 200 more were injured. The fire may have been caused by an electrical failure, though the Prime Minister of Bangladesh, Sheikh Hasina, speculated about sabotage. Less than half a year later, also in Dhaka, on April 24, 2013, an eight-story building known as the Rana Plaza, which contained several textile factories, collapsed, killing well over 1,000 people and injuring more than twice that number. That accident set the record for casualties in textile factory accidents. Management had been warned that the poorly constructed building was developing structural cracks, but the sweated workers were ordered to continue working anyway.

The garment mills in Dhaka produce clothing sold by many well-known global corporations, including Walmart and Gap. After the accidents in Pakistan and Bangladesh, some of the companies banded together to insist on careful building inspections and other safety measures in the factories. Walmart and Gap did not agree to these measures. Walmart dropped Tarzeen from its list of suppliers, but *The New York Times* reported that it negated any move to improve safety conditions in the Bangladesh factories. A "director of ethical sourcing" for Walmart asserted that the corporation refused to pay for better fire and electrical safety, because to make those improvements would be too costly: "it is not financially feasible . . . to make such investments" (Walsh and Greenhouse). The bottom line dictates that it is better to risk killing a few hundred or even a thousand impoverished workers than to risk raising prices on finished merchandise. This is just a manifestation of the world's current economic and political conjuncture. In *The Endless Crisis*, John Bellamy Foster and Robert McChesney write:

> The tendency to monopolization in the capitalist economy . . . is demonstrably stronger in the opening decade of the twenty-first century than ever before . . . . What we have been witnessing in the last quarter-century is the evolution of monopoly capital that lies at the core of the current economic system in the advanced capitalist economies—a key source of economic instability, and the basis of the current new imperialism.
>
> *(67)*

It is also the basis for the increasing millions, from slaves and debt peons to refugees fleeing war and famine, who have fallen into the abyss of disposable people.

Notes

1 The beneficiaries of capitalist globalization have been the so-called "developed" nations, but they have also experienced growing poverty and inequality within their borders. By now, there is no reason to suppose that capitalism will lead to prosperity for everyone. The Bretton Woods institutions, the International Monetary Fund (IMF) and the World Bank, were created after World War II to help alleviate poverty in the "underdeveloped" world. But for the most part, they have managed to exacerbate it. They have become partners in what George Monbiot calls the "dictatorship of vested interests," dominated by TNCs (17). There are more billionaires than ever before, but there are also millions more people living on less than $2 or even $1 a day. Only a small fraction of the world's population works for large corporations, moreover, and most of them cannot afford to buy the products the corporations produce, let alone invest in them. "Globalization" has a variety of meanings. For a good brief review of those meanings, as of 2004, see Timothy Brennan, "From Development to Globalization."
2 See, for example, Zygmunt Bauman, *Retrotopia*.
3 Ferguson's comparison between the old British and the new American empires is based on the idea that both have been propagators of a liberal and liberating version of capitalism. The British "pioneered free trade, free capital movements and, with the abolition of slavery, free labour" (304). Just what "free labour" can possibly mean he does not say, but it forms an interesting contrast to the phrase "wage slavery," often used by workers and their advocates from the nineteenth century to the present. In any event, Ferguson believes that America is following the British example, promoting capitalist "globalization" around the world.
4 Puerto Rico, the Philippines, and Guam (Cuba was an exception because the US did not hang on to it for very long).
5 Besides the authors I have already mentioned, earlier historians who recognize America's imperialistic tendencies include Charles Beard, Scott Nearing, William Appleman Williams, Sidney Lens, Richard Van Alstyne, Lloyd Gardner, and Howard Zinn, among others.

6 Labor analysts currently refer to the "precariat" instead of proletariat, and stress its "precarity" through, among other means, making it temporary and part-time.
7 In *The New Imperialism*, David Harvey addresses "that special brand of it called 'capitalist imperialism.'" This "contradictory fusion of 'the politics of state and empire'" involves both military and economic modes of domination (26). Throughout history, many nation-states have been expansive and predatory against weaker polities; capitalism is always expansive and predatory. In its current phase of globalization via TNCs, capitalism may not always need to call on military power to enforce what Smith calls "super-exploitation." That can be left to local governmental authorities, police, and armed forces. But as Michel Chossudovsky declares, "War and globalization go hand in hand" (xxiv).
8 There were, of course, many instances of cooperation between the European colonizers and first peoples around the globe. But these were overshadowed by violent conquest, slavery, and genocide.
9 See my *Dark Vanishings*. For the estimate of the population of Australian Aboriginals in 1788, see especially pp. 121–122.
10 See, for example, Eduardo Galeano, *Open Veins of Latin America*, and Greg Grandin, *Empire's Workshop*.
11 In *Violence*, Slavoj Žižek writes that "9/11 is the main symbol of the end" not of history, but of "the Clintonite happy '90s," when it briefly seemed that liberal democracy and capitalism had triumphed over all opposition, as Fukuyama claimed was the case. But after 9/11, Žižek says, the world has entered an era "in which new walls emerge everywhere, between Israel and the West Bank, around the European Union, on the US-Mexico border. The rise of the populist New Right is just the most prominent example of the urge to raise new walls." Regarding the European Union's attempt to stop the influx of immigrants from Africa and the Middle East, Žižek continues: "*This* is the truth of globalisation: the construction of new walls safeguarding prosperous Europe from the immigrant flood" (79). Meanwhile, the impoverished and war-torn lands from which the immigrants are coming, whether Iraq and Syria or Mexico, though not formal colonies of the US or the EU, are the victims of the new imperialism that is hardly the benign, peaceful globalization promised by neoliberalism. Perhaps all the new walls, like the one in Jerusalem, will be wailing walls.
12 From their origins, the sovereignty of nation-states included the authority to set boundaries, put up walls and fences, and determine weights and measures. In discourse about globalization, "flows" suggests that which cannot be contained by nation-states.
13 Negri and Hardt go on, in fact, to distinguish between their version of "Empire" and older forms of imperialism, because their version consists largely of electronic "global flows."
14 "Lumpy" may be too modest a term to describe the major patterns of inequality that have emerged globally since World War II.
15 The tourist class, able to be as cosmopolitan as they wish, visit destinations where they can take photos of picturesque natives, many of whom, unless they become refugees, will never be able to travel more than a few miles beyond their homes. As Bauman points out, like the absentee landlords of the past, today the rich belong to a globalized minority who experience an "unprecedented . . . disconnection of power from obligations: duties towards employees, but also towards the younger and weaker, towards yet unborn generations and towards the self-reproduction of the living conditions of all . . ." (*Globalization* 9). Millions more, however, are traveling because they are forced to become refugees. And still other millions remain rooted to one spot, just so long as they aren't uprooted by corporate land-grabs, storms and floods, famine, or ethnic cleansings and war.
16 Žižek cites the Marxist antithesis of "relations between things" and "relations between persons": "In the much-celebrated free circulation opened up by global capitalism, it is 'things' (commodities) which freely circulate, while the circulation of 'persons' is more and more controlled. We are not dealing now with 'globalisation' as an unfinished project

but with a true 'dialectics of globalisation': the segregation of the people *is* the reality of economic globalisation. This new racism of the developed [countries] is ... much more brutal than the previous ones ..." (*Violence* 79). I am not sure how the brutality of racisms can be measured, but there is no doubt that the "new racism" is brutal. Moreover, it does not consist merely of hate crimes and acts of terrorism committed by individuals or by groups such as the Aryan Nation or ISIS. It is also structural, which is why the phrase "global apartheid" is appropriate.

17 Marx also offers an account of Mary Anne Walkley, who died at the age of 20, as the London papers put it, of "simple over-work" (*Capital* 1: 364–355). As in her case, sweatshops are often literally death traps. The seamstress in Thomas Hood's 1843 poem "The Song of the Shirt" mournfully sings:

"Oh, Men, with Sisters dear!
Oh, men, with Mothers and Wives!
It is not linen you're wearing out,
But human creatures' lives!
Stitch—stitch—stitch,
In poverty, hunger and dirt,
Sewing at once, with a double thread,
A Shroud as well as a Shirt."

7

MANUFACTURING DISPOSABLE PEOPLE

> "Most of the world's population is becoming disposable and irrelevant from the standpoint of capital."
>
> — David Harvey

David Harvey is one of many contemporary authors now writing about "disposable" people, as it may well turn out, perhaps billions of disposable people "from the standpoint of capital." How can anyone become disposable? Under capitalism, disposability is a matter of property, or rather lack of property. During the early enclosures of land, thousands of peasants were evicted from places they and their families had occupied for generations. Many of them could no longer make a living except by begging; they were often arrested for mendicancy or vagrancy. Many others were forced to work as farm laborers or tramped into towns and cities to become wage laborers there. Today's sweatshop workers, virtually slaves, are disposable or close to it. In any society, those who occupy the lowest positions on the social hierarchy may be deemed disposable and even subject to extermination.[1]

The Black Lives Matter movement recognizes that African Americans have not mattered, or at least have not mattered enough, in majority white society. Given the history of slavery, racism, segregation, lynching, and police brutality that has led to the rise of that movement, to be poor and black in today's America also means approaching the social nadir of disposability. The white cops who have killed unarmed young black men may have viewed them as dangerous, but they also viewed them as disposable. Very few of the cops, whose lives apparently matter, have been convicted for murder or manslaughter, or even fired.

In "Busted Boy," a poem by Native American Simon Ortiz, the narrator witnesses two plainclothes cops arresting a black teenager at a bus station in Tuscon. Ortiz suggests that today, both poor African Americans and Native Americans are automatically "busted at birth" and are therefore "instantly disposable."[2] The poem does not say whether the young man is homeless, but homelessness also points toward disposability. To be homeless means you have crashed through the bottom of society's lifeboat. The homeless belong to a capacious and growing category of those typically viewed as having little or no social value. In a supposedly prosperous nation that claims to honor its military heroes, approximately 50,000 veterans experience homelessness at some time during a given year, which amounts to nearly 10 percent of the total homeless population.[3]

The view from below

Slaves and sweatshop workers, of course, have a small amount of value as property and as a cheap labor force. Prisoners have a certain value for the private prison corporations that profit from enclosing them and that also profit from prison labor, a type of slavery. But from the standpoint of capitalism, the growing categories of the homeless and unemployed are hardly worth anything—not even worth enclosing in prisons until they do something that causes them to be apprehended. Then they may be treated as less than worthless. In a capitalist economy, unless an individual has a specific economic role to play, he or she has no value. One's job and what one owns or can purchase measures one's value. Those with money have an assured place in the social hierarchy. Workers have value only as commodities—that is, only insofar as they can sell their labor. Those who can buy commodities in the marketplace also have at least that much value.

Besides workers, capitalism needs consumers with enough money to buy the products that businesses produce and sell. But if a capitalist enterprise could do so, it would dispense entirely with labor as a major cost. Maintaining a "reserve army" of the unemployed helps capitalism keep that cost as low as possible.[4] Outsourcing production to countries with cheap labor, union-busting, and automation further undermine the labor force. There is now a large and growing literature on the "jobless future," in which automation will have supplanted most forms of work that humans used to perform. Then indeed everyone may prove to be disposable.[5]

All societies, even the most egalitarian ones, produce social hierarchies. In modern societies, there are multiple hierarchies, so that, for instance, a homeless person may be highly valued by his or her friends or family. He or she may be a veteran, and so is at least nominally valued as an American hero.

Under capitalism, the hierarchy based on economic value may not be the most important one for an individual's sense of self-worth, but it is inescapable. The bottom-dwellers on the economic hierarchy, if they aren't completely cast out or killed, are nevertheless excluded from many of the rights and benefits the rest of society enjoys. They are almost always impoverished. But if one were to count as disposable all those who make less than $1 or $2 a day, that would be several billion people. Poverty, however, is just one factor that can lead to disposability.

The poor and downtrodden are frequently referred to as waste or garbage people, such as the garbage pickers of Tijuana, depicted in Luis Alberto Urrea's *By the Lake of Sleeping Children*. The phrase "white trash" also comes to mind, only the people in that category are not always so poor as Urrea's garbage pickers.[6] Today, there are garbage pickers everywhere, including my hometown. I don't know if they frequent the Bloomington landfill, but I have seen them picking through dumpsters behind restaurants and grocery stores not far from where I live. They constitute what our city officials refer to as our "homeless problem." We aren't going to drive them out of town, much less exterminate them, but we are constantly fretting about how to deal with them.

Labor history, as in E. P. Thompson's *The Making of the English Working Class* or in Philip Foner's *History of the Labor Movement in the US*, developed in contrast to the types of historiography that focus only on the rich and powerful or only on the doings of nation-states and governments. Thompson's book focused on the formation of the industrial proletariat and its emerging class consciousness around 1800 in Britain. He called it "history from below," which evokes the question of what lies beneath Thompson's "below"? Who occupies the very lowest rungs of the social hierarchy and what would a history of them look like? Besides the burgeoning population of factory workers, Thompson was well aware of the unemployed, handloom weavers, peasants, the Luddites, and the lumpen-proletariat depicted in Henry Mayhew's mid-nineteenth-century survey, *London Labour and the London Poor*. Among the street people Mayhew and his team of reporters interviewed were beggars, thieves, prostitutes, dustmen, and crossing sweepers.

One of the many fascinating characters in *London Labour* is Jack Black, rat-catcher to Her Majesty the Queen. That distinguished fellow, who obviously did not qualify as disposable because he served royalty, illustrates three facts about Mayhew's subjects. First, even Mayhew's bottom-dwelling categories—rat-catchers, for instance—form social hierarchies, mimicking the larger social class hierarchy. If Jack Black represents the apex of the rat-catching hierarchy, the sewer rat-catchers occupy the nadir. Did that lowest rank of rat-catchers qualify as disposable? Not quite, both because they lived in a relatively humane society and because what they did had some minimal social value. Along with the London dustmen,[7] the sewer rat-catchers were similar to the Dalits or Untouchables in India, who provide sanitation services to higher-caste Indians. For centuries, the Dalits have been dirt beneath the feet of the higher castes, but where would their betters be without them? Cleaning their own privvies?

Second, many of the street people in *London Labour*, even beggars, take pride in what they do, including their independence and their often-considerable skills. Jack Black, for example, proudly claims that none of the other rat-catchers in London can match his ability to snare, poison, tame, and even breed rats for sale. Jack says that he does his work almost "too well," because "wherever I went I've cleared the rats right out, and so my customers have fell off. I have got the best testimonials of any man in London . . . . I also sterminate moles for Her Majesty" (Mayhew 3: 19).

And third, Mayhew's survey illustrates one of the reasons why the industrial proletariat did not make more headway toward becoming the revolutionary vanguard that Marx and Engels hoped for. There were just too many ways to make a living in the informal economy in England, from costermongering to housebreaking, and from chimney-sweeping to prostitution. Why would someone sign up for a revolution when he or she could get along quite well as a pickpocket? Mayhew's survey yields an astonishing variety of ways the "lower orders" in Victorian London made their livings. Jack Black was a steady, reliable fellow with a wife and a home. But many of Mayhew's street people changed locations and activities at such a rate that pinning them down to steady occupations did not make much sense. The many varieties even of crime, moreover, were hugely productive. As Marx noted sarcastically, criminals produce the entire justice system: the police, lawyers, courts, prisons, wardens, and so on. We can also thank criminals for breaking "the monotony and everyday security of bourgeois life" (*Theories of Surplues Value* 1: 387–388). That was true as well for many of the others in *London Labour*—street musicians, for example.

Mayhew claimed that humans are divided into two types or, as he thought of them, "races": the civilized people, presumably like himself, and "the wandering tribes," including the street people he wrote about. Rather than a history, *London Labour* is perhaps a nomadology. "History is always written from the sedentary point of view and in the name of a state apparatus," Deleuze and Guattari declare, "even when the topic is nomads. What is lacking is a Nomadology, the opposite of a history" (23). Assuming it could account for people wandering all over the map, engaged in such specialized and often very temporary activities as mudlarking or flower-vending, a nomadology might be the antithesis even of labor history. At least it would not be teleological. It would not stress progress toward greater democracy and prosperity as liberal or Whig histories do. Nor would it stress the development of working-class consciousness leading to revolution following Thompson's Marxist model.

Anyway, Marx's investigations of capitalism and Mayhew's survey of London street people had as background and in some sense antagonist the first quasi-scientific claim that large numbers of people were disposable. The Rev. Thomas Malthus' *Essay on the Principle of Population*, originally published in 1798, was also the first text in which an early economist did not view the increase of people in a given country as a sign of progress, but the reverse. Instead of "the wealth of nations," as in Adam Smith, Malthus focused on what he viewed as the main threat to that wealth: overpopulation. Along with wealth, scarcity and starvation became central to economic thinking throughout the nineteenth century. And scarcity and starvation pointed to such issues as unemployment, vagrancy, and crime, as well as disposability.

When Malthus talks about a "superfluous" or "redundant" population, he is talking about disposable people. In the second edition of his *Essay* (1803), he asserted that there is no place at "nature's table" for such people and that they have no right even to be born:

A man who is born into a world already possessed, if he cannot get subsistence from his parents on whom he has a just demand, and if the society do not want his labor, has no claim of *right* to the smallest portion of food, and, in fact, has no business to be where he is. At nature's mighty feast there is no vacant cover for him. She tells him to be gone, and will quickly execute her own orders by exterminating him.

(531)

That remark proved so objectionable that Malthus removed it from later editions of his *Essay*.

Turning away from "the wealth of nations," Malthus turned economics into "the dismal science," as Thomas Carlyle called it. From the Malthusian perspective, the poor are always an overpopulation, a cancerous growth on the body politic that ought to be excised. Yet there is no way to do so. "To remove the wants of the lower classes" is impossible, Malthus declares; "the pressure of distress on this part of a community is so deeply seated that no human ingenuity can reach it" (38). Money only adds to the dilemma, because the more money the poor possess, the greater their inducement to overpopulate. The expenditures of the poor beyond bare subsistence can only produce more unwanted lives. Similar arguments appear today in reports from the right-wing Heritage Foundation and in rationalizations for the Trump Administration's budget proposal.

As Marx and Engels recognized, Malthus' argument was another way of saying that "the poor ye shall always have with you," no matter what the economic mode of production. According to Malthus, the tendency to overpopulate was the outcome of natural laws that had always been operative. In later editions of his *Essay*, Malthus cited Captain James Cook and other explorers to provide examples of population pressures in non-Western regions. He stressed the customs, including warfare, infanticide, widow-murder, human sacrifice, and cannibalism, that he thought limited population in "savage" societies. Malthus also argued that a "redundant population" in any society would inevitably be whittled down to the level of subsistence by the major, "positive" checks of famine, disease, and war. So indeed "redundant population" meant disposable people, because they were continually being disposed of by those positive checks or by savage customs such as infanticide.

Malthus thought that the only solution to poverty was an individual one. The poor were that way because they were "improvident." A poor man might improve his circumstances by being thrifty, having fewer children, and putting off getting married as long as possible. In *Losing Ground*, American libertarian Charles Murray echoed Malthus by contending that government anti-poverty programs are misguided, because poverty is caused by the poor themselves. They lack foresight and initiative. Stop giving them handouts, and then maybe some of them will get up enough gumption to take responsibility for their otherwise unnecessary and parasitic lives. The Heritage Foundation also tells us that there isn't any poverty in

America anyway, because the so-called poor have cars, air conditioners, big-screen TVs, and so on. They are moochers or freeloaders, willing just to live off the fat of the land. And many of the poor don't stay married and so cannot support the surplus children they keep producing.

That is supposedly how white trash becomes white trash, through their own lack of initiative and foresight. Poverty today supposedly has nothing to do with the system—that is, with capitalism—or so the right-wing argument goes. The argument was little different in nineteenth-century Britain, for example during the Great Irish Famine in the late 1840s. As an English clergyman put it in 1850, the poor were "immortal sewerage" (Osborne). The poor had souls like everyone else, but on earth they were just refuse. Like sewerage, moreover, it wasn't easy to get rid of them. Even the most obvious nineteenth-century remedy for "overpopulation"—emigration—Malthus regarded as merely "a slight palliative" (346). The only other "palliative" that Malthus could think of was no palliative at all, and that was "the total abolition of all the present parish laws" for poor relief (37). Let them eat grass.

In nineteenth-century America and Britain, there were countless representations, if not histories of the poor, and most of those representations were much more sympathetic to their plight than was Malthus. How could a good Christian treat abandoned children, for example, as garbage? Dickens' Oliver Twist comes to mind, and also the less familiar Michael Armstrong, the factory boy. Michael is the pathetic main character of an early factory novel by Anthony Trollope's mother, Frances Trollope. At one point, he escapes from the prison-like factory where he has been slaving away. Standing on the edge of a cliff, he contemplates suicide, because the conditions he has just run away from are wretched and he sees no alternative. Trollope's novel aimed at factory reform, and particularly at curtailing the hours for child workers to 10 a day. Child labor, which often led to early deaths, was one way of disposing of "immortal sewerage." It was also a way of increasing unemployment for adults.

While most nineteenth-century representations of the poor evoke pity, many of them do little else except perhaps encouraging charity. In 1850, George Frederic Watts produced a painting of a starving family during the Great Irish Famine. Most of the images and writings about the Famine are sympathetic toward its victims, and yet those depictions often present them, as does Watts's painting, in helpless isolation. It's a pity that the family in the painting is starving, but there is nothing that can be done about it. They will no doubt be dead by the time relief arrives, which apparently the artist is unable or unwilling to provide. What do you do when confronting disposable people? You can have pity on them, but supposedly that's about all you can do.

Exterminism

Irish nationalist historians have viewed the Famine as a genocide. That is because relief efforts were too little, too late, because the exporting of grain and other crops continued in the midst of mass starvation, and because English onlookers often asserted that it was a providential clearing of the land that would lead to greater prosperity for Ireland—or at least for Irish landowners. For many English observers, the million or so Irish peasants who died of starvation and the million and a half who managed to emigrate were disposable people par excellence. "The time has come when the Irish population must either be improved a little, or else exterminated." So wrote Carlyle in 1839 in *Chartism* (183), seven years before the onset of the Famine. Carlyle supported improvement rather than extermination, but there is also no doubt that he considered extermination a possibility. The Famine was a late, extreme episode in the enclosure movement that had been going on in Britain since the Tudor period. As with the earlier Highland Clearances in Scotland, for several centuries peasants were being driven off of the land, forced into wage labor, and, toward the end of the 1700s, often into the industrial proletariat.

Marx and Engels condemned Malthus as an apologist for the status quo. They saw overpopulation not as the result of the workings of the eternal laws of nature, but as the result of capitalism. In her study of totalitarianism, Hannah Arendt contends that, besides "superfluous wealth," a second "by-product of capitalist production" was "the human debris that every crisis, following invariably upon each period of industrial growth, eliminated permanently from producing society." She adds that throughout the 1800s, it was understood:

> they were an actual menace to society . . . and their export had helped to populate the dominions of Canada and Australia as well as the United States. The new fact in the imperialist era is that these two superfluous forces, superfluous capital and superfluous working power, joined hands and left the country [England or Europe] together.
>
> *(30)*

As already noted, Marx identified the early enclosure movement as the first stage of capitalism or "primitive accumulation." Moreover, Marx declared in *Capital* that "the constant production of a relative surplus population of workers is a necessity of capitalist accumulation" (*Capital* 1: 787). This "reserve army of labor" drives wages down and supplies new workers when new industries emerge. We see today how, as large corporations have gone global, they have relentlessly sought out the cheapest sources of labor, creating an economic "race to the bottom" (e.g., see Tonelson). It is this "labor arbitrage" that John Smith contends is the main factor in "imperialism in the twenty-first century." Under capitalism, moreover, there is an inverse ratio between the value of private property and the value of people. A major aspect of so-called "free trade" has been the push to eliminate as much human labor as possible, which is helping to create the pattern of "global apartheid"—rich world, poor world—that has emerged since World War II.

In the *Grundrisse*, Marx declares:

> It is a law of capital [and not of nature] to create surplus labour . . . . It is its tendency, therefore, to create as much labour as possible; just as it is equally its tendency to reduce necessary labour to a minimum. It is therefore . . . a tendency of capital to increase the labouring population, as well as constantly to posit a part of it as surplus population—population which is useless until such time as capital can utilize it.
>
> *(399)*

Marx implies the obvious: if "necessary labour" is constantly ground down "to a minimum," then "surplus population," along with unemployment and poverty, must increase. Of course, capitalism also seeks to increase the consumption of its products, so it cannot simply create "surplus population" with no spare change. Nevertheless, Marx says, capital makes "human labour (relatively) superfluous, so as to drive it . . . towards infinity" (399).

Most workers under capitalism can easily be disposed of. Recent accounts of "the precariat" (the diminished proletariat) or of the precariousness of the globalized working class sometimes fail to recognize that workers, whether employed or not, have always been in a precarious situation (Jonna and Foster). Labor historians tell many stories about strikes during which industries and corporations have thrown away the strikers and hired "scabs" to replace them. Frequently, such situations have led to violence, in which the state typically sides with the industries and corporations. Today, hotels, restaurants, and other businesses often fire workers who had been receiving only the legal minimum wage and replace them with workers from, say, Eastern Europe, who receive lower than minimum wages. The standard excuse is that they also get tips. This is just another version of sweatshop labor. In *Deported*, Tanya Golash-Boza explains how the current record number of deportations enforced by the US, sending thousands of the undocumented back to their countries of origin, enhances neoliberal economic arrangements by creating a huge pool of desperate workers who can easily be exploited by international corporations.[8]

Malthus does not advocate exterminating the poor, but his argument involves an exterminationist logic similar to the many versions of rationalizing genocides. These typically include the idea that the people being liquidated are worthless, mere vermin. As Carlyle put it in 1839, "To believe practically that the poor and luckless are here only as a nuisance to be abraded and abated, and in some permissible manner made away with, and swept out of sight, is not an amiable faith" (176). Also in the late 1830s, under the pseudonym "Marcus," someone published a small volume called *The Book of Murder!* The author claimed it was a contribution to "the Science of Population" (31). Along with Dickens' *Oliver Twist* and Carlyle's *Chartism*, it was one of many publications in England attacking Malthus and the New Poor Law of 1834.[9] According to the editor of the second edition of this "diabolical" volume, its "Demon Author" advocates limiting "population by murdering all the infants born over three in each family of the poor." Lots should then be drawn to choose one-quarter of all of the third children to destroy. Regarding the Irish poor, Marcus proposes that they "shall be allowed to rear only one child to each family until their present numbers shall have been brought down." He recommends giving the doomed infants, while they are sleeping, a "deadly gas" to render their extinctions "painless."

Marcus asserts that pauper infants do not have the right to exist (39). But he is not altogether unsympathetic to the poor. The editor notes that the Demon Author urges reconciling "Mothers to the MURDER OF THEIR INFANTS, by presenting them with gay and lively images." The mothers:

> are to be impressed with the idea that it is for the benefit of the world that they are to submit to the sacrifice, and above all, the murdered infants are to be interred in beautiful colonnades decorated with plants and flowers, which are to be called the Infants' Paradise, and which are to be the scenes of the chastened recreations of all classes!
>
> *(41)*

The passage by Marcus on "The Infants' Paradise" comes toward the end of *The Book of Murder!*; it is followed by five pages on "The Theory of Painless Extinction," which might have been written by Jonathan Swift.[10] By this time, it is apparent that *The Book of Murder!* is a satire on Malthus and the New Poor Law. Surprisingly, not everyone has seen it as a satire: Carlyle took it seriously, and so does even such an astute modern historian as Gertrude Himmelfarb.[11]

Besides exterminating them, another way that Britain discovered to get rid of disposable people was of course to promote their emigration to the colonies. That included transporting convicts to Botany Bay and elsewhere. Criminals were obviously among the people the British legal system wanted to dispose of, but also did not want simply to execute. The next best thing—send them to the antipodes. That led, however, to what became a familiar theme in Victorian literature, when convicts such as Abel Magwitch in Dickens' *Great Expectations* returned to Britain, with all sorts of threatening consequences.

Whether as convicts or free colonists, the number of European immigrants to Australia increased, and so did conflicts between them and the Aboriginal inhabitants of that continent. The losers were the Aboriginals in what amounted to a genocide lasting over a century. The last Tasmanian Aboriginal, Truganini, died in 1876. She and her people were, in effect, disposed of by those Britain had previously disposed of, through transportation and through so-called "free" emigration and colonization. On the other side of the world, in Newfoundland, supposedly the last Beothuk Aboriginal or "Red Indian" died in 1829. The Beothuk were also the victims of invasion and colonization. They belonged to the much larger population of "vanishing" Native Americans. From the Renaissance forward, by far the largest category of disposable people has been indigenous populations in many parts of the world.

Some indigenous societies were able to resist the colonizers better than others, and these groups were frequently regarded by Europeans either as partially civilized, such as the Chinese, or as noble savages, such as the Zulus. They proved capable of exterminating most of the other savage "tribes" around them and they defeated a British force at Isandlwana in 1879, so the Zulus could not be categorized as disposable. But many indigenous populations were seen as ignoble savages and treated accordingly. Their territories were frequently called "wastelands" and they themselves were regarded as "waste" populations, doomed to vanish as "civilization" advanced.[12] By some accounts, many indigenous populations had no history—they simply did not count in the annals of Western progress. According to Hegel, the entire continent of Africa had no history—in short, it did not amount to anything philosophically or in any other meaningful way. And Hegel was hardly alone in making that racist judgment.

In his *Two Treatises of Government*, John Locke identified property with the cultivation of land and its non-cultivation with waste. Property for Locke also involved the use of money. Throughout the world, he writes, "there are still great tracts of ground to be found, which the inhabitants thereof, not having joined with the rest of mankind in the consent of the use of their common money, lie waste, and are more than the people who dwell on it, do, or can make use of, and so still lie in common; though this can scarce happen amongst that part of mankind that have consented to the use of money."[13] Locke's erroneous portrayal of "the Indians" as non-industrious and ignorant both of cultivation and of money suggests that they themselves are waste or human refuse.[14] This suggestion foreshadows numerous European portrayals of supposedly uncivilized peoples around the world as waste populations occupying wastelands: if incapable of becoming "civilized," then they deserved what many came to see as their inevitable extinction while the land they had occupied was enclosed and put to what Europeans considered productive uses.

One of the major figures in the history of modern liberalism, Locke owned shares in the Virginia Company. He therefore was quite ready to defend slavery. If they survived the Middle Passage, slaves in the Americas were valuable property. Slavery in the American South or the Caribbean was different from slavery today, which is widespread but everywhere illegal. Because it is illegal, modern slavery does not treat its victims as property. Hence, modern slaves are often treated as even more disposable than the plantation slaves of the past. In *Disposable People*, Kevin Bales estimates that there are at least 27 million slaves now in the world, including in the United States, though he adds that there may be as many as 200 million. If yesterday's plantation slaves were just as valuable as livestock, today's slaves are worthless or almost so; they can always be replaced at little or even no cost. Bales writes that slaveholders today "get all the work that they can out of their slaves, and then throw them away" (14). There are many varieties of slavery, but to take just one of Bales' examples, young girls by the thousands in Thailand are sold by their impoverished parents or else kidnapped and forced into prostitution. In her book on contemporary slavery in Brazil, Alison Sutton similarly writes:

> On more than ten occasions I woke early in the morning to find the corpse of a young girl floating in the water by the barge. Nobody bothered to bury the girls. They just threw their bodies in the river to be eaten by the fish.
>
> *(cited in Bales 4)*

Sutton is talking about girls enslaved as prostitutes in mining communities along the Amazon. If they are uncooperative or sick, they get fed to the piranhas.

Besides slavery, the related phenomenon of debt peonage is both ancient and widespread. After the Civil War, many of the ex-slaves became tenant farmers and debt peons to their former owners. That is often what happened to European peasants who witnessed the commons they depended upon being enclosed by wealthy landowners. Latin American peasants today are frequently debt peons. Following the economic crisis that began in 2007, some economists began to talk about the US as having a debt peonage economy.[15] Besides the national debt, many Americans are currently worthless in monetary terms, because they have debts they may never be able to pay off. Imagine earning a PhD from a major university after amassing a student debt the graduate may never be able to repay. Being in debt does not make someone disposable, but it pushes a person in that direction.

Race science and eugenics

To return to Marcus and *The Book of Murder!*, it was a short step from there or from Malthus—take your pick—to the eugenics movement, with Darwin in between. Eugenics was an offshoot of what was considered scientific knowledge about the human races. The natural historians of the Enlightenment, including Linnaeus, Buffon, and Blumenbach, all developed racial hierarchies according to which the white or Caucasian race stood at the apex, with the other races ranged in various degrees of inferiority beneath it. It seemed evident to them that the success of Europeans from the Renaissance forward in discovering new lands and enclosing them in their burgeoning empires meant that they were the superior race, the heralds of civilization, and, of course, of Christianity. That the dark races of the world succumbed so easily to the European invaders, dying out in great numbers because of violence and disease, seemed to prove that they were, in varying degrees, both inferior and disposable. Even before Darwin's *Origin of Species* (1859) and *The Descent of Man* (1871), many self-designated experts such as Dr. Robert Knox in England and Count de Gobineau in France treated "the dark races" throughout the world as doomed to extinction.

Scientific racism proved extraordinarily useful as an ideological rationalization both for the elimination of millions of indigenous people and for the slave trade and slavery in the US, the Caribbean, and Latin America. American authorities George Glidden and Josiah Nott, co-authors of *Types of Mankind* (1854), espoused the idea of polygenesis, or the notion that the human races had different origins and were therefore distinct species. Their view drew support from craniometry and phrenology, or the pseudosciences of skull measurement and skull shapes. After

Darwin, those pseudosciences provided the groundwork for eugenics and an early version of criminology based on physical anthropology.

Darwin and most of his followers dismissed polygenesis, contending instead that the various races of humans belonged to the same species. As Darwin noted, individuals within any race varied far more than did the races themselves. Although it seemed obvious that the races evolved at very different rates and in different circumstances, there were still huge cultural gaps between them. After the American Civil War, moreover, ideas and fears about racial degeneration became widespread. The major cities of Europe and the New World were signs of the progress of civilization, but they also appeared to provide conditions in which the weakest, most unfit specimens of humanity could breed and multiply, and thus cause the deterioration of the white race. Starting in the 1860s, the British medical journal *The Lancet* published numerous articles about racial decline and fall. Also in that decade, both eugenics and criminology emerged as culminations of race science.

Francis Galton, Darwin's cousin, began the eugenics movement with a double article he published in *Macmillan's Magazine* in 1865 that he then expanded into a book, *Hereditary Genius* (Kevles 3). Daniel Pick writes that Galton's "long inquiry into heredity was perhaps the most striking example of the re-direction of questions of economic and social progress to the evolutionary problem of the body's reproduction"—in short, to biopolitics (Pick 197). Galton's project for racial improvement or "purification" was based on the fear that civilization was self-subverting, because it allowed the "weak" or "unfit," like Malthus' paupers, to survive and breed. Among ways to prevent that from happening were, first, as in Malthus, to keep the poor—that is, the unfit in social Darwinian terms—from breeding, and, second, to promote breeding among the fit—that is, the upper classes, people such as Francis Galton. In civilized conditions, the fittest did not reproduce quickly enough to outbreed the unfit. Galton believed that the key to the progress of any race was to preserve "the desirables" and eliminate "the undesirables." Elimination might come about through nonviolent persuasion, but it might also take coercive and even violent forms, ranging from forced sterilization to extermination, as in *The Book of Murder!* Also, beginning in the 1860s, the researches of Cesare Lombroso led him to claim that most criminals belonged to an atavistic, hereditary type that could be identified through physical features. Soon, many books were filled with photographs—the first mug shots—of criminals (Pick 109–139).

In its most benign form, eugenics aimed at racial progress through promoting the reproduction of the best and brightest human specimens. But it necessarily involved the opposite issue of how to dispose of the weak and unfit—the mentally defective, paupers, criminals. And this question in turn led to the supposedly scientific rationalizations for the genocidal practices of the Nazis in the twentieth century. Inspired by Galton, numerous eugenics journals, organizations, and projects sprang up between the 1880s and World War II. For many intellectuals in the early 1900s, eugenics promised social, economic, and racial progress.

To take just one example out of many, in 1901, H. G. Wells published *Anticipations*, a book of secular prophecies. His most hopeful prediction concerns the emergence of "the New Republic," consisting of engineers, scientists, and other technocrats—the future rulers. In contrast, among his pessimistic forecasts is "the rapid multiplication of the unfit" (61–62)—that is, of all those millions of individuals at the bottom of "the social pyramid" whose potentially life-sustaining labor was being superseded by machinery (63). Wells asks how will the society of the future rid itself of "these gall stones of vicious, helpless, and pauper masses"? (61–62). His answer is that they must be prevented from multiplying or, if that fails, they must be exterminated. He looks forward to a time when eugenics, involving the "merciful obliteration of weak and silly and pointless things," will be widely accepted.

Related to both eugenics and criminology between the 1860s and World War I was widespread concern over socialism, trade unionism, and labor unrest. Capitalists and their attendant intellectuals wished for a workforce made up of docile bodies. Writing about Frederick Taylor's espousal of "scientific management" for business and industry, and its connection to both capitalism and communism, Anthony Horvath stresses Taylor's relationship to eugenics. He notes that Taylor's ideas influenced what went on in Germany, adding that "the Nazis themselves borrowed heavily from American eugenicists. It was among the advocates for eugenics in America that the Nazis drew their philosophical and scientific arguments and also their practical ideas," for example from American eugenicist Madison Grant's book *The Passing of the Great Race* (Horvath; see also Edwin Black). Even before the Nazi takeover, in 1920 two German professors, Karl Binding and Aflred Hache, advocated the extermination of people with disabilities. The disabled were "empty human husks" and "useless eaters" who consumed resources without giving anything back to society. Their "'ballast lives' should be tossed overboard to better balance the economic ship of state" (Mostert; shades of Garret Hardin's "lifeboat ethics"). In the US, eugenics got a major boost from David Starr Jordan, author of *Blood of a Nation* (1902) and president of Indiana University before he moved on to Stanford. If not overtly, the basic idea in eugenics that a sizable portion of human beings such as the disabled are "unfit" and hence should somehow or other be disposed of has not disappeared.[16]

Sovereignty has evolved from older, personified versions—the emperor or king—to the modern, "biopolitical" version. Giorgio Agamben draws on Michel Foucault's ideas about "bio-power" and "biopolitics," according to which sovereignty is invested in "disciplines," notably science and technology. "Bio-power" now has authority over life and death. As both Agamben and Foucault contend, modern biopolitics is clearly exemplified by eugenics. Writing about Nazism, Agamben declares: "The principles of this new biopolitics are dictated by eugenics, which is understood as the science of a people's genetic heredity." Also discussing Nazism, Foucault writes:

> A eugenic ordering of society, with all that implied in the way of extension and intensification of micro-powers, in the guise of an unrestricted state control . . . was accompanied by the oneiric exaltation of a superior blood; the latter implied both the systematic genocide of others and the risk of exposing oneself to a total sacrifice.[17]
>
> (The History of Sexuality 150)

The biopolitics of eugenics overlooks the economic factors that produce poverty. Agamben and Foucault's analyses of biopolitics need some version of the Marxist analysis of capitalism to explain why so many people are reduced to poverty in the first place. The sovereign, even if that concept is now invested in the "micro powers" of scientific disciplines, is not the sole determinant of who winds up at the bottom or the top of the ever-shifting economic pyramid. Governmental policies of taxation, regulation, education, and distribution of revenues play a major role in shaping economies and sorting populations into social classes. Economies are relatively independent of state sovereignty, moreover, unless sovereignty is equated with capitalism. Generally speaking, though, in modern times only state sovereignty has the authority to categorize some or all members of a population as possessing only "bare life," and therefore as targets of various processes of exclusion and extermination.[18]

Around the world today, many impoverished, apparently unwanted populations *are* being exterminated, albeit often by what seem to be accidental causes—preventable diseases or malnutrition resulting in starvation, for example. Deliberate genocides are also happening in many places such as Myanmar and the Sudan. Writing in his anthology on the anthropology of genocide, Alexander Hinton declares that "to comprehend genocide fully, we must go beyond typical cases and examine [situations] in which the structural dynamics taken to an extreme in genocide are manifest in everyday life. 'Rubbish people' suffer in both times of war and peace" (31). When in the US the huge incarceration rate of African Americans and Latinos and the all-too-frequent police killings of unarmed black men and women are called genocide, that is an accurate label. Hinton mentions street children in Brazil, noting that "few people notice or care when these 'dirty vermin' disappear or die, frequently at the hands of police and death squads who describe their murder as 'trash removal,' 'street cleaning,' or 'urban hygiene'" (31). Members of death squads, often made up of off-duty cops, can earn good money for each child killed. Brazil, moreover, isn't the only country where such "street cleaning" is going on.[19]

There are also many causes of the extermination of some groups of people that fall between accidental and deliberate—for example, the "collateral damage" caused by drone strikes in Pakistan, Afghanistan, and Yemen. Claims by U.S. officials about the pinpoint accuracy of so-called smart bombs and drones are not credible. During the U.S. invasion of Iraq in 2003 and the occupation that followed, the American public got daily, presumably accurate accounts of American casualties. In the mainstream media, the far greater toll of Iraqi casualties was rarely mentioned. So, too, the estimate that half a million Iraqi children died as a result of the sanctions imposed on that hapless country after the Gulf War and the claim that those deaths amounted to genocide rarely if ever have been noted in the corporate media.

Genocides are typically events during which one population tries to eradicate another population differentiated by race, ethnicity, religion, or nationality. Where individuals rank in the social hierarchy of the targeted group does not matter: they are all treated as disposable. "The only good Indian is a dead Indian," or "The only good Jew is a dead Jew," and on through a horrific list that does not seem get any shorter. The 1900s has been dubbed "the century of genocides," though there have perhaps always been genocides, or at least genocidal massacres, and we are far from being out of the woods today.

There are even situations in which everyone in a given country or region becomes disposable, as happened in the 1990s when Yugoslavia fell apart. So-called "ethnic cleansing" became the tactic for all sides—Croats, Serbs, Albanians, Muslims, Catholics, Orthodox Christians. They all feared that they had become disposable to the others, and so they had. A general paranoia fueled virulent nationalisms that insisted on establishing ethnically purified nation-states, an impossibility in the Balkans, where different ethnic groups and religions had become so intermingled over centuries that attempts to enforce rigid boundaries between them were, to say the least, irrational.

Refugees and beyond

One of President Trump's first edicts bans immigrants from selected Islamic countries from entering the US. This has led to huge demonstrations throughout the country against the ban. The plight of refugees fleeing from war zones is an all-too-familiar phenomenon, although people can become refugees for other reasons—fleeing famines, for example. There are now increasing numbers of climate refugees such as the inhabitants of the Mariana Islands, which will soon be underwater. The estimate by the United Nations Commissioner for Refugees is that, at the end of 2015, there were 65,300,000 refugees in the world, and it is a safe bet that there will be many more in the future.

Many thousands are now fleeing the violence in Syria, Iraq, and Libya, causing a crisis in Europe as well as the US. Concerning "the Jungle," the refugee camp in Calais, France, Jane Miller writes:

> We, who can travel the world, live, work and holiday more or less where we want to, are encouraged to "debate" whether, where and how many refugees—people who, by definition, are not allowed to debate anything—should be allowed to have somewhere safe to live, to bring up their children, to work and to play.
>
> *(42–43)*

Even though France, Germany, and some other European countries have agreed to accept certain quotas of refugees, when they reach what are relatively safe havens most of them still find themselves virtually imprisoned, surrounded by "razor wire fences and other hideous barriers ... erected to keep these 'marauding hordes' out ... " (Miller 42).

The residents of the Calais Jungle managed to travel from Syria, Iraq, or North Africa all the way across Europe, hoping to travel still farther to get to Britain, and perhaps the US. But over half of the governors of the American states have refused to accept refugees from Syria, while Trump has tried to bar Syrian, Iraqi, Iranian, Sudanese, Somali, and Yemeni Muslims from entering the US. He promises as well to build an unbreachable wall along the Mexican border and make Mexico pay for it. It will no doubt also feature razor wire at the top.

That refugees are unwanted if not completely disposable anywhere they land is sadly self-evident. In *Inequity in the Global Village*, Jan Black describes the Whitehead camp in Hong Kong, which in the early 1990s "warehoused" boat-people from Vietnam. It was, she writes, "no charitable operation; it was a high security detention center, run by the colony's corrections department, surrounded by barbed wire and spikes":

> The inmates, of both sexes and all ages, were guilty only of seeking refugee status—a status that most had already been denied. And this, mind you, was in British-ruled Hong Kong, *before* the much feared Chinese takeover. If a people are to be judged by the way they treat the most helpless among them, the plight of the Vietnamese boat-people and of other refugees does not speak well for civilization . . . .
>
> *(4)*

The war in Vietnam began as a rebellion against French imperialism. After the US took over from the French, the corporate media insisted that "our boys" were fighting for freedom and democracy. It was instead a war waged on behalf of continued imperialism and capitalism. So, too, were the first Gulf War and the 2003 invasion of Iraq. A chief outcome of those wars was not freedom and prosperity for Iraqis, but the enclosure of Iraqi oil by Western corporations and, for the Iraqi people, the destruction of their country and ongoing warfare. Together with the civil war in Syria and unrest elsewhere in the Middle East, the ever-increasing refugee crisis suggests the possibility that everyone everywhere could wind up as refugees.

Even if we don't all become refugees, humanity has reached a situation in which everyone—the entire species—is threatened with annihilation in one form or another, with the two most obvious threats being a nuclear holocaust and climate catastrophe. Both of those threats have come about through what many have considered the chief engines of progress: scientific, technological, industrial, and capitalist development. There is now a third threat stemming from scientific and technological development that is connected to the specter of joblessness. Fears about automation putting humans out of work are as old as the Industrial Revolution. In the early 1800s in England, the Luddites sabotaged the new steam-powered factory machinery that they rightly saw as threatening their livelihoods. The class struggle between workers and owners was also a struggle between workers and machines. Today, there are many books and articles about the relationship between machinery and unemployment, including Nicholas Carr's *The Glass Cage*, Martin Ford's *Rise of the Robots*, and Robert McChesney and John Nichols's *People Get Ready*.[20]

The future may be a lot bleaker than merely jobless, moreover. Discourse about automation, robots, and the Internet includes speculation about the "posthuman" and also about the convergence of GRAIN, an acronym for genetics, robotics, artificial intelligence, and nanotechnology. Starting in the 1980s when nanotechnology was first developing, predictions by both scientists and science-fiction writers asserted that around 2014, as all the elements of GRAIN converge, the super technology that arises will render the entire human species obsolete. In 1988, in *Mind Children*, Hans Moravec claimed that the "intelligent robots" he was helping to create would soon replace us. Evolution would no longer need "our DNA" (2). Two years earlier in *Engines of Creation*, K. Eric Drexler predicted that "advanced technology" will soon "make workers unnecessary and genocide easy" (176). With nanotechnology in mind, Drexler also predicted that molecular nanobots, which potentially could both create and destroy anything and everything, posed a threat even greater than nuclear annihilation. This was the "gray goo" nightmare—an exponential acceleration of entropy that could turn the entire universe into mush. The new technology involved in GRAIN would be both super-intelligent and self-reproducing, and if it did not lead to "gray goo," it would nevertheless zoom on by *Homo sapiens*, throwing us on the scrapheap of evolution. Our own machinic creations would thereby have disposed of all of us.[21]

Such dystopian visions have, however, frequently been matched by a technological utopianism. Drexler, for one, thinks that nanotechnology, if carefully managed, promises a future of abundance for the entire world. Ray Kurzweil predicts that the merger of machines and humans could lead to immortality. The apocalyptic nature of his many books and articles have struck some commentators as a scientific version of the rapture. Kurzweil is also one of the founders of Singularity University in Silicon Valley, which emphasizes the creation of "exponential" technologies. For upbeat futurologists such as Kurzweil, joblessness promises to free humans into an almost unimaginable realm of leisure, where everyone can pursue whatever interests them. Nevertheless, under capitalism, human worth depends largely on one's occupation or profession and one's possessions and wealth. Hence, joblessness is threatening rather than promising. The ultimate extension of that threat is expressed by dystopian versions of GRAIN, including the "gray goo" nightmare.

To put it mildly, this would be a pessimistic note to end this chapter on, but paradoxically there may be hope in the recognition that we are all potentially disposable people and that the only way forward is to reduce or entirely eliminate the causes of that condition. From the Zapatista rebellion and the World Social Forums to Occupy Wall Street and Black Lives Matter, there are many struggles taking place to make the world a more equitable, democratic, peaceful, livable place, a world in which everyone counts, there are no refugees, and no one is disposable. Let's hope we succeed. And maybe, just maybe, the superintelligent machines on the horizon will steer us in the right direction.

Notes

1 According to Italian philosopher Giorgio Agamben, owning nothing means to have only "bare life." "The sovereign," after declaring "a state of emergency," can decide to exterminate those who have been deemed disposable. In *Means without End* and elsewhere, Agamben explores the machinery of social exclusion and therefore also of genocide. "Political power," he contends, "always founds itself... on the separation of a sphere of naked life from the context of the forms of life" (4). Complex societies, at least, make the distinction between humans who count as citizens, or who at any rate have various identifiable social qualities and abilities ("the forms of life"), and those who are excluded—"naked" or "bare life," the merely human without any other qualities or qualifications. The excluded ones fall outside the standard patterns of value based on social stratification (classes, castes, and so on) and hence are rendered disposable. Yet they are not excluded from society in the manner of aliens, the barbarians or foreigners, who of course have their own versions of sovereignty and social hierarchy. The excluded are within society and yet not of it. Summarizing Agamben, Slavoj Žižek writes that the Jews annihilated during the Holocaust belonged "to the species of what the Ancient Romans called *Homo sacer*—those who, although they were human, were excluded from the human community, which is why one can kill them with impunity—*and, for that very reason, one cannot sacrifice them (because they are not a worthy sacrificial offering)*" (*Welcome to the Desert of the Real* 141).
2 Ortiz's poem is the subject of Mark Karlin, "Busted at Birth."
3 Based on the National Alliance to End Homelessness.
4 "... if a surplus population of workers is a necessary product of accumulation ... on a capitalist basis, this surplus population also becomes ... the lever of capitalist accumulation.... It forms a disposable industrial reserve army, which belongs to capital just as absolutely as if the latter had bred it at its own cost" (Marx, *Capital* 1: 784).
5 In *Wasted Lives*, Zygmunt Bauman argues that what he calls "liquid modernity" is an immense waste disposal process in which everyone becomes disposable. It is not clear, however, that he sees modernity itself as the outcome of capitalism, even though he frequently refers to markets, consumer society, and people as commodities. Also, whether he means his title to include everyone or not, "wasted lives" carries with it an inevitability from which there is no escape: once a refugee, always a refugee. And of course, everyone winds up dead.
6 "... the white trash stereotype serves as a useful way of blaming the poor for being poor" (Wray and Newitz 1).
7 "Dustman" was a Victorian euphemism for garbage man.
8 In his *A Brief History of Neoliberalism*, David Harvey notes that "Neoliberal theory conveniently holds that unemployment is always voluntary. Labour, the argument goes, has a 'reserve price' below which it prefers not to work. Unemployment arises because the reserve price of labour is too high" (62). This is similar to the old arguments about happy slaves or that poor people have chosen to be poor, versions of victim-blaming.
9 *The Book of Murder!* was republished in the Chartist newspaper *The Northern Star*. It was familiar to Marx and Engels; the latter cites it in his 1844 *Outlines of a Critique of Political Economy* (Meek 59).
10 *The Book of Murder!* invites comparison to Swift's "A Modest Proposal."
11 Among modern commentators, Gertrude Himmelfarb in *The Idea of Poverty* takes Marcus at face value (125). See Harold Boner, *Hungry Generations* (138–141, 213 n. 28) for more on Marcus' reception. The rambling weirdness of Marcus' argument may not be a sign of his satiric intent, but there are some other, clearer signs. Apart from Marcus' proposal for "the infants' paradise" (42) and his lunatic "theory of painless extinction" (43–48), his single mention of Malthus also betrays his satiric intent. Marcus expects even "complainants" to further the work of his Association, which will receive them like "a work-factory ... ready to employ them. And since the complaint and the remedy will march hand in hand, there

will be no tone of disconsolate misery nor of angry importunity; such as that of the pauper-crowd, object of querimonious dread to MALTHUS" (29).
12 See my *Dark Vanishings*.
13 Notice Locke's two uses of "common" in this passage: land lying "in common" is waste; the use of "common" money is what can help to make it valuable.
14 Throughout the Americas, indigenous societies used various forms of money, and "cultivation" or farming was widely practiced by them. See, for example, Dunbar-Ortiz, *An Indigenous Peoples' History of the United States* (15–31).
15 See, for example, Paul Krugman, *The Great Unraveling*.
16 The protagonist in Ayn Rand's novel *We the Living* says this about eliminating millions of ordinary people for the sake of "the best" people: "Deny the best its right to the top— and you have no best left. What are your masses but mud to be ground under foot, fuel to be burned for those who deserve it? What is the people but millions of puny, shriveled, helpless souls that have no thoughts of their own, no dreams of their own, no will of their own, who eat and sleep and chew helplessly the words others put into their mildewed brains? And for those you would sacrifice the few who know life, who are life? I loathe your ideals because I know no worse injustice than justice for all" (cited in Mander 72). Many on the American right today, including Paul Ryan, current Speaker in the House of Representatives, view Rand as a political sage.
17 For eugenics in the US, see Paul Lombardo, *A Century of Eugenics in America*, and Edwin Black, *War Against the Weak*.
18 Besides direct forms of genocide such as military annihilation, processes of extermination can be and often are indirect, such as simply neglecting to come to the aid of populations affected by epidemics or famine. This is why, for example, Irish nationalists accused British authorities of genocide during the Famine of 1845–1850.
19 "Street cleaning" is going on right now in major Brazilian cities as they prepare for the 2016 Olympics (see Kaplan, "Road to Rio").
20 Two decades before the collapse of the housing bubble and the economic crisis of 2007–2008, in *The Jobless Future*, Stanley Aronowitz and William DiFazio noted that the slow recovery from the recession of the early 1990s was not restoring the permanent, high-paying jobs of the past, but was instead replacing many of those jobs with temporary, low-wage work. They quote *The New York Times* (December 1992, p. 1): "Employment agencies call them contingent workers, flexible workers or assignment workers. Some labor economists, by contrast, call them disposable and throwaway workers."
21 The "gray goo" nightmare has been the basis of a number of science-fiction novels, including Greg Bear's *Blood Music*, Wil McCarthy's *Bloom*, and Michael Crichton's *Prey*. See my examination of GRAIN and the "convergence" or "singularity" debate in *States of Emergency* (170–188).

8
THE REAL TRAGEDY OF THE COMMONS

"Natives of New England, they enclose no land."

— *John Winthrop*

When in the 1820s British colonizers began to arrive in numbers in Australia, they decided that the nomadic peoples they encountered had no concept of ownership, territorial possession, or patriotism, so they declared that the entire continent was *terra nullius*—nobody's land—before they took possession of it. They installed a regime of private property that they identified with civilization. It was not until 1992 that the High Court in the Eddie Mabo land rights case overturned *terra nullius* as the official legal doctrine of Australia (see Reynolds, *The Law of the Land*). The erroneous idea of *terra nullius* is a stark reminder that one of the effects of Western imperialism was to render notions of property more extreme than they had been in Europe. That a single individual might become the absolute owner of a piece of land that had heretofore not been owned by anybody had no precedent in European history, during which the dividing line between communal and private property, though it gradually shifted in the direction of the latter, was never very precise or absolute.[1]

What the conquerors and colonists encountered in the Americas were a wide range of indigenous societies. But no matter how diverse they were, Native Americans, like the Australian Aboriginals, did not consider land as something a single individual could own (Dunbar-Ortiz 34). Land belonged—if that is the right word—to families and communities, not individuals. "Legal theorists and historians," writes Derek Wall in his *The Commons in History*, have become increasingly aware that prior to the period of European colonialism, commons were the rule rather than the exception across much of our planet" (21).[2] Just as the enclosure of the commons was doing in Europe, imperialism and settler colonialism were destroying ancient customs and patterns of community in the Americas, Austrialia, and elsewhere in much of the non-Western world. Today, there are still many versions of commons everywhere, but they have been drastically reduced in area and are now the exception rather than the rule.

Common ground

As noted earlier, from the late Middle Ages forward, many peasants in Europe resisted the enclosure of land that they viewed as their commons or as belonging to their communities. Those who had made use of the commons for centuries—the commoners—depended on them for survival. Commons might ultimately belong to "the lord of the manor," but manorial courts recognized the usufruct rights of commoners. Besides the consolidation of small peasant holdings into larger farming units, the enclosure process in England and elsewhere in Europe turned masses of peasants away from the land, causing many of them to become paupers and vagrants if they could not find other means of support. It is no wonder, then, that resisting enclosure frequently involved violence, as in the case of Kett's Rebellion in Norfolk in 1549. There, the peasants, perhaps numbering 16,000, tore down the fences that had enclosed their commons. After they stormed Norwich, a government force was sent to defeat the rebellion, and its leader, yeoman Robert Kett, was hanged from the walls of the town.[3]

For a variety of reasons, however, peasants themselves enclosed land, which usually meant surrounding a small area with stones or hedges to keep livestock in or out. A commons, moreover, was not viewed as land open to anybody, but was rather territory that by custom or law came under the collective control of a specific community or group. Small-scale enclosures by the peasantry were usually regarded as unproblematic. The difficulty arose from lords and other large-scale landholders seeking to increase their holdings, which frequently involved evicting commoners, including entire peasant communities. Defenders of enclosures saw them as increasing agricultural productivity and profits; opponents saw them as disrupting communal ways of life and increasing rural poverty. Both sides were right.[4]

In her magisterial study of commons and commoners in England between 1700 and 1820, Jeanette Neesom demonstrates that areas deemed to be commons before they were enclosed were subject to regulation, either by custom or by law. She notes that stinting, or regulating when and how many cattle or sheep could graze on a commons, was frequently practiced. Also, although they were a major source of firewood, the commons typically had restrictions against individuals cutting timber simply for their own use (Neesom 160–162). And there were other customs and laws that regulated the use of commons.[5]

The agricultural modernizers such as Arthur Young who supported enclosure of the commons "wanted to raise productivity and to improve the supply and quality of labour" (Neesom 35).[6] The commoners, however, were largely independent of the money economy. To the well-to-do, they were a nuisance, an ignorant, backward-looking impediment to progress. To those above them in the social hierarchy, English commoners were viewed as little different from "the wilde Irish." They were "a 'sordid race', as foreign and uncultivated as the land that fed them. Like the commons they were wild and unproductive. They were lazy and dangerous. If wastes must be subdued, so must they" (32). Neesom adds that the "improving ideology was as deadly to the old system," which supported perhaps half of England's population, "as greed itself" (44).

Defenders of common right and the commoners often argued that the old system provided both self-sufficiency—"having 'enough'"—and independence for the rural poor. But, Neesom says, "Perhaps having 'enough' was unimaginable to men who wrote about crop yields, rents, improvements, productivity, economic growth, always *more*, as it has been incomprehensible to twentieth-century historians living in constantly expanding market economies, albeit on a finite planet." She goes on to surmise that the critics of the commoners and their commons might at least have sympathized with "the pride of ownership that small farmers also displayed which was the other side of self-importance. Something [the critics] missed entirely was the constantly negotiated interdependence of commoners, their need of each other" (41).

As an aspect of that constant negotiation, conflicts among its beneficiaries about how a commons was being used were frequent. It is erroneous to view all commons as either all alike or utopian. Sir Thomas More's Utopians were not burdened by any concept of property, but all types of commons are versions of shared property. Those who share in a commons do not necessarily do so equally or equitably. For a variety of reasons, in the early going women were often more reliant on what they could glean from a commons than were men; women were also often in the front lines of those opposing enclosure. Wall mentions that "women have often taken militant action, including breaking fences and demolishing hedges, to restore commons. Plumstead Commons in South London, which remains greenspace [today], was apparently rescued by angry women in the nineteenth century" (92–94).

For the defenders of the commons, Neesom points out, enclosure meant loss of both independence and interdependence, and with them "connection, sympathy and obligation. The value of the commons was their social cement. The arrogance of the critics was to think they could do without it" (46). The commons were once and still are very much about community. Perhaps more frequently today than in the past, the ideas of community and the commons evoke a nostalgia and sometimes a utopianism that expresses itself in many forms. William Morris' *News from Nowhere* (1890) depicts a post-revolutionary society that seems more medieval than modern or postmodern. In his Marxist dreamworld, there is no private property and also no poverty. Work takes the form of art. Everything is shared in common, by the entire community, and no one is threatening to enclose anything.

Morris' utopia is a culmination of a lengthy tradition of pastoral literature. Toward the end of the 1700s and into the next century, Oliver Goldsmith, John Clare, William Wordsworth, and many other British writers lamented the disappearance of the customs and practices associated with commoning. In "Emmonsales

Heath" (1819), the "peasant poet" Clare lamented the loss of freedom that he associated with the fencing of land:

> Unbounded freedom ruled the wandering scene
> Nor fence of ownership crept in between
> To hide the prospect of the following eye
> Its only bondage was the circling sky ...

Also with the enclosure movement in mind, Oliver Goldsmith penned "The Deserted Village" (1770):

> Ill fares the land, to hastening ills a prey,
> Where wealth accumulates, and men decay:
> Princes and lords may flourish, or may fade;
> A breath can make them, as a breath has made;
> But a bold peasantry, their country's pride,
> When once destroyed, can never be supplied.

In contrast to Morris who considered himself a Marxist, Goldsmith, Clare, and Wordsworth were all conservative thinkers, and yet all four were opposed to capitalist modernization.[7]

As capitalism took shape through accumulation by dispossession, the economic factors that led to the ruin of Goldsmith's "sweet Auburn" and of England's "bold peasantry" have today gone global. Much of England's economy in the 1700s was based on subsistence agriculture, but it was a communal economy that for many centuries had supported countless villages and peasants all over Europe and much of the rest of the world, and continues to do so today.

> A time there was, ere England's griefs began,
> When every rood of ground maintained its man ...

In Goldsmith's era, subsistence farming was dying a gradual, painful death, giving way from commons and small plots of ground to vast areas of tillage and pasturage, including "sheep walks" that provided wool for the burgeoning textile industry. As many critics of the enclosure movement complained, sheep seemed to be worth more than the "bold peasantry." Even "the village green" was sometimes coming under private rather than collective ownership.

> But times are altered; trade's unfeeling train
> Usurp the land and dispossess the swain ...

It was and still is easy to romanticize both the "bold peasantry" in England and elsewhere and the often-ancient versions of "the commons," as Morris does in *News from Nowhere*. Prejudicial though it may sound, it is worth recalling Marx and

Engels' comment in the first section of *The Communist Manifesto* about "the idiocy of rural life." Until well into the nineteenth century, the vast majority of peasants everywhere in Europe were illiterate and largely unaware of the wider world. But that does not mean they were stupid and unaware of what was going on around them. That he had gained an education is part of what made a peasant poet such as Clare noteworthy. In his important essay, "Custom Law and Common Right," E. P. Thompson states:

> It is not that John Clare—nor the commoners for whom he spoke—were primitive communists. Viewed from their standpoint, the communal forms expressed an alternative notion of possession, in the petty and particular rights and usages which were transmitted in custom as the *properties* of the poor. Common right, which was in lax terms coterminous with settlement, was *local* right, and hence was also a power to exclude strangers. Enclosure, in taking the commons away from the poor, made them strangers in their own land.
>
> *(184)*

In partial contrast to Thompson, R. H. Tawney saw in the pre-enclosure commons "a miniature cooperative society" and "a little commonwealth" that involved a "practical communism" (235). That is how Morris saw it. Of course, it was quite different from the totalitarian variety of communism.

Yet it has always been the case that the opponents of the enclosure of the commons have sided with the poor in favor of versions of customary, communal ownership and against the impositions of capitalism and the modern regime of private property. Feudalism was, of course, a hierarchical form of society and economy, but it supported the commoning that in turn supported the peasantry. In *The Magna Carta Manifesto*, Peter Linebaugh writes that throughout the Middle Ages, "Prophets and messiahs preached the doctrine of having all things in common, which made sense to peasants who resolutely defended their customs and communal routine against the encroachments of feudal landlords and grasping clergy" (25–26). That message also made sense to them centuries later. At the time of the English Revolution in the 1640s, for example, Gerrard Winstanley and the Diggers espoused a quite radical brand of egalitarianism that condemned the private ownership of land and of the class structure that elevated the wealthy over the poor.[8]

Two extreme nineteenth-century examples exemplifying the enclosure movement are the so-called "Highland Clearances" in Scotland and the clearing off of the peasantry from Irish estates during the Great Famine of 1845–1850. In one infamous Scottish case, between 1814 and 1820, the Duchess of Sutherland "swept" some 15,000 peasants off of nearly 800,000 acres, destroying their villages and turning their fields into sheep farms. "By 1825," writes Marx, "the 15,000 Gaels [in the Highlands] had . . . been replaced by 131,000 sheep" (*Capital* 1: 892). In Ireland, famine and diseases associated with starvation were major causes of the clearing of the land, but so was the eviction of peasants from their cottages and smallholdings even in the midst of starvation. Supposedly because his estate in County Mayo was encumbered by debt, Lord Sligo ordered the eviction of thousands during the Famine. With their cabins "tumbled" or demolished, sometimes peasants hunkered down in pits or "scalpeens" for shelter, covered with turf or sticks, while they starved. Many others hit the road, joining thousands headed for the towns and cities, and, when they could manage it, emigrating to England, Scotland, or North America. Approximately 1 million Irish peasants starved to death, while another 1.5 million managed to leave Ireland altogether.

English observers often interpreted what was happening as the necessary path of progress for agriculture in both Scotland and Ireland, and Marx, although fully cognizant of the irony of that view, did not disagree. The long history of Irish rebellion against English rule amounted to agrarian, class warfare in which the peasantry were fighting against their literal dispossession at the hands of English or Anglo-Irish landlords and their middlemen.[9] In Ireland after the Famine, the Land League and the rural violence of the 1870s, writes Mike Cronin, aimed "to protect tenants from the effects of sudden and dramatic increases in their rent, and the fear, or experience, of eviction" (158). As peasant resistance and Irish nationalism grew both more vocal and more violent, the modern fear of terrorism was born (Martin).[10]

Everywhere in Europe, cooperation and communal work among peasants gradually gave way to the new money economy that involved private property, competition, contracts, and strictly calculable relations of credit. Eventually, everything began to have a monetary value, including human relations. And once a monetary value was attached to an individual, if that value was negligible, he or she could also be seen as negligible or even disposable, as noted in Chapter 7. The peasants who became wage laborers, either in cities or still in the countryside, may not have recognized it, but they were being turned into commodities, and treated as such by their employers.

The enclosure of land is still going on around the world in a big way. Two giant agribusinesses, Cargill and ConAgra, are responsible for half of U.S. grain exports. And they are two of the three corporations that slaughter three-quarters of beef in the US (the third is Iowa Beef Processors). Citing these statistics, David Korten also notes that between 1935 and 1990, small American farms disappeared at a great rate, from nearly 7 million to around 2 million (*When Corporations Rule the World* 208). Many small country towns in the US, such as Goldsmith's "sweet Auburn," have disappeared along with the family farms that sustained them. "The top ten 'farms' in the United States are now international agribusiness corporations..." (Korten 208). Besides Cargill and ConAgra, Korten names Tyson Foods, Gold Kist, Continental Grain, Perdue Farms, and Pilgrims Pride. Big Ag not only gobbles up land, it even privatizes seeds, as does Monsanto. The World Trade Organization, doing the bidding of globalizing corporations, has ruled in favor of granting them patents over seeds and other genetic materials, including genetically modified crops or GMOs.

According to Alexander Ross, in the "new scramble" for Africa, "the quantity of land grabbed in just two years, between 2008 and 2009, amounts to an area the size of the state of California, plus much of Oregon." The main "land grabbers" in Africa and elsewhere in the world are "large transnational corporations" (Ross 20). The new corporate conquistadors may not slaughter the natives, but they have little or no use for them. Their livelihoods gone, the dispossessed natives are just more disposable people. Similarly, in *Biopiracy*, addressing "the second coming of Columbus," Shiva connects Western imperialism and its enormous land-grabs in the Americas and elsewhere to the current "theft" of the commons by corporations. She notes that John Locke in his *Two Treatises on Government* "effectually legitimized [the] process of theft and robbery during the enclosure movement in Europe" (3), as he also legitimized private property. And in *Revitalizing the Commons*, C. A. Bowers contends that to understand "current threats to the commons needs to take account of the many ways in which today's industrial culture contributes to [their] enclosure . . . ." The threats come not only from industry and corporations, moreover, but also from "international institutions such as the World Trade Organization, and [from] the Western scientific, technological, and educational approach to development" (vii).

Defining the commons today

The trilogy by Michael Hardt and Antonio Negri that began with *Empire* (2001) and was followed by *Multitude* (2004) has been completed by their publication of *Commonwealth* (2009). What do they mean by that title? In the preface, they write:

> A democracy of the multitude is imaginable only because we all share and participate in the common. By "the common" we mean, first of all, the common wealth of the material world, the fruits of the soil, and all nature's bounty . . . . We consider the common also and more significantly [to include] those results of social production that are necessary for social interaction and further production, such as knowledges, languages, codes, information, affects, and so forth. This notion of the common does not position humanity separate from nature . . . .
>
> *(7)*

In other words, according to Hardt and Negri, "the commonwealth" includes just about everything. So, too, in *Silent Theft*, David Bollier writes: "For millenia, nature has served as a commons for the human species" (61). And Vandana Shiva says that the entire planet should be treated as the commons or as our common wealth, shared by everyone (*Earth Democracy* 2). She adds that the commons are "the highest expression of economic democracy" (3).

If Hardt and Negri, Bollier, and Shiva are right, turning any aspect of nature, including land and what grows on it or lies under it (wildlife, seeds, grass, trees, crops, coal, oil, gas, uranium, etc.), as well as water (fish, rivers, lakes, wetlands, oceans) and even the atmosphere, into private property represents a loss to our—that is, everyone's—common wealth. Bollier, however, steps back from that all-encompassing position to assert that "protecting the commons is about maintaining a balance, not bashing business. It is self-evident that we need markets" (*Silent Theft* 3). Yes, of course we need markets. But what kind of markets are necessary? A neighborhood grocery store is categorically different from the labor market, which is categorically different from the stock market. Bollier is hardly an orthodox economist, but one of the problems with capitalist economics, at least as it is presented in introductory textbooks, is that it treats "the free market" as a universal and infallible machine that automatically renders capitalism the only rational way to do business. Markets, however, aren't free to those who shop in them.[11]

Today's defenders of the commons, including Bollier, equate freedom with the recognition of "our common wealth." Using that phrase as his title, Jonathan Rowe declares:

> The true story of the commons . . . explains how we lost the capacity to see our own wealth. It debunks the myth that privatization is always progress. And it shows how [economic] growth has become a form of cannibalism in which the market devours the bases of its own existence.
>
> *(100)*

The existence of a Walmart megastore in my hometown has nothing to do with freedom. It does not fulfill my wishes or express my interests. It has nothing democratic about it except prices so low that it has caused several local businesses to fold. Walmart certainly does not operate democratically in regard either to its management or to its workers. It does not permit union organizing. It forbids demonstrations protesting its policies (or anything else) even in its parking lot. The megastore and its mega parking area have enclosed land that used to be woods and farms. The farms and probably the woods were no doubt privately owned from the early 1800s onward. But at least the owners were individuals who resided in close proximity to each other, not some distant and enormous corporation, its management, or its board of directors.

Unlike Walmart and other transnational corporations, commons are ordinarily thought of as belonging to specific communities and as being under some form of local, democratic control. Yet the idea that all of nature has been and always will be our commons appears to encompass everything. If that notion seems hyperbolic, just what more specifically constitutes the commons? After "all of nature," the shortest answer may be that the commons consists of whatever belongs to the public or to us "commoners" collectively as opposed to whatever is privately owned. This dichotomy is perhaps confusing, because a publicly approved and traded corporation such as Walmart is in some sense a public entity. Yet it behaves as though it were privately owned and for the most part can do whatever its CEO and board of directors decide.

In regard to private property, moreover, most accounts about the fate of the commons are not concerned with individual ownership of such items as cars or houses, but rather with the privatization by corporations of what had been publicly owned or controlled, often-huge swaths of land, and with them the natural resources they contain such as oil and timber. Along with increasing privatization goes the weakening of governments to exercise any effective control over the behavior of corporations. Part of that weakening has come about through the outsourcing of many government services to corporations, as when the federal or a state government signs a deal with a corporation to build and run a new prison. Partly, too, it has come about through the revolving door between Congress and K Street, where many lobbying groups have their headquarters. And it has happened as well through international trade deals such as NAFTA, which sap the power of governments over many aspects of those deals.

As governments weaken and corporations gain power throughout the world, so arises the fear that everything may be privatized—enclosed and commodified—causing the disappearance of the commons. So what is left of the commons today? To explain what constitutes—or should constitute—the commons, Canadian activist Maude Barlow offers a tripartite list:

> The first category [of the commons] includes the water, land, air, forests, and fisheries on which everyone's life depends. The second includes the culture and knowledge that are collective creations of our species. The third is the social commons that guarantees public access to health care, education, and social services, including pensions and welfare.
>
> *(69)*

Once again, as in Hardt and Negri, this sounds like everything—all of nature. A minor point, no doubt, but an author based in the US would be less likely than Barlow to write that government or anything else "*guarantees* public access to health care, education, and social services." Nevertheless, her list is similar to those in Bollier, Shiva, Rowe, and others who write about the commons. Compare Barlow's list, for example, to the one in *First as Tragedy, Then as Farce*, by Slavoj Žižek:

- *the commons of culture*, the immediately socialized forms of "cognitive" capital, primarily language, our means of communication and education, but also the shared infrastructure of public transport, electricity, the postal system, and so on;
- *the commons of external nature*, threatened by pollution and exploitation (from oil to rain forests and the natural habitat itself);
- *the commons of internal nature* (the biogenetic inheritance of humanity); with new biogenetic technology, the creation of a New Man in the literal sense of changing human nature becomes a realistic prospect.

(91)

Žižek combines Barlow's first and third categories, while apparently adding another: "the commons of internal nature." In any event, such lists are meant to be inclusive, so that there is little or nothing that might not be considered part of the commons. One implication is simply that whatever is now considered private property, including everything supposedly owned and controlled by corporations, should instead be redefined as in some sense communal property. Yet under globalizing capitalism, many items included in the lists have already been enclosed or privatized, while others are threatened by privatization.

Do we continue to endorse capitalism, Žižek asks, or does today's global version of it entail contradictions that may be powerful enough to cause a massive system change? He emphasizes the obvious—that the three categories of commons he has identified are all under siege by corporations. But globalizing capitalism is in turn threatened by four "antagonisms." First, there is the growing danger of global warming and ecological catastrophe. Second, much intellectual and culture production does not fit easily into the category of private property. The Internet, for example, currently fits more readily into the category of the commons. Third, new developments in science and technology such as genetic engineering should not simply be turned over to corporations to manage, and struggles to prevent that happening are increasing. And finally, Žižek mentions "the creation of *new forms of apartheid*, new walls and slums"—in other words new, quite literal modes of enclosing or imprisoning large groups of humans, such as Greenville Penitentiary or Guantanamo (91). Implicit in the fourth antagonism is the fact that treating more and more people as disposable (see Chapter 7) is bound to lead to massive resistance, perhaps on a global scale.

Žižek notes that there is an important difference between his last antagonism—"the gap that separates the Excluded from the Included"—and the others, which refer to different categories of the commons, or "the shared substance of our social being." He adds that the privatization of any of them "which involves violent acts" should, "where necessary, be resisted with violent means." As Žižek is well aware, those who engage in "violent means" to protest the enclosure of aspects of the commons are likely to find themselves the victims of "new forms of apartheid," perhaps winding up in prison for their efforts (91). Such has been the case, for example, for environmentalists who have tried to prevent logging in state or national forests, or drilling for oil in the Arctic. Often they expect to be arrested. Many of the protesters against the Keystone XL and Dakota Access pipelines, including many Native Americans, have landed in jail. And frequently environmental activists have been labeled "terrorists" by the currently corporate-controlled U.S. government.

Barlow and Žižek's lists are so inclusive that they are not much different from the assertions by Hardt and Negri, Bollier, and Shiva that the commons include all of nature, or all of nature and culture. Is there anything these authors leave out—any category that could reasonably be identified as private property? To turn that question around, should we not restore to the commons much that has so far been enclosed or removed from our common possession? What right, for example, did Western oil corporations have to seize control of Iraqi oil, which had been state-owned, after the U.S. invasion of 2003?[12]

Again, private property on the individual level is not the main issue. It is instead everything that has been privatized or threatened with privatization by major corporations. It seems clear, moreover, that the corporate elimination of the commons also eliminates the chance of achieving widespread social justice, which, according to philosopher and labor activist Milton Fisk, "is realized by establishing and maintaining public goods" by democratic means. For Fisk, "goods" means something close to the opposite of commodities and more inclusive than that category. He adds that "the theory and the practice of [economic] neoliberalism has been to attack public goods":

> An offensive to save what public goods are left, and to create needed new ones would, if successful, undermine a key feature of neoliberalism, thereby destabilizing it as a whole. To survive in a global economy with dignity and justice calls for a concerted effort to change it from a neoliberal economy by an initial step of an offensive for public goods.
>
> *(45)*

Like Fisk, many of those who write about the commons today advocate reclaiming as much of them as possible, taking them back from the corporations that have enclosed them.

Corporations have always functioned as often highly destructive "engines of enclosure" (Anton 31), operating originally as empire-building machines, claiming vast stretches of territory and even entire continents as their or their royal sponsors' possessions. Dystopian novels and films today such as *Snow Crash*, *Blade Runner*, and *WALL-E* often feature worlds dominated by corporations and their typically despotic CEOs. In *WALL-E*, consumerism and the relentless push by the corporate powers that be to privatize whatever can make money for them have turned the world into a gigantic garbage dump. Is that what society will be like when virtually everything has been enclosed, corporatized, and commodified? A planet ruled by Walmart is a distinctly dystopian prospect. On the other hand, the restoration of community—hopefully on a global scale—would entail establishing an economic regime antithetical to corporate capitalism, an ecologically sustainable version of democratic socialism with its main sources of authority based in local and regional institutions and in people-oriented decision-making processes. Property, too, would be redefined as, in the first instance, communal. Recently, albeit on a limited scale, the communities established by the Landless Workers Movement and neighborhood experiments in participatory budgeting in Porto Alegre, Brazil, have exemplified what such an economic regime might look like.[13] Such a redefinition of property and a communal mode of governance would need to avoid the top-down, tyrannical communism of the Soviet era *and* the major failings of profiteering and piratical corporate capitalism.

A key ideological roadblock toward that sort of transformation is market populism, whose hegemony, at least in the US ever since the Cold War, has been strengthened by the notion that all forms of socialism have failed and will always fail.[14]

That is why Barlow's statement that the social commons "guarantees" such items as health care sounds so foreign in the U.S. context. An insidious corollary of this roadblock has been the idea of "the tragedy of the commons," which neoliberal economists such as N. Gregory Mankiw interpret as proving that collective ownership or any attempts to manage natural resources through communal processes will ultimately fail.[15] I suspect that most fifth-graders could figure out the fallacy of this argument, because everywhere around us are examples of the more or less successful collective management of natural resources and other aspects of the economy. What would be gained by outsourcing America's national parks, for example, to a corporation to manage? Why privatize the U.S. Post Office, which is both efficient and self-supporting? What improvements would privatized police departments bring about? Besides, both governmental and corporate modes of management are collective. But the claim that the commons are inevitably tragic has been used to contend that public assets—a city-owned water system, for instance—should be turned over to corporations. Instead of a fifth-grader, it has taken a Nobel Prize winner to dispel the tragedy of the commons argument.

Actually working commons

The late Professor Elinor Ostrom won the Nobel Prize in economics in 2009. She is the only woman to have won that prize, and she did so as a political scientist. Both facts raised the hackles of a number of economists. She became a Nobel laureate on the basis of empirical research that demonstrated how the collective management of "the commons" or of "common pool resources" need not lead to tragedy, but could instead often contribute to ecological sustainability and be productive for those participating in their use.[16] Ostrom's work and that of her husband Vincent, as well as of their numerous colleagues and students, have opened new perspectives on what constitutes the commons today and on aspects of certain resources that cannot or should not be privatized.

A key result of Ostrom's work has been to discredit the idea that communal management of resources typically has tragic results. That notion originated in a 1968 article by biologist Garrett Hardin in *Science*. Worrying about the Malthusian problem of overpopulation, Hardin argued that free access to any resource—treating it as a commons—would produce overexploitation and the depletion of that resource. One of his examples was a pasture open to anyone wishing to graze livestock there. If too many farmers took advantage of it, the result would be overgrazing and unsustainability. Obviously even a renewable resource such as a pasture can be overused. There are many examples—the clear-cutting of a forest, for example, or the extinction of codfish off the Newfoundland coast, and with it the disappearance of what had been a very large, thriving fishing industry (though it is gradually making a comeback).

Besides Hardin's "tragedy of commons" thesis, Ostrom critiqued similar arguments or conundrums that seem to show why cooperative or communal actions and ownership are likely to fail. These include the prisoner's dilemma and Mancur

Olson's theory of collective interaction. In the first case, two prisoners who cannot communicate with each other and who have been arrested for the same crime are given the choice either to claim that the other prisoner committed that crime or to remain silent. If both of them betray each other, they will both serve two years in prison. If one of them betrays the other while the other remains silent, the betrayer will go free while the silent one will serve three years in prison. And if both remain silent, both of them will only serve one year in prison. Assuming they are both strictly rational in terms of self-interest, they will both betray each other. In short, self-interest trumps collective loyalty and cooperation. Olson's theory reaches a similar conclusion: in situations demanding collective action, cooperation will be rendered difficult if not impossible by those who choose to be "free riders"—that is, those who benefit from the cooperation of others without contributing anything themselves. Yet as Ostrom's research showed, cooperation is often more rational in terms of self-interest than is strict selfishness.

In Hardin's view, private or state ownership are the only alternatives to the tragedy of the commons. But he does not see, as Vandana Shiva points out, that "the very existence of the commons implies the reality of cooperative management and ownership" (*Earth Democracy* 52). Further, David Bollier contends that the tragedy "precipitated by 'rational' individualism is not the tragedy of the commons, but the tragedy of the market" (*Think Like a Commoner* 31). "The real tragedy of the commons," writes Derek Wall, "has been the often bloody enclosure and destruction of the commons" (88). And Raj Patel argues that people don't always behave selfishly, as in Hardin's view and more generally in neoliberal economics, although corporations always behave that way—"the profit motive makes them so" (87).

Ostrom, Shiva, and many others have by now shown that Hardin and Mancur Olson oversimplify in at least two ways. First, they overlook the many ways humans have often, sometimes for centuries, cooperated locally, regionally, and globally for the collective good. An evocative exploration of this fact is Heather Menzies' "memoir and manifesto," *Reclaiming the Commons for the Common Good*, in which she recounts what life must have been like for her Scottish ancestors before the Highland Clearances. And second, Hardin reduces the alternatives to overcoming the tragedy of the commons to just two, private and governmental, whereas there are at least four. David Feeny and his co-authors call these four alternatives "open access," "private property," "communal property," and "state property." They also point out that there are combinations and intermediate variations among these four main categories. None of these alternatives, moreover, calls for the elimination of markets. But if commons "are to interact with markets," writes Bollier, "they must be able to resist enclosure, consumerism, the lust for capital accumulation and other familiar pathologies of capitalism" (*Think Like a Commoner* 122).

In the world's bestselling economic textbook, Mankiw cites Hardin's argument as if it were scientific fact. Mankiw's discussion of cooperative ownership is restricted to a few remarks about air pollution, wildlife species, and a brief account of the tragedy of the commons based on Hardin. Mankiw imagines a medieval town sharing common grazing land but allowing the sheep to overpopulate. The grazing land will soon be exhausted (232–234). However, he overlooks the methods medieval peasants used to avoid that outcome. Besides maintaining a commons in the first place, they typically practiced stinting, or limiting the number of animals that could graze there, and they frequently allotted time limits for grazing. In other words, they put the welfare of the community ahead of individual gain. E. P. Thompson remarks that in managing their commons successfully, the peasantry used "common sense." Neoliberal economists such as Mankiw believe that individuals are rational actors, but they forget that rational behavior can be cooperative. And markets, moreover, are just as much the outcomes of cooperative behavior as are commons.

To live in a community—or, better, multiple communities, as almost everyone does today—means to follow communal customs, rules, and laws. A given community may not be open to everyone. As already noted, to work effectively, commons themselves often need to be enclosed. The communities that oversee and use them follow specific customs and rules. A peasant community, for example, may gather firewood in a forest commons, but individuals who belong to it may not be free to cut down trees for their private use. A public park may be open to everybody, but drunk and disorderly conduct may be outlawed, and there may be rules against having dogs on leashes or setting off fireworks.

Besides believing that property held in common is never so well cared for as private property, Mankiw also believes that government management and regulation get in the way of the "Invisible Hand" of the market, which should be the ultimate arbiter of how resources are used. But reliance on the market can just as easily result in the sort of tragedy Hardin worries about. With few restraints, coal mining companies are removing entire mountaintops in West Virginia and Kentucky and ruining nearby streams and rivers. Forests everywhere in the world are rapidly disappearing as timber companies mow them down. With inadequate regulation and high demand for codfish, Newfoundland fishermen nearly destroyed their livelihood. They failed to treat their fishery as a well-regulated commons.

Capitalist economics has for years taught that communal ownership of resources is inefficient and will in all likelihood result in excessive exploitation. But so can individual or corporate ownership. Nothing "guarantees that the individuals who . . . pillage and raid the common wealth will act collectively in such a way as to ensure the reproduction of that common wealth," writes David Harvey; "Private individuals or corporations acting in their own short-term self-interest often undermine, if not destroy, the conditions for their own reproduction" (*Seventeen Contradictions and the End of Capitalism* 75). Raj Patel puts it even more bluntly: "Over the past thirty years, the accelerating pace of enclosure, and the increasing scale of the theft, have brought our planet to the edge of destruction" (151). This is the conclusion of many others; Noam Chomsky, for instance, declares: "As we now understand all too well, it is what is *privately* owned, not what is held in common, that faces destruction by avarice, bringing the rest of us down with it" ("Magna Carta").[17]

Ergo, common resources must be managed for the collective good to achieve environmental sustainability. Regulation can come from communities, regional or provincial governments, national governments, or international institutions. Markets are also collective institutions, of course, though they are no substitute for communities or other sources of deliberative action such as legislatures. It is largely because resources in an unrestrained capitalist system are put up for grabs to the highest bidders that the tragedy of overexploitation is occurring today in the form of environmental degradation and the climate crisis.

Ostrom's research does not lead to one answer about how all resources should be managed. Instead, it indicates that there have been and are many versions of cooperation over resource management, and that, depending on such factors as the size and availability of the resource and the nature of the group or groups making use of it, there can be many different outcomes, everything from its quick exhaustion to its long-term sustainability. Moreover, there are often no sharp dichotomies between private and public forms of management. "Institutions are rarely either private or public—'the market' or 'the state,'" Ostrom points out (33). What is more, as Bollier comments in *Think Like a Commoner*, "the Market and State, once very separate realms of morality and politics, are now joined at the hip: a tight allegiance with a shared vision of technological progress, corporate dominance and ever-expanding economic growth and consumption," which he calls "a mad utopian fantasy" (13). Although corporations are typically viewed as the epitome of private property, they are large-scale modes of cooperation and they can be publicly owned. Even when they are privately owned, they still have numerous shareholders, large boards, many employees, and numerous people in management, so they are obviously collective enterprises. But neoliberal economics valorizes private property and supposedly rational individuals as owners, entrepreneurs, and consumers (*Homo economicus*). It denigrates public ownership and control, and tends to treat anything that fits into the expansive category of the commons as uneconomical.

For economists, the commons is "a kind of inchoate mass that awaits the vivifying hand of the market to attain life. Forests are worthless until they become timber, just as quiet is worthless until it becomes advertising. In this way of seeing things, the enclosure of a commons is always a good thing" (Rowe 15). In one sense, the commons consists of whatever is not easily marketable. In another, it is whatever goods, marketable or not, make our lives together in communities possible. Rowe says that the commons "includes our entire life support system, both natural and social," and he comes up with this list:

> The air and oceans, the web of species, wilderness and flowing water. . . language and knowledge, sidewalks and public squares, the stories of childhood, the processes of democracy. Some parts of the commons are gifts of nature, others the product of human endeavor. Some are new, such as the Internet; others are as ancient as soil and calligraphy.
>
> *(14)*

Environmentalism in general is about protecting "our entire life support system" for both the present and the future.

Rowe's mention of the Internet points to a recent aspect of the cultural commons or intellectual property that Žižek, Barlow, and others mention in passing. In his 2008 book *Viral Spiral*, Bollier offers a highly enthusiastic account of "how the commoners built a digital republic of their own," as his subtitle says, via computers and the Internet. He begins by asserting that "the commons—a hazy concept to many people—is a new paradigm for creating value and organizing a community of shared interest" (4). The problem with that statement, as Bollier knows full well, is that the commons is an ancient idea. It's just that the Internet allows "commoners" to create new, digital communities where they can share all sorts of information for free, if they so choose. Bollier's enthusiasm leads him to apply political language—"digital republic," for example—as though what is happening over the Internet is revolutionary. Perhaps it is. At least social media—Facebook, YouTube, Twitter, and so forth—have aided and abetted the Zapatista rebellion, MoveOn, the Arab Spring, Occupy Wall Street, and Black Lives Matter, among other resistance movements.

It is new and important that sharing information in digital communities enables many people and organizations to avoid the pitfalls of patenting, copyright law, and privatization. Bollier is right when he states: "Through an open, accessible commons, one can efficiently tap into the 'wisdom of the crowd,' nurture experimentation, accelerate innovation, and foster new forms of democratic practice" (*Viral Spiral* 6). At the same time, the fight over "net neutrality" signals that, just as most radio and television broadcasting has fallen prey to corporate greed, so the Internet may be headed down the same dreary path. That is what the enclosure of the commons throughout history suggests.

Many other scholars have commented, often with as much enthusiasm as Bollier, about the promise of the digital commons. The Internet and other new technological capabilities make participating in the creation and the sharing of ideas and cultural products of all sorts accessible to millions. In *The Wealth of Networks*, Yochai Benkler writes that we are witnessing:

> the emergence of a new folk culture—a practice that has been largely suppressed in the industrial era of cultural production—where many more of us participate actively in making cultural moves and finding meaning in the world around us.
>
> (27)

The Creative Commons, the Open Source Initiative, and many similar projects are practicing a sharing of resources that is obviously more democratic than previous forms of cultural production that adhered to a proprietary, top-down model of ownership. While naming this development "a new folk culture" may recall the earliest forms of commons and commoning, it is dependent on technological innovations that seem to be leading in altogether "new" and unpredictable directions.

James Boyle writes that "we are in the middle of a second enclosure movement." He is referring to attempts to privatize versions of intellectual property. During the first enclosure movement, what Boyle calls "the earthy commons"—land understood as commons—was not infinitely open to everyone even when it was open to a specific peasant community to use. Facts and ideas, however, should "always remain in the public domain." Yet even these intellectual products are now threatened with privatization: "Both overtly and covertly, the commons of facts and ideas is being enclosed. Patents are increasingly stretched out to cover 'ideas' that twenty years ago all scholars would have agreed were unpatentable." Besides ideas, Boyle mentions genes and the genome project as examples that competing forces are today struggling over:

> The opponents of enclosure have claimed that the human genome belongs to everyone, that it is literally the common heritage of humankind, that it should not and perhaps in some sense cannot be owned, and that the consequences of turning over the human genome to private property rights will be dreadful, as market logic invades areas which should be the farthest from the market. In stories about stem cell and gene sequence patents, critics have mused darkly about the way in which the state is handing over monopoly power to a few individuals and corporations, potentially introducing bottlenecks and coordination costs that slow down innovation.
>
> *(37)*

Why indeed should genes and the genome project itself become the private property of corporations?

Pharmaceutical corporations have also been reaping profits from the medicinal plants they have patented. Often those plants have been used and cultivated by indigenous peoples for centuries. The UN adopted the Nagoya Protocol in 2010 under the rubric of Biological Diversity, whose goal is to share profits with the peoples who were the original discoverers and users of such plants. But so far that protocol has been rarely followed. Comparable problems arise when corporations claim exclusive ownership over genetically modified seeds and crops (e.g., see Shiva, *Biopiracy*).

The oldest examples of intellectual commons are languages. Anyone who can speak, read, or write a language is free to do so. No one "owns" a language. Specific uses of any language may be protected by copyrights, patents, or trademarks, but otherwise all languages are open-access resources. And until recently so has been the Internet, although now it too is threatened by corporate enclosure. What is more, the Internet is also threatened by various types of surveillance and hacking, as Julian Assange and Edward Snowden have vividly demonstrated.

To help avoid surveillance and also the barrage of corporate and political advertisements users of the Internet are now subjected to, various pay-to-play services are now on offer to provide individuals with some amount of protection and privacy. An online ad for Expandiverse Technology's Digital Boundaries offers "digital barbed wire that protects you with priorities, filters, paywalls, physical protection and privacy. As we build a digital world, it will be the world you choose and want—and a world that protects you in multiple ways—for the first time." The ad even refers to the fence wars between ranchers and farmers in the American West:

> When barbed wire was invented, it was new technology. For the first time farmers could protect their property. Their fences ended the cattle drives that trampled their homesteads. Could something similar happen from Expandiverse Boundary Management Services, and each person's self-chosen Digital Boundaries?

The ad goes on to liken corporations to "today's 'cattle drivers'" who don't want people to be able to filter them out or put up "digital barbed wire" fences to keep out what you don't want to see on your computer screens.

Earlier, I quoted Vijay Prashad on "the second enclosure movement," by which he means current attempts by corporations to privatize just about everything. James Boyle uses the same phrase in regard to issues of "intellectual property." Both Boyle and Prashad recognize, however, that between the first and what they call the "second" enclosure movements, there has been constant pressure by capitalist development to enlarge and enforce the regime of private property. But that means also that there has been no break between a first and second enclosure movement in the struggle to maintain the commons, whatever forms they take.

Notes

1 In her study of land ownership in Ireland, Sara Maurer, citing Sir Henry Maine's *Ancient Law* (1861), declares that "the original unit of society was the family, not the Lockean man mixing his labor with the land." Quoting Maine's assertion that "ancient law knew nothing of individuals," Maurer adds that "the traces of more primitive property arrangements could still be found alive and well in cultures where the basic social unit is the village community, 'an assemblage of co-proprietors' who assume themselves to share a common origin and who allot property rights to individual families only with the understanding that when families became extinct, their property would return to the village unit." She notes as well that the concept of "absolute property, controlled wholly by one individual without social interference, was a modern invention . . ." (128).
2 Wall also notes that historical and archaeological evidence suggests that "commons existed prior to written record" (33).
3 On Kett's Rebellion, see Stephen Land, *Kett's Rebellion*, and Darmaid MacCulloch, "Kett's Rebellion in Context."
4 "Enclosures have appropriately been called a revolution of the rich against the poor," writes Karl Polanyi; "The lords and nobles were upsetting the social order, breaking down ancient law and custom sometimes by means of violence, often by pressure and intimidation. They were literally robbing the poor of their share in the common, tearing down the houses which, by the hitherto unbreakable force of custom, the poor had long regarded as their and their heirs.'" The result was "desolate villages and the ruins of human dwellings . . . endangering the defences of the country . . . decimating its population . . . harassing its people and turning them from decent husbandmen into a mob of beggars and thieves" (75–76).

5 Similarly, according to Stephen Marglin, "contrary to the claims of ... Hardin and myriad others who have followed Hardin's lead, the open field [system of agriculture] is neither apt metaphor nor early prototype for the disaster of unbridled consumption that Hardin and his ilk see as the fate of an overpopulated planet.... [T]he open field was not governed by a regime of open access. Sensitive to the possibility of a 'tragedy of the commons'... the village community was at great pains to regulate access to the open fields, even—especially—when fallow and managed as common property" (84).
6 In *The Country and the City*, Raymond Williams quotes Arthur Young, who evidently felt some remorse for his support of the enclsoure movement: "I had rather that all the commons of England were sunk in the sea, than that the poor should in future be treated on enclosing as they have been hitherto" (67).
7 In *The Country and the City*, Williams quotes agrarian radical William Cobbett, writing in the early 1800s, on "the madness of enclosures." Agricultural improvements, including land consolidation, Cobbett declared, had "worked detriment to the labourer. It was out of his bones that the means came. It was *the deduction made from him* by the rise of prices and by the *not-rise of his wages*" (99). Cobbett's analysis is similar to Marx's in the first volume of *Capital*. Both understood that enclosures, whether it meant the privatization of the commons by sale, rackrenting, force, or other means, "worked detriment to the labourer" even as it advanced agricultural productivity and capitalism.
8 Linebaugh points out that although the Magna Carta is remembered today largely because of its stress on political and legal freedoms such as habeas corpus, its other half, the Charter of the Forest, addressed economic issues, including the "forms of commoning" on which the peasantry relied.
9 "Enclosure is usually thought of in connection with the encroachments made by lords of manors or their farmers upon the land over which the manorial population had common rights or which lay in the open arable fields," R. H. Tawney writes; "And this is on the whole correct" (150). It is this aspect of the enclosure movement that led to "agrarian warfare" (237). Such warfare has continued in many parts of the world—for example, the violence that has accompanied land reform throughout Latin America.
10 The idea that terrorism was born on 9/11 and that all terrorists are Islamic jihadists is false. The thesis that it was born in Irish struggles against English domination may also seem erroneous, but as a guerilla tactic terrorist actions in Ireland were even older than Robespierre's government by terror in France.
11 "'Free' capitalist markets means no strong governments that can check and balance the global power of corporations," write Kahn and Minnich in *The Fox in the Henhouse*; "It doesn't mean that you and I are free from the dominance of those corporations" (10).
12 When Donald Trump insisted that "we" should have taken Iraq's oil, he did not realize that Western corporations had already done so. See Larry Everest, *Oil, Power, and Empire*, and Antonia Juhasz, *The Tyranny of Oil*.
13 See Wright and Wolford, *To Inherit the Earth*, and Gret and Sintomer, *The Porto Alegre Experiment*.
14 A fallacy related to the notion that "free" markets somehow are connected to individual freedom is the notion that markets are democracy at work. In *One Market under God*, Thomas Frank calls this fallacy "market populism." According to their advocates, markets supposedly express "the popular will more articulately and more meaningfully" than do elections. Market populists believe markets are a friend of "the little guy" that bring down "the pompous and the snooty" (xiv). They fulfill our wishes; in "free markets," the customer is always right.
15 "In the belief system called economics," writes Jonathan Rowe, "it is an article of faith that commons are inherently tragic. Almost by definition, they are tragic because they are prone to overuse. What belongs to all belongs to none, and only private or state ownership can rescue a commons from the sad fate that will otherwise befall it" (18).
16 See, for example, Elinor Ostrom, *Governing the Commons*, Nives Dolšak and Elinor Ostrom, *The Commons in the New Millenium*, and John A. Baden and Douglas S. Noonan, *Managing the Commons*.

17 Chomsky prefaces this statement by writing: "Hardly a day passes without more confirmation of this fact. As hundreds of thousands of people marched in the streets of Manhattan on September 21 to warn of the dire threat of the ongoing ecological destruction of the commons, *The New York Times* reported that 'global emissions of greenhouse gases jumped 2.3 percent in 2013 to record levels,' while in the United States, emissions rose 2.9 percent, reversing a recent decline. August 2014 was reported to be the hottest on record, and *JAMA: The Journal of the American Medical Association* predicted that the number of 90-degree-plus days in New York could triple in three decades, with much more severe effects in warmer climates" ("Magna Carta"). In *This Changes Everything*, Naomi Klein agrees: capitalism is increasingly unable to cope with the disastrous consequences of global warming.

9
WHAT IS TO BE DONE?

> "At the heart of building alternatives and localizing economic and political systems are the recovery of the commons and the reclaiming of community."
> — *Vandana Shiva*

Vandana Shiva's "Living Democracy Movement" is one of many current attempts to reclaim both "the commons" and "community."[1] Today, the struggle to reverse the enclosure of land and of other aspects of our "common wealth," David Harvey also contends, is "the only viable alternative strategy" for opposing the destruction being wrought by unbridled corporate capitalism. "The absorption of private property rights into a comprehensive project for the collective management of the commons and the dissolution of autocratic and despotic state powers into democratic collective management structures [have] become the only worthy long-term objectives" (*Seventeen Contradictions and the End of Capitalism* 65). In *Earth Democracy* and elsewhere, Shiva makes the same argument, as do Michael Hardt and Antonio Negri in *Commonwealth*, Jonathan Rowe in *Our Common Wealth*, and David Bollier in *Think Like a Commoner*. They and many others emphasize the need for overthrowing the domination not just of corporations, but of the hegemony of private property, and replacing that concept with one of communal property. This is an argument for some version of democratic socialism, but it is also a profoundly conservative one—in the precise sense of conservation: restoring and saving our common wealth, which includes conserving nature and the natural resources of the planet.

At the start of a recent issue of *YES! Magazine*, the editor Sarah van Gelder writes that:

> the fetish for privatization devalues open spaces along with other commons, like public education, a stable climate, and clean air and water. Powerful corporations profit by 'enclosing,' or taking for themselves, a commons that actually belongs to all of us (or, as in the case of water and the atmosphere, by using it as a dump). It takes tenacious people's movements to push back . . . .

"Fetish" is an understatement, and so far, despite "tenacious people's movements," powerful corporations have continued to privatize or enclose—plunder—the commons. As Bill Ayers puts it, "the frantic pace of privatization, and the firesale of the public square" accelerates (18), although the mounting resistance to Trump and Trumpism, which includes the corporate takeover of the U.S. government, may prove to be a turning point.

Reports about the ongoing protest over the Dakota Access oil pipeline, undertaken mainly by Native Americans, show that struggles against Western imperialism are far from over, and that many of these struggles continue to be about land and natural resources. The enormous Women's March in Washington, DC and "sister marches" around the country on January 21, 2017 reveal the extent of opposition to newly anointed President Trump and his corporate, corrupt, and sexist agenda. These have been followed by nationwide and, indeed, international protests against Trump's attempt to ban immigration from seven majority Muslim nations. There has also been widespread opposition, and not just by Democrats in the Senate, to Trump's nominations of billionaires for cabinet positions. Those now in key positions—Betsy DeVos as Secretary of Education, for example—seem bent on undermining what they are supposed to be promoting. The recent firing of James Comey as head of the FBI has increased pressure for Trump's impeachment. And the beat goes on. The mounting resistance to Trumpism, however, is hardly the same as resistance to capitalism.

In the US at least, the Cold War led to a rejection of socialism and virtually all forms of criticism of capitalism. Margaret Thatcher famously declared that "There is no alternative." But the recent and surprisingly successful presidential campaign by Bernie Sanders, who openly calls himself a socialist, may represent a turning point. Calls for universal healthcare and the national effort to overturn *Citizens United* continue, and are perhaps growing stronger.

Regarding the corporate takeover of just about everything, Naomi Klein, in a 2001 talk she gave at UCLA, declared: "Thousands of groups today are all working against forces [aimed at] the privatization of every aspect of life, and the transformation of every activity and value into a commodity." She continued:

> We often speak of the privatization of education, of healthcare, of natural resources. But the process is much vaster. It includes the way powerful ideas are turned into advertising slogans and public streets into shopping malls; new generations being target-marketed at birth; schools being invaded by ads; basic human necessities like water being sold as commodities; basic labour rights being rolled back; genes are patented and designer babies loom; seeds are genetically altered and bought; politicians are bought and altered.

Klein went on to say that the groups fighting the corporate privatization and commodification of the world are all aiming at:

> a radical reclaiming of the commons. As our communal spaces—town squares, streets, schools, farms, plants—are displaced by the ballooning marketplace, a spirit of resistance is taking hold . . . . People are reclaiming bits of nature and of culture, and saying "this is going to be public space."
> *(Klein, "Reclaiming the Commons")*

But is "reclaiming bits of nature and culture" being too pessimistic or too optimistic? Over many centuries, there have been countless efforts, from much earlier than Kett's Rebellion in 1549 down to the fence wars in the American West and forward to the present, to oppose enclosures and reclaim commons. On most imperial frontiers, indigenous peoples from Newfoundland to Tasmania waged war against the European invaders who were seizing their territories, but nearly always the indigenous societies lost. In many cases, however, their struggles continue, as exemplified by the Dakota Access protest, or the Maori protest over the Trans-Pacific Partnership in Aukland, New Zealand (where it was nevertheless recently signed by representatives of the 12 participant nations), or the Zapatista rebellion that began in Chiapas, Mexico, in 1994, or the declaration of independence from the US by the Republic of Lakotah in 2008.[2] Native Americans and the First Nations of Canada are often in the forefront of the protests now sometimes referred to as "Blockadia," or the widespread attempts to stop more drilling, fracking, pipelines, transport, and environmental damage by Big Oil.[3]

Springing to life in 2011, Occupy Wall Street is another instance of resistance against enclosures and, more generally, against capitalism. An article dated February 3, 2016 on the Occupy website (www.occupywallst.org) calls that movement a "constructive failure" because it did not manage to alter how big business, the banks, and big government operate. But the existence of the website itself suggests that it has not been defeated. Its activist spirit lives on through Blockadia, through Black Lives Matter, and through the Moral Mondays movement that began in 2013 in North Carolina, led by the Rev. William Barber. Moral Mondays has spread to other states, including my own state of Indiana. It aims to restore voters' rights and to reverse the agenda of the radical right that espouses covert racism, the repeal of Obamacare, and corporate privatization.

Just because progressive movements such as these are not all directly related to each other and are frequently downplayed within the myopic boxes of the corporate media does not mean that they are ineffective or don't exist. Resistance to enclosures has often failed, but there are many movements today combatting corporate domination, including the attempts by Greenpeace, Sierra Club, 350.org, and other environmental groups to stop fracking and to slow down global warming by keeping the remaining fossil fuels in the ground. The upsurge among institutions such as universities, hospitals, and even the Rockefeller Foundation to divest from the fossil fuel industries and support alternative energy sources has soared into the billions of dollars and is rapidly growing.[4] Divesting multiplies the effectiveness of protests against the Keystone XL and Dakota pipelines, against fracking, and against mountaintop removal in West Virginia and Kentucky, among many similar protests throughout the US and the world. Divestment is beginning to have an impact on the profits of Big Oil and Big Coal.

Peabody Coal, the biggest coal corporation in North America, recently went bankrupt. Another divestment movement is seeking to undercut the private prison corporations and their impact on mass incarceration in the US. And still a third, calling itself the "Hedge Clippers" campaign, is urging universities and other institutions to divest from hedge funds, which profit from huge tax breaks while lobbying for right-wing goals such as privatizing schools and prisons (Lerner).

A widespread "Move to Amend" protest has also emerged that seeks to overturn the 2010 Supreme Court decision in *Citizens United*. That absurd ruling means corporations are now regarded as persons under the U.S. Constitution and that the money corporations give to election campaigns is a version of free speech (e.g., see Clements). The upshot has been the influx of additional millions into election campaigns by corporations and by billionaires such as the Koch brothers, making the US even more plutocratic than it was before that ruling. There are, moreover, "Fight for $15" and related actions by Jobs with Justice and many trade unions in support of raising the minimum wage in the US. These include recent strikes against major fast-food restaurants such as McDonald's and against Walmart. The Coalition of Imokolee Workers in Florida recently succeeded in getting several major fast-food chains to increase the earnings of tomato pickers. Rebuilding union strength, which was for several decades—World War II through the 1970s—a major factor in the prosperity experienced by many Americans, is an ongoing struggle, one that does not directly threaten the hegemony of the big corporations, but that seeks to strengthen protections for workers and to restore jobs lost to corporate outsourcing and automation.

Resistance can also include creating alternative ways to carry on economic activity, such as worker-owned enterprises, co-ops, and land trusts. Such alternatives are not necessarily antagonistic to corporations, although Richard Wolff sees them as "a cure for capitalism" and Gar Alperovitz writes that they contribute to "the next American revolution." Surveying these alternatives to business as usual, Alperovitz notes that there are approximately 11,000 worker-owned businesses of many shapes and sizes in the US, involving over 10 million people, and that this number is growing. The number would grow much faster with more governmental support on all levels. What if most businesses were worker-owned? "Repeated studies show that worker-owned firms" are more efficient, competitive, and profitable than "comparable firms," he writes (68). Cooperative enterprises of many shapes and sizes are also prevalent and growing in number. As an alternative to corporate banks, there are currently nearly 7,200 "community based credit unions with more than one-trillion dollars in total assets" in the US, including the Indiana University Credit Union to which I belong (110). And by 2012, there were over 250 community land trusts in 45 states and the District of Columbia (62), such as the Sycamore Land Trust in southern Indiana, which has acquired approximately 10,000 acres to maintain as nature preserves.

Alperovitz points out as well that many corporations are in a variety of ways partially socialized enterprises. In so doing, he isn't talking about resistance, but just indicating the extent to which corporations rely on government support of many sorts—versions of "corporate welfare." Starting with President Bush in 2007, the federal government bailed out the "too big to fail banks," which meant that it basically socialized them, at least temporarily, as later happened with the auto industry under President Obama. Cities and states give enormous tax breaks and subsidies to corporations to build factories and outlets in their localities, although this practice falls far short of providing much if any governmental control over corporate behavior.

There are far too many examples of corporations that have been given tax breaks to locate in a particular city or state, only to see them pull up stakes a few years later and move somewhere else, as happened with Thomson Electronics, Otis Elevator, and the GE plant in my hometown. Also Walmart and McDonald's, among other corporations, pay their workers so little that many rely on food stamps and other forms of public support to make ends meet. Can this be considered a perverse form of socialism? Of course, corporate welfare is just how capitalism ordinarily operates: scam the workers and the taxpayers in order to boost profits. Why not, then, simply nationalize the banks, GM, GE, and ExxonMobil?

In the debates leading up to the 2016 presidential election, the Republican candidates behaved like mindless troglodytes snarling and snapping at each other, while the two Democratic candidates, Hillary Clinton and Bernie Sanders, argued over whether any of Sanders' "democratic socialist" ideas were realistic or not. But all of Sanders' ideas—universal healthcare, for example—have been successfully adopted in other countries. Without Sanders' competition, Secretary Clinton would no doubt have sounded even more moderate—or conservative—than she did, which would place her in the range of what used to be considered Republican moderation. She is, in other words, an advocate of a certain brand of hopeless realism or centrism: we may be able to do a little better, but not too much better, since the only way forward is through compromise. It has at least been heartening to hear Sanders speak openly and forcefully not only about breaking up the major banks and against "the billionaire class," but also in favor of socialism. Democratic variations of socialism have worked perfectly well in many places, including the Scandinavian countries. Nation-states that have retained aspects of their social welfare programs, despite the global hegemony of neoliberalism and its austerity programs, have much better results in healthcare and education than does the US.

Quite often a specific corporate privatization or enclosure backfires, as when in 2000 Cochabamba, the second largest city in Bolivia, turned over its water works to Bechtel Corporation. Water bills soared, quickly leading to a rebellion by Cochabamba's residents. The city sent Bechtel packing and reclaimed municipal control over its water supply. Another episode involving a municipal water supply is the poisoning of it in Flint, Michigan, caused by the misguided attempt of

Republican governor Rick Snyder and an unelected city manager appointed by Snyder. The governor's treatment of Flint, Detroit, Benton Harbor, and other largely African American cities as if they were corporate properties has generally been reprehensible. So-called "water wars" are being waged in many parts of the world for many reasons—for example, the fight by Indian peasants in drought-stricken Rajasthan against the appropriation of water by Coca-Cola and other mega-bottling corporations.

Several state and municipal governments in the US are now reversing or at least beginning to question the wisdom of privatizing both prisons and schools. As noted in Chapter 3, the safety record of privately run prisons for both prisoners and guards is abysmal. The pursuit of profits by prison corporations, moreover, is one of the causes for the mass incarceration of nearly 2.5 million American citizens, most of them black or Latino. And charter schools, though some are excellent, have by and large proven no better and are often less effective than public ones, while they draw funds, teachers, and students away from their public counterparts. Unfortunately, Betsy DeVos favors charters and voucher programs over public education.

The idea that the privatization of public institutions such as schools, toll roads, or the postal service will save taxpayers' money is more often false than not. Privately run institutions typically cut corners in order to increase their profits. When the state of Indiana, under Republican governor Mitch Daniels, turned over the management of much of its welfare system to IBM, supposedly as a way to save money, that company made such a mess of it that the contract was rescinded after only a couple of years. But so far, bad experiences with privatization have not led many local, state, or federal officials to avoid past mistakes or to recognize the flaws in neoliberal economic practices.

On an international level, what is frequently called the "anti-globalization" movement received a big dose of media attention in the US with the Battle of Seattle in 1999. On that occasion, various groups from labor unions to environmentalist organizations to anarchists to churches to representatives of indigenous peoples managed to shut down a World Trade Organization ministerial meeting (e.g., see Thomas). Many similar demonstrations have occurred around the world at meetings of the major global arbiters of so-called "free trade" agreements and of the WTO, the IMF, and the World Bank. Whether mounting resistance, such as the Maori protest mentioned earlier, against the Trans-Pacific Partnership, led to President Trump's executive order causing the US to withdraw from it is unclear. But it is at least clear that he thinks such trade agreements have in the past been "bad deals."

A year after the WTO meltdown in Seattle, the first World Social Forum (WSF) convened in Porto Alegre, Brazil, announcing that "another world is possible." One of its aims was to provide a counter to the corporate agenda of the World Economic Forum. In 2005, the program of the WSF, which again met in Porto Alegre, included 155,000 participants. It began with a march through that city estimated at 200,000 people. Although many different groups and causes were represented by the marchers, including all 17 of Brazil's political parties, a main emphasis was opposition to the U.S. invasion of Iraq. The WSF has continued to meet annually in different countries: in 2015 it met in Tunisia, and in 2016 in Montreal. Although well publicized in many parts of the world, the social forum "movement of movements" is almost never mentioned in the mainstream media in the US. It is a safe bet that most Americans have never heard of it. In any event, its website reads, in part:

> The goal of the WSF . . . is to gather tens of thousands of people from groups in civil society, organizations and social movements who want to build a sustainable and inclusive world, where every person and every people has its place and can make its voice heard.

There are also regional and national versions of the WSF in Europe, North America, and elsewhere, such as the U.S. Social Forum and the People's Assembly Movement. Their gatherings bring together global justice activists and NGOs under the general banner, "Another world is possible."

In *Multitude*, Michael Hardt and Antonio Negri view the WSFs and their offshoots as exemplary of the sort of resistance civil society will continue to mount against what, in their earlier book, they call "Empire." By that term, they basically mean the current domination of transnational corporate capitalism. They have followed up their argument in their third book, *Commonwealth*. In the foreword to *Another World Is Possible*, Hardt and Negri write that the organizations and presentations at the annual WSFs "reveal the horrible state of our present form of globalization, the scandal of neoliberal capitalist power, and the misery of the majority of the world's populations" (xviii). They call the WSFs "the movement of movements," and add that only movements aiming at global justice "can destroy the fascisms, fundamentalisms, and imperialisms however and wherever they appear in the world. Porto Alegre is thus the symbol of a new internationalism . . . born and reborn against the war" in Iraq and elsewhere (xix).

The southern Brazilian city of Porto Alegre was the site of the first of several WSFs, including the one in 2005 that I attended, partly because of the leadership of several Brazilian activists, partly because of that city's experiment with participatory budgeting, and partly because it was there that the Landless Workers Movement began (see the Introduction). Land reform, helping to reverse centuries of land enclosures under colonialism and capitalism, is also a major aspect of the work of La Via Campesina, founded in 1993 to be the "international voice" of peasants and small farmers. Its website says that it:

> brings together millions of peasants, small and medium-size farmers, landless people, women farmers, indigenous people, migrants and agricultural workers from around the world. It defends small-scale sustainable agriculture as a way to promote social justice and dignity. It strongly opposes corporate driven agriculture and transnational companies that are destroying people and nature.

While land reform is one of its goals, another is food sovereignty, or the right of all peoples to produce and consume food that is locally grown using agriculturally sustainable methods. Food sovereignty also involves farmers' control over seeds and opposition to GMOs, or genetically modified organisms. La Via Campesina is one of the many organizations affiliated with the WSFs.

The new anti-corporate internationalism that is expressed in the WSF and its offshoots is not "anti-globalization," despite what its opponents say. Rather, as Susan George points out, it is "deeply engaged with the world as a whole and the fate of everyone who shares the planet." It is "easily more 'pro-globalisation' than its [neoliberal capitalist] adversaries" (ix). Its supporters call their movement's aim "global justice"; it is, hence, an "alterglobalization" movement. Whether they participate in the WSFs or not, many NGOs now find themselves in opposition to neoliberal economic policies, to transnational corporate domination, and to the neo-imperialisms of the US, the EU, China, and other powerful nations.

A short list of changes that could radically democratize affairs among nations and peoples would include reforming the United Nations into a truly representative and effective world government. It would also include worldwide disarmament, and not just of nuclear weapons, but of all weapons. Right now, there are 21 small, independent countries such as Costa Rica that do not have standing armies. Why not all countries? And how is it that, since World War II, the US has allowed the "military-industrial complex" to mushroom to such an extent that it is now caught in a gigantic trap of seemingless endless war, nuclear proliferation, munitions development and international gun-running, and a mass culture that promotes violence as the solution to virtually everything? The anti-war movement both in the US and abroad has been nonstop at least since the war that American anti-communism waged in Vietnam, Cambodia, and Laos.

Although no doubt minor in importance compared to resistance to war, the U.S. war machine, and Western imperialism, advocacy of fair trade instead of so-called "free trade" as the norm seems to be gaining ground. Yet a corporation such as Starbucks is busily undermining it by establishing "fair trade" brands of its own. And the Tobin tax or something like it would help curtail international financial flows and out-of-control speculation in stocks, currencies, and real estate. There should also be cancellation of the major debts supposedly owed by the poor nations to the rich ones. "That the colonized world, whose wealth has been plundered for 500 years," writes George Monbiot:

> should be deemed to owe the rich world money, and that this presumed debt should be so onerous that every year $382 billion, which might have been used to feed the hungry, to house the poor, to provide healthcare, education, clean water, transport and pensions for people who have access to none of these amenities, is transferred from the poor world to the banks and financial institutions of the rich world in the form of debt repayments is an obscenity which degrades all those of us who benefit from it.

(158)

So far, there has been some debt relief for the poorer nations of the world, but there needs to be much more.

The anti-corporate, anti-enclosure efforts and goals that I have mentioned are piecemeal, and right now most of them can be evaded or ignored by both corporations and nation-states. But the "movement of movements" and its allies are growing, and it is impossible, especially given the pushback in the US and the world against Trumpism, to predict what the result will be. Perhaps results, plural, is more likely. Given the crisis of climate change, surely the fossil fuel industries will soon be going the way of the dinosaurs—or else we all are going that way. Dismantling the major financial institutions from banks to hedge funds to insurance companies may prove more difficult, as will toppling the military-industrial complex in the US and in many other countries. There may be many possibilities and forces working toward global justice that I am not aware of that could well result in what David Korten calls "the great turning." The turning—or revolution—will involve the formation of a global community in which corporate capitalism and the hegemony of private property are replaced by a new regime of communal property, peace, democracy, environmental sustainability, and prosperity for all. What is certain is that corporate capitalism in its present form, especially as it is centered in massive financial speculation, the military-industrial complex, and the fossil fuel industries, is unsustainable.

In his book on the WSF, José Corrêa Leite declares that today there is:

> a paradoxical multiplication and crisis of utopias. Utopian aspirations erupt everywhere, highlighting the material abundance achieved by humanity and the possibility of general well-being, the equality . . . of genders, the recognition of different cultures, the enjoyment of sexual diversity, the search for perfect health, total communication, or of a society reconciled with nature.

Leite adds, however, that "the desired society, which could effectively provide these objectives, seems more distant than ever" (36). Paradoxically, that distance may be a sign of its approaching birth. The unpredictability of history encourages the utopianism Leite refers to. Who could have predicted the fall of the Soviet Union or of the apartheid regime in South Africa? To most observers, the Zapatista rebellion and the Battle of Seattle and the Arab Spring and Occupy Wall Street all came as surprises. So, too, did the American and French Revolutions and the abolition of slavery. It is at least conceivable that the convergence of numerous end-time crises—of capitalism, of global warming, of the various liberating movements I have mentioned—history will alter its course in the direction of universal liberation, prosperity, peace, and equality. And at least some of the commons will be reclaimed, along with a new emphasis on community and communal property. Or so I and countless others hope.

Notes

1 The epigraph comes from a paper Vandana Shiva delivered at the World Social Forum in 2002. It is reproduced under her name in "The Living Democracy Movement."
2 Led by Russell Means, the American Indian Movement's attempt to establish an independent Lakotah nation protested the breaking of many treaties over the centuries and the seizure of land from Native Americans by non-indigenous settlers. It was one of many protests by AIM and other Indian rights organizations both in the US and Canada. There are similar movements all over Latin America, such as the Zapatistas in Chiapas, Mexico (e.g., see Collier; Mander and Tauli-Corpuz).
3 On "Blockadia," see Naomi Klein, *This Changes Everything*, 293–336. The Idle No More movement in Canada that began in 2012, like the Lakotah nation movement, exemplifies protests by indigenous peoples.
4 "'We are quite convinced that if he were alive today, as an astute businessman looking out to the future, he would be moving out of fossil fuels and investing in clean, renewable energy,' said Stephen Heintz about John D. Rockefeller, as he announced that the heirs to one of America's most famous dynasties, which was built on oil, were pulling their philanthropic funds out of fossil fuels" (Vaughan, "Fossil Fuel Divestment").

BIBLIOGRAPHY

Abu-Jamal, Mumia. *Writing on the Wall: Selected Prison Writings of Mumia Abu-Jamal.* San Francisco, CA: City Lights Books, 2015.
Adler, Moshe. *Economics for the Rest of Us: Debunking the Science that Makes Life Dismal.* New York: The New Press, 2009.
Adorno, Theodor. *The Culture Industry: Selected Essays on Mass Culture.* New York and London: Routledge, 2001.
Agamben, Giorgio. *Means Without End: Notes on Politics.* Minneapolis, MN: University of Minnesota Press, 2000.
Alexander, Michelle. *The New Jim Crow: Mass Incarceration in the Age of Colorblindness.* Rev. ed. New York: The New Press, 2012.
Allen, Terry J. "Global Land Grab: Fear of Unrest and Hunger for Profit are Sparking Massive Acquisitions of Farmland." *In These Times* 35:9 (September 2011): 14–19.
Alperovitz, Gar. *What Then Must We Do? Straight Talk About the Next American Revolution.* White River Junction, VT: Chelsea Green, 2013.
Althusser, Louis. "Ideology and Ideological State Apparatuses." *Lenin and Philosophy and Other Essays.* Ben Brewster, trans. New York and London: Monthly Review Press, 1971: 127–186.
Amin, Samir. *The Implosion of Contemporary Capitalism.* New York: Monthly Review Press, 2013.
Anton, Anatole. "Public Goods as Commonstock: Notes on the Receding Commons." Anatole Anton et al., eds. *Not for Sale: In Defense of Public Goods.* Boulder, CO: Westview Press, 2000: 3–40.
Anzaldúa, Gloria. *Borderlands/La Frontera: The New Mestiza.* San Francisco, CA: Aunt Lute Book Company, 1987.
Appadurai, Arjun, ed. *Globalization.* Durham, NC: Duke University Press, 2001.
Arendt, Hannah. *Imperialism.* Part 2 of *The Origins of Totalitarianism.* New York: Harcourt Brace & World, 1968.
Aronowitz, Stanley, and William DiFazio. *The Jobless Future: Sci-Tech and the Dogma of Work.* Minneapolis, MN: University of Minnesota Press, 1994.
Atan, Ira. *Six and One-Half Years in Ranger Service.* Texas Ranger Hall of Fame. www.texasranger.org/halloffame/Aten_Ira.htm.

Ayers, Bill. *Demand the Impossible! A Radical Manifesto.* Chicago, IL: Haymarket Books, 2016.

Baden, John A., and Douglas S. Noonan, eds. *Managing the Commons.* 2nd ed. Bloomington, IN: Indiana University Press, 1998.

Bakan, Joel. *The Corporation: The Pathological Pursuit of Profit and Power.* New York: Free Press, 2004.

Bales, Kevin. *Disposable People: New Slavery in the Global Economy.* Berkeley, CA: University of California Press, 2000.

Barlow, Maude. *Blue Future: Protecting Water for People and the Planet Forever.* New York: The New Press, 2013.

Bauman, Zygmunt. *Globalization: The Human Consequences.* New York: Columbia University Press, 1998.

———. *Wasted Lives: Modernity and Its Outcasts.* Cambridge: Polity Press, 2004.

———. *Retrotopia.* Cambridge: Polity Press, 2017.

Bello, Walden. *Deglobalization: Ideas for a New World Economy.* London: Zed Books, 2002.

Benjamin, Rich. "The Gated Community Mentality." *The New York Times.* March 29, 2012. www.nytimes.com/2012/03/30/opinion/the-gated-community-mentality.html?mcubz=3.

Benkler, Yochai. *The Wealth of Networks: How Social Production Transforms Markets and Freedom.* New Haven, CT: Yale University Press, 2006.

Bennis, Phyllis. *Challenging Empire: How People, Governments, and the UN Defy US Power.* Northampton, MA: Olive Branch Press, 2006.

Berkhoffer, Robert F. *The White Man's Indian: Images of the American Indian from Columbus to the Present.* New York: Vintage Books, 1979.

Billington, Ray Allen. *Westward Expansion: A History of the American Frontier.* 4th ed. New York: Macmillan, 1974.

Black, Edwin. *War against the Weak: Eugenics and America's Campaign to Create a Master Race.* New York: Four Walls Eight Windows, 2003.

Black, Jan Knipper. *Inequity in the Global Village: Recycled Rhetoric and Disposable People.* West Hartford, CT: Kumarian Press, 1999.

Black, William K. "(Mis)understanding a Banking Industry in Transition." Gerald Friedman et al., eds. *The Economic Crisis Reader: Readings in Economics, Politics, and Social Policy from Dollars & Sense.* Boston, MA: Economic Affairs Bureau, 2009: 65–76.

Blakely, Edward, and Mary Gail Snyder. "Divided We Fall: Gated and Walled Communities in the United States." Nan Ellin, ed. *Architecture of Fear.* New York: Princeton Architectural Press, 1997: 85–99.

———. *Fortress America: Gated Communities in the United States.* Washington, DC: Brookings Institution, 1999.

Bollier, David. *Silent Theft: The Private Plunder of Our Common Wealth.* New York: Routledge, 2003.

———. *Viral Spiral: How the Commoners Built a Digital Republic of Their Own.* New York: The New Press, 2008.

———. *Think Like a Commoner: A Short Introduction to the Life of the Commons.* Gabriola Island, British Columbia: New Society Publishers, 2014.

Boner, Harold A. *Hungry Generations: The Nineteenth-Century Case against Malthusianism.* New York: King's Crown Press, Columbia University, 1955.

Bose, Purnima. "General Electric, Corporate Personhood, and the Emergence of the Professional Manager." Purnima Bose and Laura Lyons, eds. *Cultural Critique and the Global Corporation.* Bloomington, IN: Indiana University Press, 2010: 28–63.

Bowers, C. A. *Revitalizing the Commons: Cultural and Educational Sites of Resistance and Affirmation*. Lanham, MD: Rowman & Littlefield, Lexington Books, 2006.
Boyle, James. "The Second Enclosure Movement and the Construction of the Public Domain." *Law and Contemporary Problems* (Winter 2003): 33–74.
Bracken, Christopher. *The Potlatch Papers: A Colonial Case History*. Chicago, IL: University of Chicago Press, 1997.
Brantlinger, Ellen. *Dividing Classes: How the Middle Class Negotiates and Rationalizes School Advantage*. New York: Routledge, 2003.
Brantlinger, Patrick. *Rule of Darkness: British Literature and Imperialism, 1830–1914*. Ithaca, NY: Cornell University Press, 1988.
———. *Crusoe's Footprints: Cultural Studies in Britain and America*. New York: Routledge, 1990.
———. *Dark Vanishings: Discourse on the Extinction of Primitive Races, 1800–1930*. Ithaca, NY: Cornell University Press, 2003.
———. *Victorian Literature and Postcolonial Studies*. Edinburgh: Edinburgh University Press, 2010.
———. *Taming Cannibals: Race and the Victorians*. Ithaca, NY: Cornell University Press, 2011.
———. *States of Emergency: Essays on Culture and Politics*. Bloomington, IN: Indiana University Press, 2013.
Brennan, Timothy. "From Development to Globalization: Postcolonial Studies and Globalization Theory." Neil Lazarus, ed. *The Cambridge Companion to Postcolonial Literary Studies*. Cambridge: Cambridge University Press, 2004: 120–138.
Brockway, George. *The End of Economic Man: Principles of Any Future Economics*. New York: Norton, 1995.
Buell, John. "Why Myths of the 'Free Market' Survive—and How to Resist Them." *Common Dreams*. November 19, 2014. www.commondreams. org/views/2014/11/19/why-myths-free-market-survive-and-how-resist-them.
Burbach, Roger, and Jim Tarbell. *Imperial Overstretch: George W. Bush and the Hubris of Empire*. London and New York: Zed Books, 2004.
Carlyle, Thomas. "Chartism." In *English and Other Critical Essays*, London: Dent, 1964: 165–238.
Carr, Nicholas. *The Glass Cage: Automation and Us*. New York: Norton, 2014.
Carswell, John. *The South Sea Bubble*. London: Cresset, 1960.
Chomsky, Noam. "Magna Carta Messed Up the World, Here's How to Fix It: The Logic of Capitalist Development Has Left a Nightmare of Environmental Destruction in Its Wake." *The Nation*. April 6, 2015.
Chossudovsky, Michel. *The Globalization of Poverty and the New World Order*. 2nd ed. Montreal: Global Research Publishers, 2003.
Clear, Todd R. *Imprisoning Communities: How Mass Incarceration Makes Disadvantaged Neighborhoods Worse*. New York: Oxford University Press, 2007.
Clements, Jeffrey D. *Corporations Are Not People: Reclaiming Democracy from Big Money and Global Corporations*. San Francisco, CA: Berrett-Koehler Publishers, 2014.
Collier, George. *Basta! Land and the Zapatista Rebellion in Chiapas*. 3rd ed. Oakland, CA: Food First, 2005.
Coyle, Andrew, Allison Campbell, and Rodney Neufeld, eds. *Capitalist Punishment: Prison Privatization and Human Rights*. Atlanta, GA: Clarity Press; London: Zed Books, 2003.
Cronin, Mike. *A History of Ireland*. New York: Palgrave, 2002.
Davis, Mike. *City of Quartz: Excavating the Future in Los Angeles*. 1990. New York: Vintage Books, 1992.
———. *Planet of Slums*. London: Verso Books, 2006.

Davis, Mike, and Daniel Bertrand Monk, eds. "Introduction." *Evil Paradises: Dreamworlds of Neoliberalism*. New York: The New Press, 2007: 9–18.

Deleuze, Gilles, and Félix Guattari. *A Thousand Plateaus: Capitalism and Schizophrenia*. Brian Massumi, trans. Minneapolis, MN: University of Minnesota Press, 1987.

Derber, Charles. *Corporation Nation: How Corporations Are Taking over Our Lives and What We Can Do About It*. New York: St. Martin's, 1998.

Desmond, Matthew. *Evicted: Poverty and Profit in the American City*. New York: Crown Publishers, 2016.

Dickson, P. G. M. *The Financial Revolution in England: A Study in the Development of Public Credit, 1688–1756*. London: Macmillan, 1967.

Dolšak, Nivas, and Elinor Ostrom, eds. *The Commons in the New Millennium*. Cambridge, MA: MIT Press, 2003.

Drexler, K. Eric. *Engines of Creation*. Garden City, NY: Doubleday, 1986.

Drug Policy Alliance (DPA). "A Brief History of the Drug War." 2014. www.drugpolicy.org/new-solutions-drug-policy/brief-history-drug-war.

Duchrow, Ulrich, and Franz Hinkelammert. *Property for People, Not for Profit: Alternatives to the Global Tyranny of Capital*. London: Zed Books, 2004.

Dunbar-Ortiz, Roxanne. *An Indigenous Peoples' History of the United States*. Boston, MA: Beacon Press, 2014.

Eagleton, Terry. *Ideology: An Introduction*. London: Verso Books, 1991.

Ehrenreich, Barbara. *This Land Is Their Land: Reports from a Divided Nation*. New York: Henry Holt, 2008.

Ellin, Nan, ed. *Architecture of Fear*. New York: Princeton Architectural Press, 1997.

———. "Shelter from the Storm or Form Follows Fear and Vice Versa." *Architecture of Fear*. New York: Princeton Architectural Press, 1997: 13–45.

Elsner, Alan. *Gates of Injustice: The Crisis in America's Prisons*. Upper Saddle River, NJ: Prentice Hall, 2006.

Engels, Friedrich. *The Condition of the Working Class in England*. 1844. Stanford, CA: Stanford University Press, 1968.

Everest, Larry. *Oil, Power and Empire: Iraq and the U.S. Global Agenda*. Monroe, ME: Common Courage Press, 2004.

Fairness and Accuracy in Reporting (FAIR). "No Debate and the New War: Study Finds Little Opposition to US Attacks on Iraq, Syria." November 14, 2014. http://fair.org/press-release/no-debate-and-the-new-war/.

Fang, Lee. "Where Have All the Lobbyists Gone?" *The Nation*. March 10, 2014.

Feeny, David, Fikret Berkes, Bonnie J. McCay, and James A. Acheson. "The Tragedy of the Commons: Twenty-Two Years Later." John A. Baden and Douglas S. Noonan, eds. *Managing the Commons*. 2nd ed. Bloomington, IN: Indiana University Press, 1998: 76–94.

Ferguson, Charles H. *Predator Nation: Corporate Criminals, Political Corruption, and the Hijacking of America*. New York: Crown Publishing, Random House, 2012.

Ferguson, Niall. *Colossus: The Rise and Fall of the American Empire*. New York and London: Penguin, 2004.

Fisher, William, and Thomas Ponniah, eds. *Another World Is Possible: Popular Alternatives to Globalization at the World Social Forum*. London: Zed Books, 2003.

Fisk, Milton. "Surviving with Dignity in a Global Economy: The Battle for Public Goods." Anatole Anton et al., eds. *Not for Sale: In Defense of Public Goods*. Boulder, CO: Westview Press, 2000: 41–63.

Flusty, Steven. "Building Paranoia." Nan Ellin, ed. *Architecture of Fear*. New York: Princeton Architectural Press, 1997: 47–59.

Foner, Philip S. *History of the Labor Movement in the United States*. 10 vols. New York: International Publishers, 1947–1994.
Ford, Martin. *Rise of the Robots: Technology and the Threat of a Jobless Future*. New York: Basic Books, 2015.
Foster, John Bellamy, and Brett Clark. "Marxism and the Dialectics of Ecology." *Monthly Review* 68:5 (October 2016): 1–17.
Foster, John Bellamy, and Robert McChesney. *The Endless Crisis: How Monopoly Finance Capital Produces Economic Stagnation and Upheaval from the USA to China*. New York: Monthly Review Press, 2012.
Foucault, Michel. *Discipline and Punish: The Birth of the Prison*. Alan Sheridan, trans. New York: Vintage Books, 1979.
———. *The History of Sexuality. Vol. 1, An Introduction*. Robert Hurley, trans. New York: Vintage Books, 1980.
Frank, Thomas. *One Market under God: Extreme Capitalism, Market Populism, and the End of Economic Democracy*. New York: Anchor Books, 2001.
Friedman, Gerald, Fred Moseley, Chris Sturr, and the Dollars & Sense Collective, eds. *The Economic Crisis Reader: Readings in Economics, Politics, and Social Policy from Dollars & Sense*. Boston, MA: Economic Affairs Bureau, 2009.
Friedman, Milton. "The Role of Government in Education." Robert A. Solo, ed. *Economics and the Public Interest*. New Brunswick, NJ: Rutgers University Press, 1955: 123–144.
Friedman, Thomas. *The Lexus and the Olive Tree*. New York: Farrar, Strauss, Giroux, 2000.
Fuentes, Annette. *Lockdown High: When the Schoolhouse Becomes a Jailhouse*. London and New York: Verso, 2013.
Fukuyama, Francis. *The End of History and the Last Man*. New York: Free Press, 1993.
Gagnier, Regina. *The Insatiability of Human Wants: Economics and Aesthetics in Market Society*. Chicago, IL: University of Chicago Press, 2000.
Galbraith, James K. *The Predator State: How Conservatives Abandoned the Free Market and Why Liberals Should Too*. New York: Free Press, 2008.
Galeano, Eduardo. *Open Veins of Latin America: Five Centuries of the Pillage of a Continent*. Cedric Belfrage, trans. New York: Monthly Review Press, 1973.
George, Susan. *Another World Is Possible If . . . .* New York and London: Verso, 2004.
Gibler, John. *Mexico Unconquered: Chronicles of Power and Revolt*. San Francisco, CA: City Lights Books, 2009.
———. *To Die in Mexico: Dispatches from inside the Drug War*. San Francisco, CA: City Lights Books, 2011.
Giroux, Henry. "Beyond Pedagogies of Repression." *Monthly Review* 67:10 (March 2016): 57–71.
Golash-Boza, Tanya. *Deported: Policing Immigrants, Disposable Labor and Global Capitalism*. New York: New York University Press, 2015.
Gordon, Jennifer. *Suburban Sweatshops: The Fight for Immigrant Rights*. Cambridge, MA: Harvard University Press, 2007.
Gould, Stephen J. *The Mismeasure of Man*. New York: W. W. Norton, 1981.
Gramsci, Antonio. *Prison Notebooks*. New York: International Publishers, 1971.
Grandin, Greg. *Empire's Workshop: Latin America, the United States, and the Rise of the New Imperialism*. New York: Henry Holt, 2006.
Greene, Judith. "Banking on the Prison Boom." Tara Herivel and Paul Wright, eds. *Prison Profiteers: Who Makes Money from Mass Incarceration*. New York: The New Press, 2007: 3–26.
Gret, Marion, and Yves Sintomer. *The Porto Alegre Experiment: Learning Lessons for Better Democracy*. London: Zed Books, 2005.

Habermas, Jürgen. "Modernity: An Incomplete Project." Hal Foster, ed. *The Anti-Aesthetic: Essays on Postmodern Culture*. Port Townsend, WA: Bay Press, 1983: 3–15.
Hardin, Garrett. "The Tragedy of the Commons." *Science* 162: 3859 (1968): 1243–1248.
———. "Lifeboat Ethics: The Case Against Helping the Poor." *Psychology Today*. September, 1974. www.org/articles/art_lifeboat_ethics_case_against_helping_poor.html.
Hardt, Michael, and Antonio Negri. *Empire*. Cambridge, MA: Harvard University Press, 2000.
———. "Foreword." William Fisher and Thomas Ponniah, eds. *Another World Is Possible*. Blackpoint, Nova Scotia: Fernwood, 2003: xvi–xix.
———. *Multitude: War and Democracy in the Age of Empire*. New York: Penguin, 2004.
———. *Commonwealth*. Cambridge, MA: Harvard University Press, 2009.
Harman, Chris. *Zombie Capitalism: Global Crisis and the Relevance of Marx*. Chicago, IL: Haymarket Books, 2009.
Harrison, Guy P. *Race and Reality: What Everyone Should Know about Our Biological Diversity*. New York: Prometheus Books, 2010.
Hartmann, Thom. *Unequal Protection: How Corporations Became "People" and How You Can Fight Back*. San Francisco, CA: Berrett-Koehler Publishers, 2010.
Harvey, David. *The New Imperialism*. Oxford: Oxford University Press, 2003.
———. *A Brief History of Neoliberalism*. Oxford: Oxford University Press, 2005.
———. *The Enigma of Capital and the Crisis of Capitalism*. Oxford: Oxford University Press, 2010.
———. *Seventeen Contradictions and the End of Capitalism*. Oxford: Oxford University Press, 2014.
Henwood, Doug. *After the New Economy: The Binge . . . and the Hangover That Won't Go Away*. New York: The New Press, 2003.
Herivel, Tara. "Introduction." Tara Herivel and Paul Wright, eds. *Prison Profiteers: Who Makes Money from Mass Incarceration*. New York: The New Press, 2007: ix–xviii.
Herivel, Tara, and Paul Wright, eds. *Prison Nation: The Warehousing of America's Poor*. New York: Routledge, 2003.
———. *Prison Profiteers: Who Makes Money from Mass Incarceration*. New York: The New Press, 2007.
Hightower, Jim. *Thieves in High Places: They've Stolen Our Country—and It's Time to Take It Back*. New York: Viking, 2003.
———. "America *Isn't* Broke. There's Plenty of Money to Build an Economy Worthy of Our Ideals and Can-Do Spirit." *The Hightower Lowdown*. December 2013: 1–4.
———. "New Trade Pacts Create Secret, Pro-Corporate Tribunals That Use Their Powers to Eviscerate Our Democratic Laws." *Hightower Lowdown*. January 2015: 1–4.
Himmelfarb, Gertrude. *The Idea of Poverty: England in the Industrial Age*. New York: Knopf, 1984.
Hinton, Alexander Laban. "The Dark Side of Modernity: Toward an Anthropology of Genocide." Alexander Laban Hinton, ed. *Annihilating Difference: The Anthropology of Genocide*. Berkeley, CA: University of California Press, 2002: 1–40.
Hoenig, Jonathan. *Greed Is Good: The Capitalist Pig Guide to Investing*. New York: Harper Business, 1999.
Horvath, Anthony. "Frederick Taylor and the Connection Between Eugenics, Capitalism, and Communism: Scientific Management." http://eugenics.us/frederick-taylor-and-the-connection-between-eugenics-capitalism-and-communism-scientific-management/67.htm.
Houppert, Karen. "No Safe Haven: A Special Report on Domestic Violence." *Mother Jones*. July/August 2005. www.motherjones.com/politics/2005/07/base-crimes.

Howe, Daniel Walker. *What Hath God Wrought: The Transformation of America, 1815–1848*. Oxford: Oxford University Press, 2007.
Huffington, Ariana. *Pigs at the Trough: How Corporate Greed and Political Corruption Are Undermining America*. New York: Three Rivers Press, 2003.
Hughes, Robert. *The Fatal Shore: The Epic of Australia's Founding*. New York: Alfred A. Knopf, 1986.
Jameson, Fredric. *Postmodernism, or, the Cultural Logic of Late Capitalism*. Durham, NC: Duke University Press, 1991.
Johnson, Chalmers. *The Sorrows of Empire: Militarism, Secrecy, and the End of the Republic*. New York: Metropolitan Books, 2004.
Jonna, R. Jamil, and John Bellamy Foster. "Marx's Theory of Working-Class Precariousness." *Monthly Review* 67:11 (April 2016): 1–19.
Juhasz, Antonia. *The Tyranny of Oil: The World's Most Powerful Industry—and What We Must Do to Stop It*. New York: Harper, 2008.
———. "Why the War in Iraq Was Fought for Big Oil." April 15, 2013. www.cnn.com/2013/03/19/opinion/iraq-war-oil-juhasz.
Kahn, Si, and Elizabeth Minnich. *The Fox in the Henhouse: How Privatization Threatens Democracy*. San Francisco, CA: Berrett-Koehler Publishers, 2005.
Kaplan, Michael. "Road to Rio: Police Sweep Away 'Street Children' Ahead of Brazil Olympics." *International Business Times*. April 18, 2016. www.ibtimes.com/road-rio-police-sweep-away-street-children-ahead-brazil-olympics-2353865.
Karlin, Mark. "Busted at Birth: Becoming Instantly Disposable in the United States." December 18, 2015. www.truth-out.org/buzzflash/commentary/busted-at-birth-the-irony-of-being-born-and-becoming-instantly-disposable-in-the-united-states.
Keen, Steve. *Debunking Economics: The Naked Emperor Dethroned?* London: Zed Books, 2011.
Kevles, Daniel. *In the Name of Eugenics: Genetics and the Uses of Human Heredity*. Cambridge, MA: Harvard University Press, 1995.
Kilgore, James. *Understanding Mass Incarceration: A People's Guide to the Key Civil Rights Struggle of Our Time*. New York: The New Press, 2015.
Kim, Catherine Y., Daniel J. Lasen, and Damon T. Hewitt. *The School-to-Prison Pipeline: Structuring Legal Reform*. New York and London: New York University Press, 2010.
Kimmett, Colleen. "The Myth of New Orleans' Charter School 'Miracle.'" *In These Times* October 2015: 18–23.
Klein, Naomi. "Reclaiming the Commons." *New Left Review* 9 (May–June 2001). http://newleftreview.org/II/9/naomi-klein-reclaiming-the-commons.
———. *Shock Doctrine: The Rise of Disaster Capitalism*. New York: Henry Holt, 2007.
———. *This Changes Everything: Capitalism vs. the Climate*. New York: Simon & Schuster, 2014.
Kohn, Margaret. *Brave New Neighborhoods: The Privatization of Public Space*. New York: Routledge, 2004.
Kolko, Gabriel. *World in Crisis: The End of the American Century*. London: Pluto Books, 2009.
Korten, David C. *When Corporations Rule the World*. 2nd ed. San Francisco, CA: Berrett-Koehler Publishers, 2001.
———. *The Great Turning: From Empire to Earth Community*. San Francisco, CA: Berrett-Koehler Publishers, 2006.
Kotz, David M. *The Rise and Fall of Neoliberal Capitalism*. Cambridge, MA: Harvard University Press, 2015.
Kovel, Joel. *The Enemy of Nature: The End of Capitalism or the End of the World?* London and New York: Zed Books, 2013.

Kowinski, William S. *The Malling of America: An Inside Look at the Great Consumer Paradise.* New York: W. Morrow, 1985.

Krell, Alan. *The Devil's Rope: A Cultural History of Barbed Wire.* London: Reaktion Books, 2004.

Krugman, Paul. *The Great Unraveling: Losing Our Way in the New Century.* New York: W. W. Norton, 2004.

Land, Stephen K. *Kett's Rebellion: The Norfolk Rising of 1859.* Totowa, NJ: Rowman & Littlefield, 1977.

Lapavitsas, Costas. *Profiting without Producing: How Finance Exploits Us All.* London: Verso, 2013.

Lawrence, D. H. *Studies in Classic American Literature.* Ezra Greenspan, Lindeth Vasey, and John Worthen, eds. Cambridge: Cambridge University Press, 2003.

Leech, Garry. *Capitalism: A Structural Genocide.* London: Zed Books, 2012.

Leite, José Corrêa. *The World Social Forum: Strategies of Resistance.* Chicago, IL: Haymarket Books, 2005.

Lerner, Stephen. "Clipping America's Hedge Funds." *Inequality.org.* February 8, 2016. http://inequality.org/clipping-hedge-funds.

Lewis, Michael. *The Big Short: Inside the Doomsday Machine.* New York: W. W. Norton, 2011.

Linebaugh, Peter. *The Magna Carta Manifesto: Liberties and Commons for All.* Berkeley, CA: University of California Press, 2007.

———. *Stop, Thief! The Commons, Enclosures, and Resistance.* Oakland, CA: PM Press, 2014.

Linklater, Andro. *Owning the Earth: The Transforming History of Land Ownership.* New York: Bloomsbury, 2013.

Lombardo, Paul. *A Century of Eugenics in America: From the Indiana Experiment to the Human Genome Era.* Bloomington, IN: Indiana University Press, 2011.

Locke, John. *Two Treatises of Government.* London: Dent, 1991.

Louie, Miriam Ching Yoon. *Sweatshop Warriors: Immigrant Women Workers Take on the Global Factory.* Cambridge, MA: South End Press, 2001.

Loury, Glenn C. *Race, Incarceration, and American Values.* Cambridge, MA: MIT Press, 2008.

Low, Setha. *Behind the Gates: Life, Security, and the Pursuit of Happiness in Fortress America.* New York: Routledge, 2003.

Lowenstein, Antony. *Disaster Capitalism: Making a Killing out of Catastrophe.* London and New York: Verso Books, 2015.

Lutz, Ashley. "These 6 Corporations Control 90% of the Media in America." *Business Insider.* June 14, 2012. www.businessinsider.com/these-6-corporations-control-90-of-the-media-in-america-2012-6.

Lyotard, Jean-François. *The Postmodern Condition: A Report on Knowledge.* Minneapolis, MN: University of Minnesota Press, 1984.

MacCulloch, Diarmaid. "Kett's Rebellion in Context." *Past & Present* 84:1 (August 1, 1979): 36–59.

MacEwan, Arthur. "The Greed Fallacy." Gerald Friedman et al., eds. *The Economic Crisis Reader: Readings in Economics, Politics, and Social Policy from Dollars & Sense.* Boston, MA: Economic Affairs Bureau, 2009: 58–60.

Madrick, Jeff. *Age of Greed: The Triumph of Finance and the Decline of America, 1970 to the Present.* New York: Alfred A. Knopf, 2011.

Maine, Sir Henry. *Ancient Law; Its Connection with the Early History of Society and Its Relation to Modern Ideas.* 1861. Gloucester, MA: P. Smith, 1970.

Making Change at Walmart. www: makingchangeatwalmart.org/walmart-and-workers/.

Mallett, Christopher A. *The School-to-Prison Pipeline: A Comprehensive Assessment.* New York: Springer, 2016.

Malthus, Thomas. *On Population.* New York: Modern Library, 1960. First edition: *Essay on the Principle of Population.* London: Joseph Johnson, 1798.

Mander, Jerry. *The Capitalism Papers: Fatal Flaws of an Obsolete System.* Berkeley, CA: Counterpoint, 2012.

Mander, Jerry, and Victoria Tauli-Corpuz, eds. *Paradigm Wars: Indigenous Peoples' Resistance to Economic Globalization.* San Francisco, CA: International Forum on Globalization, 2006.

Mankiw, N. Gregory. *Principles of Economics.* 5th ed. Mason, OH: South-Western Cengage Learning, 2008.

"Marcus." *The Book of Murder! Vade-Mecum for the Commissioners and Guardians of the New Poor Law throughout Great Britain and Ireland . . . .* 2nd ed. London: John Hill, 1839.

Marcuse, Peter. "Walls of Fear and Walls of Support." Nan Ellin, ed. *Architecture of Fear.* New York: Princeton Architectural Press, 1997: 101–121.

Marcuse, Peter, and Robert van Kempen. "Introduction." *Globalizing Cities: A New Spatial Order?* Hoboken, NJ: John Wiley & Sons, 1999.

Marglin, Stephen A. *The Dismal Science: How Thinking Like an Economist Undermines Community.* Cambridge, MA: Harvard University Press, 2008.

Martin, Amy. *Alter-Nations: Nationalism, Terror, and the State in Nineteenth-Century Britain and Ireland.* Columbus, OH: The Ohio State University, 2012.

Marx, Karl. *Theories of Surplus Value.* 3 vols. London: Lawrence & Wishart, 1967.

———. *Capital.* 3 vols. New York: Penguin, 1990.

———. *Grundrisse.* London: Penguin, 1993.

Marzec, Robert P. "Enclosures, Colonization, and the *Robinson Crusoe* Syndrome: A Genealogy of Land in a Global Context." *Boundary* 2:1 (June 2002): 129–156.

Mason, Paul. *Postcapitalism: A Guide to Our Future.* New York: Farrar, Strauss & Giroux, 2015.

Massey, Douglas S., and Nancy A. Denton. *American Apartheid: Segregation and the Making of the Underclass.* Cambridge, MA: Harvard University Press, 1993.

Mauer, Marc. *Race to Incarcerate.* New York: The New Press, 1999.

Maurer, Sara. *The Dispossessed Estate: Narratives of Ownership in 19th-Century Britain and Ireland.* Baltimore, MD: Johns Hopkins University Press, 2012.

Mayhew, Henry. *London Labour and the London Poor.* 4 vols. 1862–1864. New York: Dover, 1968.

McChesney, Robert W., and John Nichols. *The Death and Life of American Journalism.* New York: Nation Books, 2011.

———. *People Get Ready: The Fight Against a Jobless Economy and a Citizenless Democracy.* New York: Nation Books, 2016.

McKibben, Bill. "Exxon: No Corporation Has Ever Done Anything This Big and This Bad." First published in *Ecowatch.* Republished by *Buzzflash at Truthout.* October 16, 2015. www.truth-out.org/buzzflash/commentary/exxon-no-corporation-has-ever-done-anything-this-big-and-this-bad.

Meek, Ronald, ed. *Marx and Engels on the Population Bomb.* Berkeley, CA: Ramparts Press, 1971.

Menzies, Heather. *Reclaiming the Commons for the Common Good.* Gabriola Island, BC: New Society Publishers, 2014.

Meronek, Toshio. "Privatizing Public Housing: 'The Genocide of Poor People.'" *Truthout.* March 13, 2013. www.truth-out.org/news/item/29483-privatizing-public-housing-the-genocide-of-poor-people.

Midnight Notes Collective. *The New Enclosures*. New York: Midnight Notes 10, 1990.
Miller, Jane. "Fences for Thee—but Not for Me." *In These Times* 39:12 (December 2015): 42–43.
Mills, C. Wright. *The Sociological Imagination*. New York: Oxford University Press, 1959.
Miner, Barbara. "Why the Right Hates Public Education." *Rethinking Schools*, Summer 2002. www.rethinkingschools.org/specialreports/ bushplan/righPRO.shtml.
Mohn, Tanya. "America's Most Exclusive Gated Communities." *Forbes Magazine*, August 3, 2012.
Monbiot, George. *Manifesto for a New World Order*. New York: The New Press, 2003.
Moravec, Hans. *Mind Children: The Future of Robot and Human Intelligence*. Cambridge, MA: Harvard University Press, 1988.
Moskowitz, Peter. *How to Kill a City: Gentrification, Inequality, and the Fight for the Neighborhood*. New York: Nation Books, 1917.
Mostert, Mark P. "Useless Eaters: Disability as Genocidal Marker in Nazi Germany." *The Journal of Special Education*. 36:3 (2002): 155–168.
Munck, Ronaldo. *Globalization and Contestation*. New York: Routledge, 2007.
Murray, Charles. *Losing Ground: American Social Policy, 1950–1980*. New York: Basic Books, 1984.
National Alliance to End Homelessness. "Fact Sheet: Veteran Homelessness." April 22, 2015. www.endhomelessness.org/library/entry/fact-sheet-veteran-homelessness.
Neesom, J. R. *Commoners: Common Right, Enclosure, and Social Change in England*. Cambridge: Cambridge University Press, 1993.
Netz, Reviel. *Barbed Wire: An Ecology of Modernity*. Middletown, CT: Wesleyan University Press, 2004.
Nkrumah, Kwame. *Neocolonialism: The Last Stage of Imperialism*. London: Thomas Nelson, 1965.
Norris, Frank. *The Octopus: A California Story*. 1901. West Roxbury, MA: B&R Samizdat Express, n.d.
Onuf, Peter S. *Jefferson's Empire: The Language of American Nationhood*. Charlottesville, VA: University Press of Virginia, 2001.
Osborne, Sidney Godolphin. "Immortal Sewerage." Viscount Ingestre, ed. *Meliora; or, Better Times to Come*. 1st series, 1853: 7–17. London: Frank Cass, 1971.
Ostrom, Elinor. *Governing the Commons: The Evolution of Institutions for Collective Action*. Cambridge: Cambridge University Press, 1990.
Pager, Devah. *Marked: Race, Crime, and Finding Work in an Era of Mass Incarceration*. Chicago, IL: University of Chicago Press, 2007.
Palast, Greg. *The Best Democracy that Money Can Buy*. New York: Penguin, 2003.
Parenti, Christian. *Against Empire*. San Francisco, CA: City Lights Books, 1995.
———. *Lockdown America: Police and Prisons in the Age of Crisis*. New ed. New York: Verso, 2008.
———. "Privatized Problems: For-Profit Incarceration in Trouble." Andrew Coyle et al., eds. *Capitalist Punishment: Prison Privatization and Human Rights*. Atlanta, GA: Clarity Press; London: Zed Books, 2003: 30–38.
Partnoy, Frank. *Infectious Greed: How Deceit and Risk Corrupted the Financial Markets*. Rev. ed. New York: Public Affairs, Perseus Books, 2009.
Patel, Raj. *The Value of Nothing: How to Reshape Market Society and Redefine Democracy*. New York: Picador, 2009.
Perelman, Michael. *Railroading Economics: The Creation of the Free Market Mythology*. New York: Monthly Review Press, 2006.

Persson, Jonas. "CMD Publishes Full List of 2,500 Closed Charter Schools." September 22, 2015. *Center for Media and Democracy's PR Watch*. www.prwatch.org/node/12936#sthash.M4yIleSq.dpuf.
Petras, James, and Henry Veltmeyer. *Globalization Unmasked: Imperialism in the 21st Century*. London: Zed Books, 2001.
Pieterse, Jan Nederveen. *Globalization or Empire?* New York: Routledge, 2004.
Pinnacle List. www.thepinnaclelist.com/blog/directory/the-biltmore-estate-george-vanderbilt-mansion-is-the-largest-privately-owned-home-in-america.
Pick, Daniel. *Faces of Degeneration: A European Disorder, c.1848–c.1914*. Cambridge: Cambridge University Press, 1989.
Pilkington, Doris. *Follow the Rabbit-Proof Fence*. Brisbane: University of Queensland Press, 1996.
Pizzigati, Sam. "The Epitome of U.S. Corporate Success?" April 28, 2016.http://inequality.org/epitome-american-corporate-success/#sthash.on68cF6e.dpuf.
Polanyi, Karl. *The Great Transformation: The Political and Economic Origins of Our Time*. Boston, MA: Beacon Press, 2001.
Posner, Richard. *A Failure of Capitalism: The Crisis of '08 and the Descent into Depression*. Cambridge, MA: Harvard University Press, 2009.
POV: Documentaries with a Point of View. *Prison Town, USA*. www.pbs.org/pov/prisontown/film_description.php.
Prashad, Vijay. *Fat Cats and Running Dogs: The Enron Stage of Capitalism*. Monroe, ME: Common Courage Press, 2003.
Raban, Jonathan. *Soft City*. London: Hamilton, 1974.
Ramnath, Maia. *Decolonizing Anarchism: An Antiauthoritarian History of India's Liberation Struggle*. Oakland: AK Press, 2011.
Ravitch, Diane. *Reign of Error: The Hoax of the Privatization Movement and the Danger to America's Public Schools*. New York: Alfred A. Knopf, 2013.
Reynolds, Henry. *The Law of the Land*. 2nd ed. Ringwood, Victoria: Penguin Books Australia, 1992.
Richards, Eric. *Debating the Highland Clearances*. Edinburgh: Edinburgh University Press, 2007.
Ridgeway, James, and Jean Casella. "America's 10 Worst Prisons: Pelican Bay Where a Christmas Card Might Land You in the Hole." *Mother Jones*. May 8, 2013. www.motherjones.com/politics/2013/05/10-worst-prisons-america-pelican-bay.
Riis, Jacob. *How the Other Half Lives*. 1890. New York: Barnes and Noble, 2004.
Ross, Alexander Reid, ed. *Grabbing Back: Essays Against the Global Land Grab*. Oakland, CA: AK Press, 2014.
Ross, Andrew. *The Celebration Chronicles: Life, Liberty and the Pursuit of Property Values in Disney's New Town*. New York: Ballantine, 1999.
Ross, Robert. *Slaves to Fashion: Poverty and Abuse in the New Sweatshops*. Ann Arbor, MI: University of Michigan Press, 2004.
Rowe, Jonathan. *Our Common Wealth: The Hidden Economy That Makes Everything Else Work*. Peter Barnes, ed. San Francisco, CA: Berrett-Koehler Publishers, 2013.
Rowley, C. D. *The Destruction of Aboriginal Society*. Canberra: Australian National University Press, 1970.
Roy, Arundhati. *An Ordinary Person's Guide to Empire*. Boston, MA: South End Press, 2004.
———. *Capitalism: A Ghost Story*. Chicago, IL: Haymarket Books, 2014.
Scheer, Robert. *The Great American Stickup: How Reagan Republicans and Clinton Democrats Enriched Wall Street While Mugging Main Street*. New York: Nation Books, 2010.

Shiflett, Dave. "Mexican Border Fence Cost $3 Billion, Does Nothing." *Bloomberg News.* September 15, 2010. www.bloomberg.com/news/2010-09-15/idiotic-mexico-border-fence-cost-3-billion-does-nothing-dave-shiflett.html.
Shipler, David K. *The Working Poor: Invisible in America.* New York: Vintage Books, 2005.
Shiva, Vandana. *Biopiracy: The Plunder of Nature and Knowledge.* Boston, MA: South End Press, 1997.
———. "The Living Democracy Movement." DAGAinfo. February 28, 2002. www.daga.org.hk/res/dagainfo/di129.htm.
———. *Earth Democracy: Justice, Sustainability, and Peace.* Cambridge, MA: South End Press, 2005.
Silko, Leslie Marmon. *Ceremony.* New York: Penguin, 1977.
Smith, Adam. *The Wealth of Nations.* 2 vols. In 1. Chicago, IL: University of Chicago Press, 1976.
Smith, John. *Imperialism in the Twenty-First Century: Globalization, Super-Exploitation, and Capitalism's Final Crisis.* New York: Monthly Review Press, 2016.
Sorkin, Michael. *Variations on a Theme Park: The New American City and the End of Public Space.* New York: Hill & Wang, 1992.
St. Clair, Jeffrey. *Grand Theft Pentagon: Tales of Corruption and Profiteering in the War on Terror.* Monroe, ME: Common Courage Press, 2005.
Stephenson, Neal. *Snow Crash.* New York: Bantam Books, 1993.
Stiglitz, Joseph. *Globalization and Its Discontents.* New York: W. W. Norton, 2002.
———. *Freefall: America, Free Markets, and the Sinking of the World Economy.* New York: W. W. Norton, 2010.
———. *The Price of Inequality.* New York: W. W. Norton, 2012.
Swift, Jonathan. *Poetical Works.* Herbert Davis, ed. London: Oxford University Press, 1967.
Tawney, R. H. *The Agrarian Problem in the Sixteenth Century.* 1912. New York: Burt Franklin, 1961.
Thomas, Janet. *The Battle in Seattle: The Story Behind and Beyond the WTO Demonstrations.* Golden, CO: Fulcrum Publishing, 2000.
Thompson, E. P. *The Making of the English Working Class.* New York: Vintage Books, 1966.
———. "Custom, Law and Common Right." *Customs in Common: Studies in Traditional Popular Culture.* New York: The New Press, 1993: 97–184.
Tonelson, Alan. *The Race to the Bottom: Why a Worldwide Worker Surplus and Uncontrolled Free Trade Are Sinking American Living Standards.* Boulder, CO: Westview Press, 2002.
"Trump's Irreversible Threat." Editorial in *The Nation* 303: 23–24 (December 5, 12, 2016): 2.
Urbina, Ian. "Prison Labor Fuels American War Machine." Tara Herivel and Paul Wright, eds. *Prison Profiteers: Who Makes Money from Mass Incarceration.* New York: The New Press, 2007: 120–129.
Urrea, Luis Alberto. *By the Lake of Sleeping Children: The Secret Life of the Mexican Border.* New York: Random House, 1996.
Van Gelder, Sarah. "The Urban Common Spaces That Show Us We Belong to Something Larger." *YES! Magazine.* April 17, 2017.
Varga, Joseph J. *Hell's Kitchen and the Battle for Urban Space: Class Struggle and Progressive Reform in New York City, 1894–1914.* New York: Monthly Review Press, 2013.
Vaughan, Adam. "Fossil Fuel Divestment: A Brief History." October 8, 2014. *The Guardian.* www.theguardian.com/environment/2014/oct/08/fossil-fuel-divestment-a-brief-history.
Venturi, Robert. *Learning from Las Vegas.* Cambridge, MA: MIT Press, 1972.
Vine, David. *Base Nation: How the U.S. Military Bases Abroad Harm America and the World.* New York: Metropolitan, 2015.

Wall, Derek. *The Commons in History: Culture, Conflict, and Ecology*. Cambridge, MA: MIT Press, 2014.
Walljasper, Jay, ed. *All That We Share: A Field Guide to the Commons*. New York: The New Press, 2010.
Walsh, Declan, and Steven Greenhouse. "Inspectors Certified Pakistani Factory as Safe Before Disaster." *The New York Times*. September 20, 2012: A6.
Washington, John. "Coal and Unusual Punishment." *In These Times* 40:8 (August 2016): 10–11.
Watson, Bruce. "High Crimes: Military Towns Are Among the Country's Most Dangerous." *Daily Finance*. November 16, 2009. www.dailyfinance.com/2009/11/16/most-dangerous-military-towns.
Weber, Max. *The Protestant Ethic and the Spirit of Capitalism*. 1904–1905. Talcott Parsons, trans. New York: Scribners, 1958.
Wells, H. G. *Anticipations of the Reaction of Mechanical and Scientific Progress on Human Life and Thought*. 1901. New York: Harper, 1902.
Wikipedia. "Pakistan Factory Fires." https://en.wikipedia.org/wiki/2012_Pakistan_factory_fires.
Williams, Raymond. *The Country and the City*. New York: Oxford University Press, 1973.
Wolff, Richard. *Democracy at Work: A Cure for Capitalism*. Chicago, IL: Haymarket Books, 2012.
Wolfson, Marty. "Derivatives and Deregulation." Gerald Friedman et al., eds. *The Economic Crisis Reader: Readings in Economics, Politics, and Social Policy from Dollars & Sense*. Boston, MA: Economic Affairs Bureau, 2009: 135–138.
Wolin, Sheldon S. *Democracy Inc.: Managed Democracy and the Specter of Inverted Totalitarianism*. Princeton, NJ: Princeton University Press, 2008.
Wolpert, Stanley. *India*. 3rd ed. Berkeley, CA: University of California Press, 2005.
Wood, Ellen Meiksins. *Empire of Capital*. London: Verso Books, 2003.
Wood, Phillip J. "The Rise of the Prison Industrial Complex in the United States." Andrew Coyle et al., eds. *Capitalist Punishment: Prison Privatization and Human Rights*. Atlanta, GA: Clarity Press; London: Zed Books, 2003: 16–29.
Wray, Matt, and Annalee Newitz, eds. *White Trash: Race and Class in America*. New York: Routledge, 1997.
Wright, Angus, and Wendy Wolford. *To Inherit the Earth: The Landless Movement and the Struggle for a New Brazil*. Oakland, CA: Food First, 2008.
Wright, Paul. "The Cultural Commodification of Prisons." Tara Herivel and Paul Wright, eds. *Prison Profiteers: Who Makes Money from Mass Incarceration*. New York: The New Press, 2007: 98–106.
Zangwill, Israel. *Children of the Ghetto*. Black Apollo Press, 1892.
Žižek, Slavoj. *Welcome to the Desert of the Real*. London: Verso, 2002.
———. *Violence: Six Sideways Reflections*. New York: Picador, 2008.
———. *First as Tragedy, Then as Farce*. London: Verso, 2009.
———. *Living in the End Times*. London: Verso, 2010.
———. *The Year of Dreaming Dangerously*. London: Verso, 2012.

INDEX

Abizaid, John 86
Abu-Ghraib 6, 39
Abu-Jamal, Mumia 34, 43
Adorno, Theodor 61
Affordable Care Act 74
Afghanistan 62, 81, 84, 86, 112
Africa x, 2, 6, 14, 81, 83, 109, 114, 125
African-Americans 19, 22, 24, 28, 29, 32, 36, 37, 42, 100–101, 113, 144
Agamben, Giorgio 6, 112, 113
Ahmad, Eqbal 14
Alexander, Michelle 2, 36, 39
Ali Enterprises 95
Alperovitz, Gar 142–43
Al-Qaeda 62, 85
Althusser, Louis 57
American Revolution xiv, 14, 51, 147
Anglo-Boer War ix, 6, 14
Anti-Drug Abuse Act 37
Anzaldúa, Gloria 13, 14
Appadurai, Arjun 88
Apple 93
Arab Spring xiv, 147
Arbenz, Jacob 84
Arendt, Hannah 51, 106
Assange, Julian 135
Aten, Ira 9
Attica prison riot 7
Auden, W. H. ix
Australia; Australian Aboriginals 7, 14, 15, 106, 108, 119–20
auto industry *see* GM
automation 101, 115–16, 142
Ayers, Bill 41, 140

Bakan, Joel 72
Bales, Kevin 109
barbed wire ix–x, xiv, 1, 6, 10–11, 14, 20, 38, 69, 89, 95, 114, 115, 136
Bauman, Zygmunt 22, 30, 91
Bangladesh 26, 83, 93, 96
Barber, Rev. William 141
Barlow, Maude 127, 128, 130, 134
Battle of Seattle 93, 144, 147
Bechtel 143
Benjamin, Rich 22
Benkler, Yochai 134
Bennis, Phyllis 70
Bentham, Jeremy 35
Berkhoffer, Robert 11
Biddle, Nicholas 69
Big Oil xiii, 3, 8, 59, 85–86, 141–42, 147; *see also* BP; Chevron; Exxon-Mobil
Billington, Ray 8
Bill Moyer's Journal 58
Bindé, Jerome 22
Binding, Karl 112
Biopolitics *see* eugenics; racism
Black, Jan 115
Black Lives Matter 2, 19, 42, 100, 116, 141
Black, William 55
Blackstone, William 67
Blackwater 2, 86
Blake, William 49
Blakely, Edward 19, 22
Blockadia 141
Boeing xiii, 38, 88
Bolivia 143

Index

Bollier, David 4–5, 89, 125–6, 128, 131, 133, 134, 139
Booz Allen Hamilton 2
Bonaventure Hotel 17–19
Boston Tea Party 65
Bowers, C. A. xi, 125
Boyle, James 135, 136
BP 86
Brantlinger, Patrick 54
Brazil xiv, 27, 91, 93, 109–10, 113, 129, 144–45
Britain x, xi, 3, 7, 14–15, 106, 120, 124; *see also* England
British East India Company xi, 3
Brown, Michael 2, 19, 42
Burbach, Roger 82
Bush, George W. 45, 81, 85, 86, 92, 143

Cahokia Mounds 7
California 40, 41, 69, 125
Canada 3, 106, 141
CCA (Corrections Corporation of America) 38
Cargill 3, 124
Carlyle, Thomas 104, 106, 107
Carr, Nicholas 115
Carter, Jimmy 37
Celebration, FL 23, 25
Center for Media and Democracy 46
Center for Public Integrity 86
Ceremony 10–11
Cheney, Dick 62, 81, 85, 86
Cherokees 10
Chevron 86
Chicago 19, 28, 30, 32, 45
China xiii, 4, 29, 57, 74, 93, 109, 115, 146
Chinese Exclusion Act 29
Chomsky, Noam 132
CIA 6, 36, 84
Citizens United 5, 69, 77, 140, 142
Civil War ix, 110, 111
Clare, John 121–23
Clark, Brett xii
Clark, Kenneth 29
class conflict xi, 7, 8, 19, 30, 39, 43, 56, 115, 124
Clements, Jeffrey 5, 69
climate change *see* global warming
Clinton, Bill 34, 35, 92
Clinton, Hillary 143
Clive, Robert 68
Coca-Cola 144
Columbine High School 42, 43

Columbus, Christopher 125
Comey, James 140
commons x–xi, xii, xiv, 1, 3, 4, 8, 9, 15, 22, 30, 45, 59, 67, 89, 91, 109, 110, 119–36, 139–47
commonwealth 125–26, 139, 145
communal property *see* commons
communism xiv, 9–10, 57, 84, 112, 123, 129, 146
Community Education Partners 42
Community Mental Health Centers Act 39–40
concentration camps ix, 6, 10, 11 14
Cook, Captain James 104
Corbi, Al V. 20
corporations x, xii, xiii, xiv, 1, 2, 3, 17, 34–47, 53, 54–62, 65–78, 119–36
Creative Commons 134
credit unions 142
Cronin, Mike 124
Cuba 6, 14, 57

Daniels, Mitch 144
Darwin, Charles 50, 111
Davis, Mike 17–18, 21, 26–27, 31, 89
Davis, Robert 24
decolonization 81–82, 84
Deleuze, Gilles 87–88, 103
DeLillo, Don 27, 30–31
Dell, Michael 19
Denton, Nancy 29, 30
Derber, Charles 70
"Deserted Village" 122
Detroit 18, 28, 30, 144
DeVos, Betsy 45, 140, 144
Dickens, Charles 27, 105, 107
Disney World 23, 59
disposable people 97, 100–18, 125, 128; *see also* genocide; unemployment
divestment 141–42
Drexler, K. Eric 116
Drug Enforcement Agency 36
Drug Policy Alliance 37
Duncan, Arne 45
Dutch East India Company 65, 68
DynCorp 2, 86

East India Company 65, 68
Eddie Mabo land rights case 119
education *see* ideology; schools
Ehrenreich, Barbara 18, 19, 24, 25, 39, 74
Eisenhower, Dwight xiii
Ellin, Nan 18, 22
Elsner, Alan 37, 38, 39, 40, 41
Emmanuel, Rahm 45

Index

empire x, xi, xii, xiii, xiv, 3, 8–11, 12, 13, 14, 41, 50, 51, 65–68, 80–106, 109, 119–20, 125, 129, 141, 145, 146
enclosure (privatization) ix, x, xii, 1, 2, 5, 8, 10–11, 22, 24, 26, 27, 29, 31, 39, 41, 44, 55, 59, 67, 74, 76, 83–86, 88, 89, 91, 92, 93, 100, 106, 110, 119–20, 125, 127–27, 128, 129, 131, 135, 139, 140, 144, 145
Engels, Friedrich 51, 52, 94–95, 103, 104, 106, 123
England xiii, 14, 81, 94, 105, 114; *see also* Britain
Enron 1, 5, 55, 70, 76
EPA 5
eugenics 50, 110–14
European Union 76, 92, 146
Expandiverse Technology 135–36
ExxonMobil xii, 86, 87, 143

Facebook 134
Fair Housing Act 29
Fairn Sentencing Act 37
Fannie Mae 26, 75
FBI 140
FCC 59
Federal Reserve 52, 54
Feeny, David 131
fence-cutting wars 9, 136, 141
fencing the American West ix, 7–11, 136, 141
Ferguson, Charles 77
Ferguson, MO 2, 19, 42
Ferguson, Niall 81–82
feudalism x, 8, 87, 123
Fight for $15 142
financialization xii, xiv, 5, 53, 57, 70–78, 88–89, 92, 147
Fisk, Milton 129
Flint, MI 143–44
Florida 23–24, 67, 142; *see also* Disney World
Foner, Philip 102
food sovereignty 146
Ford 38
Ford, Martin 115
Fort Bragg 25
Foster, John Bellamy xii, 97
Foucault, Michel 1, 6, 35, 112, 113
Fox network 35, 57–58
France iii, 35, 51, 81, 114
Freddie Mac 26, 75
French East India Company 65
French Revolution xiv, 51, 147

Friedman, Milton 46
Friedman, Thomas 84, 85
Fuentes, Annette 43
Fukuyama, Francis 57, 84, 85

Galton, Francis 111
Gap 96
gated communities xiii, 19, 20–24, 26, 37
Gates, Bill 88
GE 72, 73, 77, 143
General Motors 38, 143
genocide x, 11, 14, 50, 80–81, 83, 84, 85, 89, 100, 105–14, 125
genome project 135
Geo prison corporation 38
George, Henry 51
George, Susan 146
Germany 12, 81, 91, 112, 114
ghettoes xiii, 28–30, 36, 37, 43
Gibler, John 13–14
Glidden, Joseph 8
Global Exchange xiv
globalization xiii, 8, 49, 68, 72, 75, 80–100, 106, 124, 128, 129, 144, 145, 146
global warming xiii, 57, 58, 59, 60, 62, 87, 115, 128, 133, 147
Golash-Boza, Tanya 107
Gold Kist 124
Goldman Sachs xii
Goldsmith, Oliver 121–22
Google 73
GRAIN 116
Gramsci, Antonio 51, 57
Grandin, Greg 82
Grant, Madison 112
Gray-Garcia, Tiny 32
Great Depression 72
Greece 14, 76, 92
Green Valley, NE 22
Greene, Judith 38, 40
Greenpeace 141
Greenspan, Alan 54, 86
Greenville College 35, 44
Greenville, IL 1–2, 5, 6, 7, 34–35, 37, 128
Greenville prison *see* Greenville, IL
Guantanamo 6, 39
Guatemala 84, 85
Guattari, Félix 87–88, 103
Gulf War 113
Guthrie, Woody 32

Habermas, Jürgen 52–53, 57
Hache, Alfred 112

Hagel, Chuck 86
Haldeman, Eric 36
Halliburton xiii, 62, 86
Hamilton, Alexander 68
Hardin, Garrett 89–90, 91, 112, 131–36
Hardt, Michael xiii, 88, 125, 127, 128, 139, 145
Harman, Chris 88–89
Hartmann, Tom 5
Harvey, David 3, 4, 53, 75, 83, 100, 132, 139
Hasina, Sheikh 96
Hastings, Warren 68
Hawaii 14, 19
Hegel, G. W. F. 109
hegemony 51–52
Heilig, Julian Vasquez 46
Heritage Foundation 104–105
Herivel, Tara 35
Hidden Hills, CA 21–22, 25, 26
Highland Clearances xi, 123, 131
Hightower, Jim 77, 92
Himmelfarb, Gertrude 108
Hinton, Alexander 113
Hirsch, Arnold 30
Hobson, J. A. 51
Holocaust 113–14; *see also* genocide; Nazism
homelessness 101, 102
Hong Kong 23, 115
Horvath, Anthony 112
Houppert, Karen 25
housing and mortgage crisis xii, xiii, 5, 26, 54, 55, 72, 75, 76, 77, 78
housing projects 20, 30, 32
Hudson Bay Company 65–66
Hurricane Katrina 32, 46, 62
Hussein, Sadam 86

IBM 144
Ideology xiii, 49–62, 85, 121, 129–30
IMF 55, 90–91, 92, 144
Immigration and Naturalization Service 95
immigration 11–15, 28, 29, 76, 89, 95, 105, 106, 107, 114, 124, 140
Imokolee Workers Coalition 142
Incas 14
India x, 4, 65, 68, 102, 144
Indiana 10, 37, 46, 47, 60, 141, 144
Indiana University x, 2, 112
Indianapolis 18, 19, 30
Indian Removal Act 10
Indian reservations 10–11, 14
Indonesia 68, 85

Industrial Revolution x, 5, 8, 15
Ihofe, James 60
Internet 4, 57, 61, 116, 128, 133, 134, 135
Iran 115
Iraq 2, 59, 60, 62, 81, 84, 86, 112, 114–15, 128, 145
Ireland 7, 14–15, 83, 108, 121
Irish Famine 15, 105–06, 123–24
Islam 7, 114, 140
ISIS 60, 62
Israel xiii
Italy 8

Jackson, Andrew 10
Jameson, Fredric 17–18
Japan 91
Jefferson, Thomas 14, 67, 70
Jensen, Robert 82
Jobs with Justice 142
Johnson, Chalmers 82
Johnson, Lyndon 36
Jordan, David Starr 112
journalism 5, 57–62
Judis, John 82
Juhasz, Antonia 86
Justice Department 42

Karachi 26, 95
Kesey, Ken 39
Kett's Rebellion 3, 120, 141
Kimmett, Colleen 46
Klein, Naomi 46, 140–41
Koch brothers 68, 88, 142
Kohn, Margaret 20, 23
Kolko, Gabriel 82
Korten, David 3, 49, 124, 147
Kowinski, William 30
Krell, Alan ix, 6, 9–10
Kurzweil, Ray 116

labor x, xii, xiv, 3, 6, 13, 14, 38, 53, 54, 67, 71, 73, 74, 77, 83, 89, 91, 93, 95, 100, 101, 102–03, 106–07, 112, 115, 120, 126, 142, 144 *see also* automation; sweatshops; unemployment
Laguna-Pueblo Indians 10
Lakotah, Republic of 141
Land League (Ireland) 124
land trusts xiv, 142
Landless Workers Movement (Brazil) xiv, 91, 129, 145
Lapavitsas, Costas 75–76, 77
Latinos 7, 19, 24, 37, 113, 144
Lauterdale paradox xii

law of diminishing returns xii
Leech, Gary 89
Lewis, Michael 71
Leite, José Correa 147
Libya xiv, 114
Lichtenstein, Roy 18
Linebaugh, Peter 123
lobbyists 68, 127
Locke, John 67, 109, 125
Lockheed Martin xiii
Lombroso, Cesare
London Labour and the London Poor 102–03
Long Term Capital Management 76–77
Los Angeles, CA 12, 17–24, 43, 92, 95
Louisiana Purchase 14, 82
Loury, Glenn 41
Lowenstein, Antony 12, 62, 86
Luddites 102, 115

MacEwan, Arthur 71
McCallum, Henry and Frances ix
McChesney, Robert 62, 97, 115
McDonald's 84, 142, 143
McKibben, Bill 87
McLuhan, Marshall 57, 80, 85
Mad Art 1–2, 5, 7, 19
Madison, James 67, 70
Madoff, Bernard 76
Madrick, Jeff 70, 74
malls 30, 31
Malthus, Thomas 90, 103–04, 106, 110, 111, 130
Mander, Jerry 72
Mandeville, Bernard 78
Manifest Destiny 14
Mankiw, N. Gregory 55–56, 57, 130–32
Mann, Michael 82
Maori 141, 144
"Marcus" 107–08, 110
Marcuse, Peter 28
Marglin, Stephen 5
Martin, Trayvon 22
Marx, Karl x, xi, xii, 3, 4, 51, 52, 53, 57, 61, 71–72, 77, 78, 89, 93, 94, 103, 104, 106–07, 122–23, 124
Marxism 51, 90, 103, 112, 121
mass media xi, 7, 23–24, 35, 52, 54, 57–62, 113, 134, 141, 145, 146
Massey, Douglas 29, 30
Mauer, Marc 34, 37, 39
Mayer, Marissa 73
Mayhew, Henry 102–03
Menzies, Heather 131
Mexican-American War 82

Mexico 10, 12–14, 53, 73, 91, 92, 115, 141
military-industrial complex 13, 82, 146, 147
Millennium Declaration (UN) 92
Miller, Jane 114
Mississippi Bubble 54
modernization ix, xiv, 5, 6, 11, 17–18, 52–53, 86, 87, 121, 122
Mohn, Tanya 21
Monbiot, George 146
Monk, Daniel Bertrand 17
Monsanto 3, 124
Moral Mondays movement 141
Moravec, Hans 116
More, Sir Thomas 121
Morris, Mollie 9
Morris, William 121–122
Move to Amend (Citizens United) 142
MoveOn 134
Munck, Ronaldo 80
Murray, Charles 104
Murrow, Edward R. 58
Muslims *see* Islam

Nader, Ralph 74
NAFTA 68, 91, 92, 127
Napolitano, Janet 12–13
nationalism 80–81, 85, 86, 114, 124
Native Americans 8–11, 14, 15, 30, 67–68, 83, 100–01, 108, 109, 113, 119, 128, 140, 141
NATO 86
Nazism ix, 29, 50, 111, 112
Neesom, Jeanette 120–21
Negri, Antonio xiii, 88, 125, 127, 128, 139, 145
neoliberal economics x, xiii, 4, 46, 49, 51, 53–57, 70, 75, 78, 80–81, 82, 89, 91, 92, 93, 107, 126, 129, 131–32, 143, 146
Netherlands x, 81
Netz, Reviel ix, 8–9
Newfoundland 108, 130, 132, 141
Newhouse, John 82
New Orleans 32, 46
New York City 27, 28, 92, 95
The New York Times 96–97
New Zealand 15, 76, 141, 144
NewsCorp 59
Nicaragua 36, 92
Nichols, John 62, 115
Nike 93
Nintendo 38
Nixon, Richard 35, 36
Nkrumah, Kwame 84

No Child Left Behind 45
No Sweat 93
Norris, Frank 78
North Carolina 67, 141
Nova, Scott 96
NRA 58
nuclear war 115, 146

Obama, Barack xiii, 45, 56, 92, 143
Occupy Wall Street 77, 91, 116, 141, 147
Oklahoma 10, 60
Olmes, Dana 21
Olson, Mancur 130–31
Omnibus Anti-Drug Act 37
Open Source Initiative 134
Opium Wars x
Ortiz, Simon 100–01
Osborne, S. G. 105
Ostrom, Elinor x, 51, 130–31, 133
Ostrom, Vincent x, 130
Otis Elevator 143
Owen, Robert 51

Paine, Tom 57
Pakistan 95, 96, 113
Parenti, Christian 6, 38, 39, 82, 84
Partnoy, Frank 76–77
Patel, Raj 131, 132
PBS 58
Peabody Coal 142
peasantry x–xi, xiv, 1, 3, 5, 8, 14, 27, 83, 89, 91, 100, 102, 106, 110, 120, 123, 124, 132, 135, 145
Pelican Bay penitentiary 40
Pence, Mike 46
Pentagon 68, 86
People's Assembly Movement 145
Perdue Farms 124
Perelman, Michael 56
Petras, James 74–75
Philippines 6, 14
Pieterse, Jan Nederveen 82–83
Pick, Daniel 111
Pilgrims Pride 124
Pinnacle List 124
Pittsburgh 28
Pizzigati, Sam 73
Polanyi, Karl xi
Porto Alegre, Brazil xiv, 93, 129, 144, 145
Portugal 81
Posner, Richard 55
postcolonialism xiii
postmodernity 6, 17–18, 85

poverty see disposable people; Heritage Foundation; homelessness; Malthus, Thomas
Powell, Colin 81
Prashad, Vijay 1, 74, 136
primitive accumulation x, 3, 4, 106
prisons ix, 1–2, 5–7, 11, 14, 20, 34–41, 50, 88, 89, 101, 105, 114, 115, 127, 128, 142, 144
private property x, xi, xiv, 3, 4, 8, 9, 32, 67–68, 100, 101, 119–20, 121, 123, 124, 125–26, 128, 129, 131, 132, 135, 136, 139, 147
privatization see enclosure

Raban, Jonathan 18
racism 2, 8–11, 19, 28, 30, 36, 39, 41, 42, 43, 44, 47, 50, 51, 83, 89, 100, 102, 109, 110–14, 119–20, 121, 141; see also slavery
"Race to the Top" 45
Ramnath, Maia 91
Rana Plaza (Bangladesh) 96
Rand, Ayn 70
Raptor Residence 19
Ravitch, Diane 45–47
Raytheon xiii
Reagan, Ronald 35, 37, 93
Recovery School District (New Orleans) 46
refugees 114–16
Reich, Robert 44
Reid, Harry 25
religion 51–53, 114
Renaissance xii, 3, 81, 108
Republican Party 36, 46, 60, 70, 143, 144
Reynolds, Malvina 43–44, 49
Riis, Jacob 95
Rockefeller Foundation 141
Ross, Alexander xi, 3, 125
Ross, Andrew 23
Ross, John 10
Ross, Robert 92
Rowe, Jonathan xiii, 126, 133–34, 139
Rowley, C. D. 15
Roy, Arundhati 4, 90
Royal Exchange and London Assurance Act 67
Rumsfeld, Donald 81
Rural King 31
Russia xiii, 55; see also Soviet Union
Russian revolution xiv
Rwanda 85, 86
Ryan, Paul 70

Safe House Estate 20
Said, Edward 81, 82
Saint Louis, MO 1–2, 6, 7, 11, 19, 30, 34
Saint Simon (Simonianism) 51Salvation Army 74
Sam's Club 31
San Diego, CA 12, 25
San Francisco, CA 29, 32
Sanders, Bernie 140-43
Sandy Hook School massacre 42
Scheer, Robert 72, 77
schools 2, 6, 34–47, 140, 144
Scotland 7, 106, 123, 131; *see also* Highland Clearances
Scott, H. Lee 73
Seaside, FL 24
Securities and Exchange Commission 70
Semel, Terry 73
Serbs 114
Shell 86
Shiflett, David 12
Shipler, David 95
Shiva, Vandana 125, 127, 128, 131, 135, 139
Sierra Club 141
Silko, Leslie Marmon 10–11
Simpson, O. J. 35
slavery x, xiv, 2, 6, 14, 28, 38, 50, 51, 83, 84, 92, 93, 94, 97, 100, 101, 109, 110, 147
slums 17, 26–30
Smith, Adam xi, 54, 66, 103
Smith, John 82–83, 89, 93, 106
Snow Crash 23, 129
Snyder, Mary Gail 19, 22
Snyder, Rick 144
socialism xiv, 51, 76, 112, 129, 139, 140, 143
Sorkin, Michael 18
South Africa xiii, 6, 28, 147
South Sea Bubble 54, 66–67
Southern Pacific Railroad 69
Soviet Union xii, xiv, 6, 35, 57, 84, 129, 147
Spain x, 6, 81, 82, 92
Spanish-American War ix, 6, 82
Stalin, Joseph 35
Starbucks 38, 146
Stephenson, Neil 23
Stiglitz, Joseph 55, 78
Stone, Oliver 70
Straight Outta Compton 36
Subcomandante Marcos 80
Sudan 85, 113, 115
Susanville, CA 41
Sutton, Alison 109
sweatshops 56, 83, 92–97, 100, 101, 107

Swift, Jonathan 66, 108
Sycamore Land Trust 143

Tancredo, Tom 12
Tarbell, Jim 82
Tarzeen Fashion 96
Tawney, R. H. x, 123
Taylor, Frederick 112
telegraph 69
terra nullius 119–20
terrorism 124; *see also* Al-Qaeda; Isis; war on terror
Thailand 95, 109
Thatcher, Margaret 140
Thompson, E. P. x, 102, 103, 123, 132
Thompson, Scott 73
Tijuana, Mexico 12, 13, 27, 102
Tillerson, Rex 87
Time Warner 59
Tobin tax 146
Tönnies, Ferdinand 72
"tragedy of the commons" x, 89, 119, 130–36
Trans-Pacific Partnership 68, 141, 144
Treaty of Guadalupe 13
Triangle Shirtwaist fire 95
Trollope, Anthony 105
Trollope, Frances 105
Truman Show 23–24
Trump, Donald xi–xii, 2, 12, 17, 19, 41, 45, 58, 59, 86, 87, 104, 114–15, 140, 144, 147
Tunisia xiv, 145
Turner, Frederick Jackson 7–8
Twin Lakes, FL 22
Tyson Foods 124

UN Commisioner for Refugees 114
unemployment xiii, 5, 54, 57, 73, 76, 89, 100–01, 105, 115
United Nations xiv, 2, 135, 146
urbanization 17–32, 89
Urrea, Luis Alberto 12, 27, 102
US military xiii, 6, 10, 11, 24–26, 86, 101; *see also* military-industrial complex
US Post Office 130, 144
US Social Forum 145

Van Gelder, Sarah 139–40
Van Kempen, Robert 28
Vanden Heuvel, Katrina 60
Varga, Joe 28, 30
Veblen, Thorstein 51
Veltmeyer, Henry 74–75
Venturi, Robert 18

Vera Institute of Justice 44
Via Campesina 91, 145
ViaCom 59
Virginia Company 109

Waite, Morrison Remnick 69
Wall, Derek 119, 131
Wall Street *see* financialization; Occupy Wall Street
Walmart 31, 38, 73–74, 96–97, 126, 129, 142, 143
Walton family 73
war on drugs 2, 12, 13–14, 35, 36, 37
war on terror xiii, 6, 12, 56, 60, 81, 85
Warhol, Andy 18
water xi, xiii, 2, 4, 9, 130, 140, 143
Watson, Bruce 25–26
Watts, George Frederick 105
Weber, Max xiv, 6, 52–53
Welch, Jack 72, 77
Wells Fargo 5
Wells, H. G. 66
West Virginia 53, 132
Williams, Raymond x
Winstanley, Gerard 123
Wolff, Richard 142
Wolfson, Marty 75
Wolin, Sheldon xi–xii
Women's March 140

Wood, Ellen Meiksins 83
Wood, Phillip 37
Wordsworth, William 121–22
Workers Rights Consortium 96
World Bank 91, 92, 144
World Economic Forum 144
World Social Forum xiv, 93, 116, 144–45
World Trade Center 86
World Trade Organization 68, 92, 124
World War I 28
World War II ix, xii, 2, 10, 30, 81, 83, 85, 91, 106, 111, 142, 146
WorldCom 55
Wright, Paul 7
WTO 91, 92

Yahoo 73
Yang, Jerry 73
Yemen 113, 115
Young, Arthur xi, 120
Young, Todd 60
Youngstown Correctional Center 38
YouTube 134
Yugoslavia 85, 114

Zangwill, Israel 29
Zapatistas 91, 116, 141, 147
Žižek, Slavoj 71, 127–28
Zulus 109

Taylor & Francis eBooks

Helping you to choose the right eBooks for your Library

Add Routledge titles to your library's digital collection today. Taylor and Francis ebooks contains over 50,000 titles in the Humanities, Social Sciences, Behavioural Sciences, Built Environment and Law.

Choose from a range of subject packages or create your own!

Benefits for you
- » Free MARC records
- » COUNTER-compliant usage statistics
- » Flexible purchase and pricing options
- » All titles DRM-free.

Benefits for your user
- » Off-site, anytime access via Athens or referring URL
- » Print or copy pages or chapters
- » Full content search
- » Bookmark, highlight and annotate text
- » Access to thousands of pages of quality research at the click of a button.

REQUEST YOUR FREE INSTITUTIONAL TRIAL TODAY

Free Trials Available
We offer free trials to qualifying academic, corporate and government customers.

eCollections – Choose from over 30 subject eCollections, including:

Archaeology	Language Learning
Architecture	Law
Asian Studies	Literature
Business & Management	Media & Communication
Classical Studies	Middle East Studies
Construction	Music
Creative & Media Arts	Philosophy
Criminology & Criminal Justice	Planning
Economics	Politics
Education	Psychology & Mental Health
Energy	Religion
Engineering	Security
English Language & Linguistics	Social Work
Environment & Sustainability	Sociology
Geography	Sport
Health Studies	Theatre & Performance
History	Tourism, Hospitality & Events

For more information, pricing enquiries or to order a free trial, please contact your local sales team:
www.tandfebooks.com/page/sales

 | The home of Routledge books

www.tandfebooks.com